11 in '11

11 in '11

A HOMETOWN HERO,
LA RUSSA'S LAST RIDE IN RED,
AND A MIRACLE WORLD SERIES
FOR THE ST. LOUIS CARDINALS

Benjamin Hochman

TRIUMPH
BOOKS

Library of Congress Cataloging-in-Publication Data
Names: Hochman, Benjamin, author.
Title: 11 in '11 : a hometown hero, la Russa's last ride, and a miracle World Series for the St. Louis Cardinals / Benjamin Hochman.
Other titles: Eleven in eleven
Description: Chicago, Illinois : Triumph Books, [2021] | Includes bibliographical references. | Summary: "This book documents the St. Louis Cardinals' World Series-winning season of 2011"—Provided by publisher.
Identifiers: LCCN 2021000394 (print) | LCCN 2021000395 (ebook) | ISBN 9781629378732 (hardcover) | ISBN 9781641256049 (epub)
Subjects: LCSH: St. Louis Cardinals (Baseball team)—History—21st century. | World Series (Baseball)—History—21st century. | La Russa, Tony. | Baseball—United States—History—21st century.
Classification: LCC GV875.S3 H63 2021 (print) | LCC GV875.S3 (ebook) | DDC 796.357/640977866—dc23
LC record available at https://lccn.loc.gov/2021000394
LC ebook record available at https://lccn.loc.gov/2021000395

This book is available in quantity at special discounts for your group or organization. For further information, contact:
Triumph Books LLC
814 North Franklin Street
Chicago, Illinois 60610
(312) 337-0747
www.triumphbooks.com

Printed in U.S.A.
ISBN: 978-1-62937-873-2
Design by Sue Knopf
Photos courtesy of AP Images

To my wife, Angela Hochman,
my pretty baby.
You are the human exclamation point.

To my daughter, Olsen Hochman,
my literal pretty baby.
You make the sun shine inside.

CONTENTS

FOREWORD

Why were the 2011 Cardinals so special? Well, first, it's the group of guys. I think the expectation every year, coming in as a St. Louis Cardinal, is to win a world championship—and it was no different that year. We had a great group of talented guys, we had a great front office, we had a great coaching staff. The whole deal was put into place for us by ownership to give us a chance once again. As everybody knows, we didn't succeed as well as everybody hoped in the first part of the season. So I think that part of what makes it special is the road that it took us on—the journey throughout the whole season that culminated with us winning the world championship. We were so far out of it. Everybody wrote us off. But we fought and fought and fought and were able to sneak in on the last day of that season. And then, every single series we were underdogs. We just kept winning. We were a group of guys who continued to push and fight. And it was pretty neat.

Game 162 at Houston, that was definitely a special night, one that I'll hold on to forever. I was just thankful to get the ball in that situation and to have an opportunity to be part of the outcome. That's what you live for.

Part of what made that team successful was because we just loved being with one another not only around the ballpark, but also off the field. We got together multiple times. It didn't matter who you were or where you were from on that ballclub. We were all friends and really enjoyed being around each other. And that included families, too. There were a lot of family interactions, a lot of wives and kids who hung out. It was just an awesome group of people who came together for one goal and to support each other during that season. It was just a lot of fun.

As for David Freese, you can talk about Game 6 because that's going to go down as the epic game of the whole season, but he did that all playoffs long. It just showed what kind of run he was on, what kind of place he was in mentally. To be able to do everything he did throughout that postseason is incredible, and he deserved every single bit of it. The guy is an amazing teammate and an amazing player. He's someone who you couldn't be more happy for to have had those great things happen to him.

The 2011 team is an amazing part of my life. I was fortunate and blessed to be a part of it. I came from a small town in New Hampshire where hockey is the main sport, not baseball. And to be able to have a journey throughout my life and go through all the injuries and other things that got me to that moment with the group of guys is something I'll always continue to think about, especially when I watch a playoff game. There are times I walk around the house, and I've got pictures up of my kids from those moments when they were able to celebrate with me and our teammates. You never forget it. You never forget the guys you were with, the guys who supported you the whole time. I wouldn't have been able to do anything that I did if it wasn't for the group of dudes who were around me. We really cared about one another and were rooting for each other more than ourselves.

We're all human, and I've been in situations in the past where guys weren't pulling for you; they were pulling against you, even though they were on your team. That's not a healthy situation. On that Cardinals team, we had guys who—no matter what—would do anything for you. That's what made it work and that's what made the year so special. And it's all fleshed out in detail here in Benjamin Hochman's book.

—*Chris Carpenter*
St. Louis Cardinals starting pitcher (2004–12)

CHAPTER 1

HOMETOWN HERO

In St. Louis so many people have stories about the time they met David Freese. Jeff Swatek's story is about the night he arrested him.

As Freese did, Swatek grew up in St. Louis, raised on ravioli that was toasted, pizza crust as flat as Topps, and the belief that best of all the berries was Chuck. Officer Swatek, who later became Sergeant Swatek, loved the Cardinals, but he didn't recognize David Freese when he pulled him over at Page and Lindbergh in Maryland Heights that night in December of 2009. Then again, David Freese wasn't David Freese yet. At the time Freese had only played 17 games in the majors but was earmarked to start at third base for St. Louis in 2010.

Except here he was a couple months before spring training with a blood alcohol content level that looked like a batting average. "He was pretty intoxicated—he was a 0.232," Swatek said in 2020. "Three times the legal limit would be a .24. So he was up there...Once we got to the station, we kind of ran through the course of what we do with someone with a DUI. So he's remorseful. Very humble. Never arrogant. Never antagonistic in any way. That can play out differently when people are drinking because they kind of take on different personalities. He seemed like a decent guy by everything I saw."

The 26-year-old Freese, though, had already been arrested twice for alcohol issues: once when he was 19 and the other when he was a San Diego Padres minor leaguer in 2007. Like Freese that December night, his career was stopped at an intersection. "He really had to have gone through a process to get from the point where I saw him that night to where everyone saw him in the future," Swatek said of Freese, who went through a 30-day treatment for alcohol abuse, stopped drinking at the time, and took advantage of mentoring from Cardinals star Matt Holliday. "It takes a lot of hard work and determination to get from a place that you don't want to be in your life to a place where you're feeling successful and productive."

Swatek had a particularly personal appreciation for perseverance. While in the line of duty back in 2006, he approached a stolen car on foot when the suspect suddenly drove off and hit the officer. The impact caused Swatek's left leg to be forced under the front tire of the vehicle, which dragged him into the street. Swatek's leg broke in multiple places. "I couldn't sleep after getting hit by the car," he said. "I was prescribed a couple of different sleep medications. It wasn't working. I found out my wife was pregnant with our second a week after. I had been in good shape, and that was taken away from me. I lost 30 pounds in one month."

But the officer found inner strength to fuel outer strength. Watching the Cards win it all in 2006 helped, too. After nearly half a year of physical therapy, he returned to work. And in 2011 Swatek was honored with the Law Enforcement Purple Heart.

That autumn, Swatek was alone, working an off-duty shift at Ranken Jordan Pediatric Bridge Hospital. His beloved Cardinals had made an improbable run deemed by some in late August—when the Birds were 10½ back—as impossible. There they were in the 2011 World Series, trying to win the franchise's 11th championship. As the St. Louis saying went that fall, it would be 11 in '11.

But the Cardinals were down 3–2 to the Texas Rangers in the World Series.

And down 7–5—at home—in Game 6.

And with two runners on, down to their last out.

And down to their last strike.

And…David Freese became David Freese.

He tripled to tie the game.

And in the 11ᵗʰ, he homered to win the game.

"I was looking around because you want it to be a shared experience, but it was just me and the TV," Swatek said as the man he once arrested saved the season. "Like every other St. Louisan, I celebrated. He literally and figuratively stepped up to the plate and led the Cardinals to victory. I think there's always good and bad in everything. I think that balance of what he went through, certainly, there's a lot of it there. Being a World Series MVP, what else could a little kid hope for in life? And I think going through some trials and tribulations probably got him to this point. We see that with officers at work. Sometimes if I've been doing a background check of a police applicant and they have nothing that I can find that really stands out, it causes you more concern than somebody who has gone through some things. It gives them more to reflect on, more to relate to others…He made a mistake that night and moved on from it."

• • •

This is a story of a feeling. It's a story about a team, sure, and a city, of course, but it's a story about the culmination of a journey, which created this feeling inside you that you'd never felt before. It was almost like this delirious bliss. When David Freese hit the triple, it took Cardinals fans to a place your mind didn't think it could go, sent chills up your body, shook up your heart, and laughed at your imagination for thinking it had the ability to come up with crazy thoughts, when this turn-of-events in real life proved crazier than anything the imagination could've cooked up. Ninth inning, down two, two on, two outs, two strikes, and he triples? "You're going from the depths of hell to euphoria," said St. Louis native Tim McKernan, a longtime morning radio host, "in a matter of a second."

And the guy who did it is the guy who's actually from St. Louis? "The way I look at it, he is living what so many of us wanted to live—not just hundreds of us, a million of us," McKernan said. "He is representing so many kids who have grown up in St. Louis because all of us wanted to be in that spot and pretended we were going to be in that spot. And he actually was in that spot. And he came through. And he came through in what is considered, not only by St. Louisans, but by people around baseball as arguably the greatest World Series game ever played. And then you surround it with all of these things going on in his life leading up to it? It truly is a movie."

The triple. Freese slid into third headfirst and popped up on his knees, unleashing this great glare. The emotions it stirred in fans, this perfect mix of elation and astonishment and relief, was a once-in-a-lifetime feeling. Not just for Cardinals fans. This specific turn of events had never happened in baseball before. And then it happened again! Twice in a lifetime. Heck, twice in an hour! After Josh Hamilton hit a two-run homer in the top of the 10th, the Cards scored once in the bottom but were still down one and down to one last strike again… when Lance Berkman singled to tie it!

It was the first time a team was ever one strike away twice from winning the World Series in a game and blew it. A Texas-sized feat. But the game was still tied. The Texas Rangers could still win the World Series and end the Cards' season that very night. But in the bottom of the 11th, just as your body had recovered and wondered what the hell it just went though, Freese resuscitated the ecstasy.

He drilled the Game 6 walk-off homer, and you felt the feelings, yet again—emotions that created body motions you never thought you'd do. The Cardinals' bodies, too. "I'm getting chills right now just talking about it," 2011 World Series champ Skip Schumaker said in 2020. "I watched the video recently, I watched myself. I'm running around with my hat in my hand doing a windmill motion. What the hell was I doing? But it was such a little kid, can't-believe-what-just-happened-moment. These emotions that I've never had—and never will have again on the baseball field—happened. And we didn't even win the World Series. We got to Game 7. We had another game to play still. I'll never forget him hitting it. It was also a blur for me. I don't remember windmilling my hat all around and jumping up and down. I don't know what that was about. Never did that before, never done it again. Emotions came out that we'd never had before."

And since you, the St Louis fans, got to feel the feelings, you're in a club that no one else can join. You experienced the Freese triple and the Freese homer, something that no money can buy nor any drug recreate. And it's a shared experience with all your friends from St. Louis—and, really, all of St. Louis. And what's cool about the David Freese feelings is that it can never be taken from you. You experienced it, you can always think back, it happened. It's like a first kiss, graduating from school, seeing your spouse walk down the aisle, or the birth of your first child. This feeling is right up there—if not in its own unique aura orbit—because unlike graduating or getting married, not everyone can or gets to experience this. A fellow parent can relate to the birth of a baby, but most sports fans can't relate to what Cardinals fans went through the night of Game 6.

Of course, the 2011 Cardinals had to win the next night, too. And when they won Game 7—remember who tied the game with a two-run double in the bottom of the first?—there was the final euphoric confluence of love and pride for a team and a town and family and friends. And adults of all ages felt 11 in '11. Even a decade later in a quiet moment, you think of the extraordinary things that happened that October night and suddenly you're getting that about-to-cry feeling, which rushes up your throat and face and toward your eyes.

Now, St. Louis is a big city but a smaller big city, which makes the fandom almost intimate. There are similarities between what the Cardinals mean to St. Louis and what the Saints mean to New Orleans or even the Packers to Green Bay. New York and Boston and Chicago are tremendous sports towns. They're the standards; they check all the boxes. But there's something more personal about a ballclub in a smaller burgh, where the team is part of the fiber and the fabric and other things that sound like they're sold at Michael's. St. Louis is small enough that athletes are spotted around town in local haunts, and they show up in local commercials for heating and cooling, and depending on your tax bracket, perhaps their children even go to elementary school with your kids.

St. Louis has a chip on its shoulder, but at least St. Louis admits it has a chip on its shoulder. Some towns just deny it, and it's a bad look, but St. Louis is at least honest that it is, realistically, just St. Louis. But it's authentically St. Louis. It's got quirks and cracks and flaws. But they're our quirks and cracks and flaws.

And there is an astonishing amount of pride for St. Louisans who make it big. When the 2020 pandemic kept fans from MLB games, teams put cardboard cutouts behind home plate. But few teams honored their local celebs as often and grandly as St. Louis, the home of Jon Hamm and John Goodman, Andy Cohen and Sterling K. Brown, Nelly and Ellie Kemper, Jenna Fischer and Phyllis Smith. In St. Louis there is a disproportionate pride—compared to other cities—for all things St. Louis. So when a player on the Cards or Blues is from St. Louis? It's like he's everybody's guy. Even if you didn't grow up with him, you feel a connection, which leads us back to Freese and another fellow, Patrick Maroon, the pride of Oakville, the grinding, gritty hockey player who signed with the Blues for the 2018–19 season.

Maroon even got engaged to a St. Louis girl, Francesca Vangel, from a St. Louis family. They're the folks who own Charlie Gitto's, the estimable Italian restaurant on The Hill (with mouth-watering toasted ravioli). There were plenty of similarities between that 2018–19 Blues team and the 2011 Cardinals. For starters, they both were in bad shape for a while there. The Blues had the fewest points in hockey on January 3 yet ascended to make the playoffs. But in the second round just like the Cards in the 2011 World Series, they were down 3–2 to the team from the Dallas area. So, Francecsa Vangel gave a pep talk to some of the Blues' better halves. "I told them about Game 6, Cardinals vs. Texas Rangers," she recalled. "I said, 'Guys, this can happen. Trust me. This happens in St. Louis. Here's this video [of Freese on YouTube]. This happens.' And it does."

The Blues, of course, won Game 6.

The next night, Patrick Maroon pulled a David Freese.

He scored the Game 7-winning goal in double overtime in St. Louis. The Blues went on to win their first Stanley Cup. "They're both made men," McKernan said. "The rest of your life, you're a made man. It's like that ceremony. They can never do any wrong in St. Louis. And the thing about it is they're both great guys. It isn't like, well, take your pick of whatever assholes we've covered over the years. They're both just great guys. And how their lives changed just because of one swing of the bat or one slap of the puck sitting on the ice? Now they're made men. It's an incredible thing."

Or as MLB Network journalist and St. Louis native Dani Wexelman put it: "We don't deserve those people in our lives."

• • •

As a ballplayer in elementary school, David Freese was so talented, teams didn't just pitch around him. "We intentionally walked him—twice—in the fourth grade," said Matt Landwehr, a lifelong friend who lived with Freese during Freese's early days with the Cardinals. "We played against each other. He'd get so mad because he didn't get to hit...In retrospect, it's like did we really intentionally walk somebody in the fourth grade? *Really? We did that?* But he always had something special. He really did."

Freese was a schoolboy star. He lived in Wildwood, Missouri, out in St. Louis County, about 30 miles from Busch Stadium. His mom, Lynn, was a teacher. His dad, Guy, was a civil engineer. Freese attended Lafayette High, where his metal bat's swings would ping pitches out of the park. He could've played college ball at a lot of schools but decided not to play college ball at any school. He had been overwhelmed by all that went into year-round baseball. The game consumed him to the point that it didn't feel like a game. "He was legitimately burnt out. He needed some time away to just be a kid," said Landwehr, who graduated with Freese from Lafayette in 2001.

Just like Landwehr, Freese attended the University of Missouri as a regular undergrad, even though Mizzou's baseball coaches had recruited Freese to be a Tiger. "I've often thought how much he could've helped had the timing been a bit different," said Tim Jamieson, who was Mizzou's coach from 1995 to 2016.

But as the famous story goes—after more than a year away from the game, Freese slowly and surely rediscovered why he loved the game. "A couple of the West County guys asked me if I remembered David Freese," recalled Tony Dattoli, Freese's coach at Meramec Community College in St. Louis. "I said, 'Of course.' They told me he was interested in coming by and talking to me about coming back and playing ball…You knew from Day One that there was something special and different about him as far as his ability. The way he moved around the diamond and his actions. Being around baseball for so many years, you can just tell about a guy with something as simple as seeing him play catch and the way the ball leaves his hand when he's stretching out the throws. And you can always tell the difference between a legitimate pro hitter. There's a special crack of the bat when they hit it. When a pro guy hits it, it sounds like an aluminum bat even when he's using wood. It's that violent coming off the bat. I told him after his first year: 'You're going to be the first major leaguer I ever coached.' He was."

Freese transferred to South Alabama. On the team's website, Freese's bio said: "the St. Louis Cardinals are his favorite professional sports team." He played two seasons at the school in Mobile, belting homers across the Sun Belt. And in June of 2006, the San Diego Padres selected David Richard Freese in the ninth round of the Major

League Baseball draft. In his first full pro season, Freese hit .302 in A ball in 2007.

A couple months later, Landwehr was at Mulligan's Grill in Ellisville when he got the call. "We had just beaten Marquette that night—big rivalry basketball game," said Landwehr, who became a coach at Lafayette. "He calls me and says, 'So, I'm coming home.'

"I said, 'What are you talking about, dude?'

"He tells me he just got traded to the Cardinals. '*What?*' I'm yelling it in Mulligan's. We're there with some Marquette people and Lafayette people and everything. And it hadn't come across the news yet. Even then [in December of 2007], breaking news and social media wasn't quite as heavy. So I'm telling people that Dave was coming home!"

Pretty cool news, but then the Cards fans found out who they were giving up in the trade: Jim Edmonds. "Jim Edmonds and cash for Freese? Okay, big guy!" Landwehr said. "It was pretty funny seeing people's reactions. It ended up working out okay."

At that point Edmonds was a St. Louis legend. He was also one of Freese's favorite Cardinals. But a season after winning the World Series, Edmonds hit .252 in 2007 with just a .728 OPS. And he was 37.

Freese spent a splendid 2008 season with the Cards' Triple A team. Then on Opening Day the following year—April 6, 2009—he made his MLB debut with the St. Louis Cardinals. (He grounded out to third off Paul Maholm in his first at-bat.) But Freese was continually hobbled and impeded by foot and ankle injuries, some stemming from a January of 2009 single-car accident. He played in 17 games for the Cards in 2009 and 70 in 2010, though he hit a combined .299.

In the offseason before 2011, during a Cardinals winter event, newly acquired infielder Ryan Theriot had dinner with manager Tony La Russa. "I remember him asking if I knew this Freese kid," Theriot recalled. "I said, 'Not really, I've watched him play. He's a decent player.' He looks at me, dead in the eyes, and he says: 'Ryan, he's a tiger. He's a jungle tiger.' He kept going on and on about him. This is before the season starts. And boy, did he ever live up to that."

• • •

Dan Kriegshauser, David Freese's old teammate from Meramec, moved back to St. Louis in the summer of 2010. He got a place in the Central West End area. "Dave had just moved into a condo there, too, right at the same time," Kriegshauser said. "He was sober, and it was just a great time for us to reconnect and see each other. It had been texts for like five years, seeing each other once a year. But then in 2011, I ended up moving into Brentwood Forest. And he was moving to a new place in the beginning of September."

Alas, it was going to take a couple weeks for Freese to get cable in his new place. "So he stayed at my place for a couple of nights," Kriegshauser said of September of 2011, as the Cardinals went on an epic run to make the playoffs. "He still didn't have cable. So he kept crashing. And then they went to Houston and clinched [the wild-card]. Even when he got the cable, he stayed. Why change it? We just kept it going."

During the 2011 postseason, the St. Louis Cardinals' third baseman was literally sleeping on his buddy's couch. In September and October. "It was awesome, it was kind of like college again minus the partying," Kriegshauser said. "He would come over whenever they were in town. I'd get off work, he'd come over, and every night, we would go to Farotto's and do take-out or we'd go to Joey B's. There was never a night where we weren't eating like animals and just bullshitting. Toward the end of the year, you could tell things might possibly happen. It was cool just to be around it and being able to take it all in. You wake up and you've got your buddy of 10, 15 years just hanging out, sleeping on your couch and coming back after playing in Cardinals games. And then it just took off in the playoffs. I think we all thought the Phillies would win. And then after Game 4, when he hit the home run against

Roy Oswalt, me and his uncle actually drove to Philly the next day. We went and saw Game 5 in person, which was incredible. There were a couple of guys around just screaming obscenities at us. That night was just incredible. The whole game was pins and needles after the first inning."

The Cards won Game 5 and the National League Division Series. And then they won the National League Championship Series. And then down 3–2 in the World Series, Kriegshauser's house guest contributed with a couple big hits in Game 6. That night seemingly everyone in St. Louis was out celebrating David Freese, except David Freese. When Kriegshauser returned home with some friends, "He was still up," Kriegshauser said. "He was just watching a movie."

That image is incredible: Kriegshauser opens his door after the most epic night in St. Louis sports history, and the man who was responsible for the epicness is just sitting there. "Yeah, that's exactly it," Kriegshauser said. "So we sat there with him. We were all just kind of in disbelief. What just happened? We were all just laughing. We might have yelled at him and asked, 'What the hell did you just do? Can you believe this?' Thinking back on it, it was just awesome to be around your good buddies and all that. You realize [the hugeness], but you don't really realize it. It's just like a movie. You just don't really grasp what's going on when it's going on."

St. Louis had its share of sports heroes and icons, but this was different. Someone like Lou Brock, Brett Hull, or Ozzie Smith had provided a mosaic of happy: years and years of high-level sport, entertaining St. Louis, invigorating St. Louis, representing St. Louis. But Freese's instant legend was about two moments, two indelible hits that specifically provided unparalleled joy with the highest of stakes on the table. Won them the damn World Series. Ask anyone—priests to prisoners—about Game 6, and they'll have a story you've just got to hear. In a way it's almost like St. Louis is forever indebted to Freese, forever inferior, forever in awe.

Has that been healthy for Freese? Sometimes yes, sometimes no.

The day after the Cardinals won Game 7, Freese and friends went to Johnny's in Soulard at 5:00 PM. "Nobody was in there," Kriegshauser said. "And by the time we left two hours later, the place was packed, and there was a line out the door of people trying to get autographs. That's when I knew."

The following day was the parade, and in the coming days, Freese's life felt like a parade. He appeared on *The Tonight Show with Jay Leno*, was a guest on *Ellen*, presented an award with Erin Andrews at the Country Music Association Awards, filmed a scene on a new ABC comedy called *Work It*, and was a guest at the *GQ* Man of the Year event, which featured other luminaries such as Justin Timberlake, Jay-Z, Jimmy Fallon, Kerry Washington, and Jon Hamm. In St. Louis he received the key to the city and St. Louis County (if there was anyone who could bridge the divide between the city and county, it was Freese). And at Six Flags St. Louis, the popular Mr. Freeze ride was renamed, of course, Mr. Freese.

Four nights after the World Series, fans waited overnight at the St. Louis Galleria to get wristbands for a Freese event at Macy's. "They asked me to emcee it," said Tom Ackerman of KMOX radio. "It was crazy. It was like Elvis was in the building. The biggest rock star you could ever imagine had walked in. It was completely packed. Freese had to be brought in. They radioed to us that he was on his way. They had some people escorting him in some side entrance...And if you had David Freese today, he'd still draw the same attention. If you said David Freese is going to show up somewhere, he'd still draw a huge crowd like 10 years later. That's the impact that the Cardinals have on St. Louis and what winning a World Series can do for your legend status—especially if you contribute a home run that may go down as not only the greatest in Cardinals history, but also as one of the handful of greatest in World Series history."

On November 12 Freese returned to Mizzou, his old school (though even he admitted over the years that there wasn't much actual schooling during his time there). "There were five of us there when he got honored at Mizzou," Matt Landwehr said. "Mizzou wanted to honor him at a football game. So I was with him on the field, and one of our other buddies said, 'This had to be what The Beatles kind of felt like.' It was just crazy. People wanted to touch his car and everything. We walked around the field, and anyone from a teenage girl to a college girl to a 75-year-old man was yelling at Dave. And once again to see him handle that was so cool. I couldn't have handled it. To see him handle that and sign autographs and to take probably a million pictures honestly? He went up for pictures in front of all the different fraternity and sorority blocks of seats there at the stadium. He wasn't just there to be a dude who waved and went up to a suite to get away from everyone. He walked around the whole sideline to say 'hi' to fans."

And that was, and is, the beauty of Freese being the guy who won Game 6. He wasn't already this multi-millionaire, huge-contract baseball star. He'd only played in 184 MLB games in three seasons. (In 2011 he broke his hand and battled other injuries, finishing with 97 games played and a .297 batting average.) He was a big leaguer, but he still had that aura of being a regular dude, which made him appreciate everything even more—and thus made everyone appreciate him even more. St. Louisans felt like he was one of them. There was a relatableness to it all. You knew his high school or people from his high school, you knew where he grew up or the type of childhood he had, you knew the culture of Mizzou and the status of the Cardinals. And he loved Imo's Pizza! You knew this guy—even if you hadn't met him.

That winter, Lafayette wanted to honor Freese at a basketball game. They would've taken any Freeseness they could get—even if he just showed up at halftime to wave to the crowd and left. "And he was all in on doing it," Landwehr said. "He said, 'I've got to do a signing for the kids.' I was thinking, *Seriously? We do not expect that. We want to honor you. We don't want to make you do anything.* But he was all in. So he sat there for 45 minutes, probably an hour, before our game, signing autographs and he took a picture with every kid, too. We brought in a photographer so they could do it quickly. And those kids got their World Series or Cards memorabilia signed. David didn't want it to just be some stock photo. 'If they have some Lafayette stuff, I want to sign that for them and have it be special for them.' There are still kids that I talk to, to this day, who talk about that moment. He went over and took a picture in front of our student section, and it's blown up in our school. And he came and spoke to our team and actually brought a gift for each one of our basketball players that was personalized. I shared all the names with him, and then he brought a little signed thing for each guy. It was really neat to see him embrace the community that supported him and where he came from. He was able to say, 'I was in your shoes once.' You never know what can happen…I know Dave. He's such a humble guy, chill dude who had this incredible thing happen in his life from all of his hard work. What people miss is how much he gets those people."

• • •

The little girl was born with a hole in her heart. "It's called ASD (atrial septal defect), and it was one of the largest ones they had seen," said Shannon Kozeny, the mother of Vivien, who was seven in 2011.

The doctors tried different methods and medications, but nothing worked. Vivien would have to undergo open heart surgery and later two other surgical procedures. "It was terrifying, to be honest with you," the mother said. "I stayed in the hospital 24/7. I barely slept. We had gone through one procedure, and it didn't work. They were like, 'Let's try this and see if this works.' There was a lot of uncertainty at the time. I think we were there for two-and-a-half weeks. It's a long time."

One day at SSM Health Cardinal Glennon Children's Hospital, Vivien's doctor came into the room. He said he had another doctor to see her. "Well, it was David Freese, and he was dressed up with a doctor's coat," said Vivien, who was 17 in 2021. "Meeting him actually really changed my life. I'm always telling people that I've met him and how it made me a lot stronger and gave me a lot more hope headed into the surgeries...I did play softball for a bit because David Freese inspired me. Now I actually play ice hockey."

Tom Ackerman was there that day for KMOX, reporting on Dr. Freese's shift at the hospital. "I got to see a person affect somebody else's life in a very private moment and setting," Ackerman said. "That was incredibly special. I remember he and I texting afterward about how affected we were by it positively and emotionally. It was a very human moment."

As the 2012 season approached, Dan Kriegshauser recalled how driven Freese was because everyone only knew him for his playoff heroics. He wanted to have productive and full seasons for the Cards. "He took that personally," Kriegshauser said. "We were all like, 'Don't worry about that.' But he took that personally. He ended up having a great career."

Freese was an All-Star in 2012, hitting .293 with a career best .839 OPS. And most importantly, he played 144 games. Sure enough, the Cards made the playoffs in 2012. And in 2013 Freese and the Cards returned to the World Series but lost to the Boston Red Sox. His OPS that year dropped to .721, though.

By 2013 the reality was that Freese was suffocating in the same storm his heroics created. Tim McKernan recalled seeing a close Freese confidant at a bar. McKernan asked how Freese was doing. "He said to me, 'Dude, we have to get him out of here.'" McKernan recalled. "I asked, 'Is he here?' He says, 'No, we have to get him out of St. Louis. He is in bad shape.'"

Freese was fragile. He had numerous issues with drinking. He was too nice of a guy to turn down offers from people—be it public appearances or social gatherings. Baseball, just like it did after high school, had caused Freese to be overwhelmed. Submerged. Game 6 made him seem superhuman, but he was human. "It got pretty heavy," Freese said three years later in a sit-down interview for a *St. Louis Post-Dispatch* column in 2016. Asked what he meant by heavy, Freese said, "Something that got to me and affected me after that was trying to please everybody. That was something I didn't really understand how to deal with, especially being a single guy, not having a family, you're going home to nobody. You kind of build off that. And you try to make people happy to make yourself happy in a way. There's a lot of people who deal with that type of stuff. So it got heavy. It definitely got a little much at times. I wish I had that one person who had been through something like that, that I could've talked to. And the whole hometown thing was just a little much at times. But like I said, I'm grateful for all of that, not even to individually do what I did but because the effect [the Game 6 aftermath] had on me then sped up a maturation process that I needed."

He was traded in November of 2013, along with Fernando Salas, to the Los Angeles Angels for Randal Grichuk and Peter Bourjos. He'd later play for the Pittsburgh Pirates and Los Angeles Dodgers. "I know I had the alcohol issues in the past, but you come to realize it's a lot deeper than that. It's depression and anxiety issues," Freese revealed to *USA TODAY*'s Bob Nightengale in 2017. "I was depressed. I was always depressed. I never tried to do anything to myself, but I didn't care about my life. I didn't care what would happen to me. It was almost to a point that if this is my time, so be it? There was definitely a lack of care about my well-being at certain times, for sure."

Nightengale mentioned the arrests but also referred to "the countless mornings he awoke and had no recollection of even getting into bed. The blackouts."

Said Freese to Nightengale, "I've had moments like that since high school…It's been 15-plus years of, 'I can't believe I'm still here.' You win the World Series in your hometown, and you become this guy in a city that loves Cardinal baseball, and sometimes it's the last guy you want to be. So you start building this façade, trying to be something I was not."

And while some might say the greatest save in St. Louis history was by Bruce Sutter, Adam Wainwright, or Jason Motte, one could argue it was by Mairin O'Leary for saving St. Louis' savior. Freese met Mairin while visiting a St. Louis production studio called Rukus. She wasn't a huge sports fan. She hadn't even watched Game 6 when it happened. But she connected with Freese. They fell in love. He proposed in New Zealand in December of 2015. "She's kind of the first person I've ever had in my life that I wanted to change for," Freese told the *St. Louis Post-Dispatch* in 2016, while sitting in a quiet room at the Pirates' spring training facility. "You want to look at yourself in the mirror and you want to do it for yourself, but when you see the wonderful things that life brings you, it kind of knocks you in the face. It makes you realize some things. So I'm grateful for that…I'm grateful she walked into my life. Obviously, I've had my obstacles in life. She's been wonderful."

In 2020, the year after Freese retired, his childhood friend Matt Landwehr was asked about Freese's legacy. Of course, it's Game 6, yes. But it's not just Game 6. Landwehr spoke about Freese going public to discuss depression and drinking. "To see a guy who did struggle and he's come out and said he battled depression and battled some demons, the way he tackled it head on, I admire it so much," Landwehr said. "And then to share your story? It could be so easy to just let it fade away a little bit and go away from it. But man, he tackled it head on. And to have the attitude of: if I can save someone's life and tell them that even the superhuman person can have these feelings…What happened in 2011 will be a special moment forever. But he probably legitimately saved lives. And we'll never know who those people were since it was such a widespread story."

Game 6 Story No. 1

On the day after Game 6, Game 6 began in Shanghai. At 8:07 AM on the morning of October 28, 2011, Tim Nowak and Dan Mehan gathered in a business lounge in the Ritz-Carlton Shanghai, hoping no one important spotted them. They had missed much of the 2011 World Series on this diplomatic trade mission, traveling from Beijing to Hangzhou to Shanghai, but this was different. This was Game 6, damn it.

Nowak was the executive director of the World Trade Center St. Louis, which worked to connect St. Louis companies with global opportunities. Mehan was the president and CEO of the Missouri Chamber of Commerce. And in 2011 they were knee deep in the China Hub initiative, working with Chinese air carriers to establish direct air freight, as well as passenger connection, between St. Louis and Shanghai. This particular weeklong trade mission included 30 important Missourians involved with economic development. There was a big speech planned that morning at the Ritz. But as the guys set up shop in the business lounge, guess who showed up? Missouri governor Jay Nixon. "Caught playing hooky," Mehan said.

Nixon served as Missouri's 55th governor from 2009 to 2017, but he is a Cardinals fan for life. "I was supposed to speak in what's called the AmCham—the American Chamber of Commerce—and I was ready to go to that brunch," Nixon said. "As I was walking through the hotel, I was thinking about seeing the beginning of the Cardinals game and showing up a little late. I told my body guy: 'Game 6, we've got to win.'"

So the Missouri contingency was in the business lounge and began watching Game 6 that Shanghai morning 13 hours ahead of St. Louis. Mehan and the governor chatted about rookie outfielder Jon Jay and his minor league stats. They watched the early innings—the score was 2–2 after two innings—in a busy area with international travelers, "And we're hooting and hollering a little bit," Mehan said. "Nixon gets up and says, 'Oh man, I've got to go give this speech.' He looks at me, looks at us, and says, 'You guys have seen enough of my speeches.'"

This implied he was okay with the boys skipping the brunch. "Then this is what I remember: he says, 'I've seen enough of my speeches!'" Mehan said. "And he sits back down and watches another inning or so."

Finally, Nixon made it to the ballroom to deliver his keynote address. Afterward, the governor made an important call to his chief of staff—to see how the Cards were doing. "He was at the game," Nixon said of John Watson, who passed away in 2020. "So, I asked John what's going on, and he says the Cardinals are going to lose. I said, 'What do you mean?' He said, 'It's just one of those games. I mean, Freese dropped a pop-up.' We're in the World Series, and the St. Louis kid dropped the pop up?…So I get off the phone thinking we're going to lose."

Back at their little alcove in the business lounge, Nowak and Mehan were riding the emotional waves of Game 6. "We found ourselves yelling at the TV while the other Chinese lounge patrons looked on with a mix of confusion and curiosity," Nowak said.

Both fellows were born and raised in St. Louis. Nowak, who was 41 in 2011, recalled fond memories of sleeping overnight in line for playoff tickets. Back in 1985 and 1987, he and his brother camped out near Busch Stadium on Market Street in downtown St. Louis, playing stickball in what was "like a party atmosphere" of Cards fans, hoping to snag some seats. (They ended up landing standing-room-only tickets.) Mehan, 47 in 2011, played catcher as a kid like his hero Ted Simmons did. During the recent heated political climate, Mehan wore a shirt that read: "WAINWRIGHT–MOLINA, 2020." And Mehan will never forget a previous Game 6—the Don Denkinger game in 1985. "My roommate at the time at the University of Pennsylvania said: 'Don't worry. You've got Joaquin Andujar going tomorrow night!'"

The Cards, of course, lost Game 7 in 1985, and thus that Game 6 will forever live in infamy. As for the Game 6 in 2011, Mehan and Nowak watched from Shanghai, as David Freese came to bat with two outs, two on, and, soon, two strikes in the bottom of the ninth.

Triple to right. "We went," Nowak said, "absolutely nuts."

The greatest moment ever was on tap. But Nowak had to stop watching.

It was one thing to miss the governor's speech, but it would be quite another if he missed his final lunch with potential Chinese business partners. Nowak hustled to the restaurant near the Ritz, along with Steve Johnson from the St. Louis Regional Chamber. "Steve is seated directly across from me at a large round table," Nowak said. "He knows that I am receiving text updates from Dan, and I am quietly passing these updates across the table, so as to not alert our business guests."

Back at the Ritz, Mehan was alone in the alcove, trying to take in the enormity and absurdity that was Game 6. "People are coming over and asking what I'm watching," he said. "I distinctly remember having a conversation with some guy from Germany. I said, 'Let me try to tell you about this.' And then you try to ramp up somebody, who has no concept of baseball, by explaining how mediocre we were, how we got into the playoffs by the hair of our chinny-chin-chins, and that here we are. This is Game 6, so if we lose, we're out."

Then, it happened.

To this day, nearly a decade later, both Nowak and Mehan can recite Mehan's text verbatim: "Winner, winner, chicken dinner! Freese Dinger! On to Game 7!"

After his speech at the brunch and his phone call to his chief of staff, Governor Nixon headed to a lunch meeting. Jeff Gettys, a former linebacker for the Mizzou Tigers, worked for the governor and was on the trip. "I'm sitting there with a group of Chinese educators and mayors, and Jeff taps me on the shoulder," Nixon said, "which he didn't do very often—especially in a formal meeting like that. He just hands me a note on a piece of paper, which is generally to let me know I need to call someone or something. It read: 'Cards win.' All these Chinese business guys had no idea what I was thinking about. I go, 'Yeah!' And all these guys are so confused. What's this guy doing?"

Meanwhile, Nowak and Mehan had to catch a plane. Most of the Missouri contingency was flying back to the states. "Dan and I are in the taxi and we're just high-fiving and screaming, 'We got a Game 7!'" Nowak said.

But would they even get to watch it?

Their flight departed Shanghai Pudong International Airport on the evening of Friday, October 28, 2011. And it landed in Chicago in the late afternoon of…Friday, October 28, 2011. Sure enough, Game 7 began as they flew the second leg from Chicago to St. Louis. But Nowak had a Slingbox at home, connected to his laptop, so they watched the early innings on the plane while at one point literally flying over Busch Stadium, making for a surreal moment. "We land in St. Louis, make our way to baggage claim," Nowak said, "and we see Allen Craig blast his third-inning homer on a TV at an airport bar."

The home run put St. Louis up 3–2. Nowak headed home while Mehan called his brother. Mehan lived in Jefferson City, so he parked his car at his brother's St. Louis home. "I call him as planned," Mehan said. "He's obviously watching Game 7. I ask him to come and get me. His response: 'You're fucked.'"

His brother did indeed pick him up. Mehan took to Interstate 70 home and took in Game 7 on KMOX radio. He remembered stopping for gas at the Highway 19 junction, and the sign at the gas station read: "Our Cardinals are World Serious."

He kept driving and was 10 minutes from home, as he soaked up the broadcast of the Cardinals winning No. 11 in '11. When he pulled up to the house, he recalled, "My 12-year-old daughter comes running out of the garage, yelling that 'David Freese is the MVP!'"

The series had a lasting impact on Nixon's plans. "This trip changed my procedures in my office," Nixon said. "We never scheduled a year in advance again. I hated to be out of state for the World Series. It's the only time it ever happened to me. I said, 'It'll never happen again. Even the national championship in football or basketball.'"

After serving two terms as governor and 30 years in public service, Nixon worked as an attorney with the St. Louis firm Dowd Bennett. Nowak's office was in the same building, and in the fall of 2020, the two ran into each other in the lobby on a Friday afternoon. "We laughed about everything again," Nowak said. "I had just picked up my nine-year-old daughter, Clare, from school, and she went with me to the office to pick up a few things. He looked at Clare as we reminisced together and he said, 'You know, Clare, I let your dad play hooky in China.' I laughed out loud. I told him, 'Do you have any idea how many times I have sung your praises over the last nine years that you let us do that?' When we left, Clare asked me, 'What does hooky mean?'"

CHAPTER 2

CAJUN ROOTS

When the boisterous Boudreaux D. Nutria finally decided to settle down, it was news in New Orleans. He'd been an indubitable staple of the city's sports scene and social swirl, constantly surrounded by admirers. He was quite the character. So in 1998 Boudreaux's wedding was the event of the summer. He married Clotile Picou, a Southern charmer. And the matrimony naturally made the pages of *The Times-Picayune*. Harry Lee, the renowned Jefferson Parish Sheriff himself, officiated the ceremony, proclaiming Clotile and Boudreaux Nutria's nuptials by "the power vested in me by the Louisiana Department of Wildlife and Fisheries."

Boudreaux was the beloved mascot of the minor league baseball team in New Orleans. With his brown furry body, puffy cheeks, and two long, orange front teeth, he was a lovable 7' tall nutria. The Triple A franchise hosted the faux wedding on August 16, 1998, and the buildup was so silly and clever that it became the talk of the town. The team, the New Orleans Zephyrs, set a then-record for attendance that night. There were 11,012 on hand to watch the pregame ceremony at home plate. Created by the team to be Boudreaux's belle, the mascot Clotile wore a white gown with a veil; Boudreaux was draped in a black tuxedo with a cane and top hat.

Called up to the New Orleans club that very month was Lance Berkman, the young slugging prospect for the Houston Astros, the Zephyrs' parent club in the major leagues. That next spring Berkman was back with New Orleans in Triple A. But he underwent minor meniscus surgery. "After two weeks I was ready to play, but because I was a young player, they wanted to be extra cautious," he said. "So they made me basically stay on the DL about a couple of weeks longer than I wanted to. So I was going kind of stir crazy."

During the school year, the Zephyrs occasionally held 11:00 AM games and coordinated it so that busloads of boys and girls could come to the ballgame. "And so Boudreaux was there," Berkman said of a particular spring game, "but for whatever reason, Clotile was not there that day. Her costume was just sitting there under the bleachers. So I said, 'You know what, I'm going to put this sucker on.' So I put it on and paraded around the stands and messed around with the kids. Tony Pena was our manager. And nobody knew it was me, but I guess I have a distinctive way of walking because one of the one of the players was like, 'Hey, that's Berkman!' And then when word got around to Tony, he was not happy. So he told me in no uncertain terms to get out of that costume. I was actually on top of our dugout. I was bouncing around, and he stuck his head over the rail and told me to get down!"

Berkman's spontaneous antics as a nutria captured the big personality of "Big Puma." Not all ballplayers are bred this way. Berkman was just this likable loon who was comfortable in his own skin. He was comedian-quick, though not actually quick, one of the only baseball traits he lacked.

And in that 1999 season, he made his major league debut with Houston, christening a decade-plus of dominance in orange. Although the perennial All-Star was an equal-opportunity tormentor, he sure hit the heck out of Cardinals' pitching. As it was, he played 154 games in his career against St. Louis, so essentially a full season's worth. And Berkman hit .313 with a .415 on-base percentage and a .601 slugging percentage boosted by his 39 homers. So, yeah, for his career against the division-rival Cardinals, he basically put up an MVP-type season.

But Berkman was beleaguered in 2010. That nagging knee got to him again. He finished with career lows in basically any relevant stat category. Traded at the deadline to the New York Yankees, he performed even worse than he had with the Astros that year. He was 34 and unsure.

But there had to be some Lance Berkman still left inside of Lance Berkman. So the Cardinals offered him a one-year deal for $8 million. "So many great series battles with them," Berkman said, "and having seen the way that the Cardinal organization [operates] from across the field, I had a great deal of respect for Tony and for the players that were there like Adam Wainwright, Chris Carpenter, Yadier Molina, Skip Schumaker, and, of course, Matt Holliday. They just had a great group of guys, and I kind of wanted to see what it was like from that side of things. And everybody that I've ever talked to, who had played in St. Louis, said, 'Man, if you ever get a chance, you got to play there because it's the best.'"

General manager John Mozeliak knew that not only did his club need an upgrade but so did his clubhouse. The 2010 Cards went 86–76 and just didn't have the right makeup, so Mozeliak went out to get new ingredients for the gumbo he was cooking. He nabbed the Baton Rouge-bred Ryan Theriot and got rid of the loud personality that was Brendan Ryan. He signed well-liked veterans Nick Punto and Gerald Laird. And after acquiring Jake Westbrook in a 2010 trade, Mozeliak signed the popular Georgian to a two-year deal in the offseason.

All of these guys were between 31 and 34. All had winning personalities, to which guys just gravitated. None had won a World Series. So they were sure hungry to win one before their careers were done—especially Berkman, who had tasted the World Series in Houston's 2005 loss to the Chicago White Sox. "Lance Berkman was a culture changer," Schumaker said. "I remember meeting him on one of the Cardinal Caravans in the winter and I'm thinking right away that he was going to change the dynamic in our clubhouse. The year before, we had some interesting personalities who were traded away."

Ask a casual sports fan—the one who might not know the difference between Holliday and Halladay—about the franchise of the St. Louis Cardinals and you'll get a similar response: "Aren't they in the playoffs, like, every year?"

And while the 21st century Cardinals were in the playoffs, like, most every year—from 2000 to 2020, they made the playoffs 14 times—consider this about the club entering the 2011 season. The last time they won a playoff round—or for that matter a playoff game— was when they won the 2006 World Series. And they only made the playoffs once in that span: 2009 when they were swept by the Los Angeles Dodgers. That was the division series when the potential 27th out of Game 2 literally bounced off Holliday in left field. "And in 2010 we didn't make the playoffs," Holliday said. "So coming into 2011, we signed Lance and we'd made some additions, and there was this expectation that we were loaded and ready to go…One of the draws to playing for the Cardinals is the commitment to winning. Call it what you want. 'The Cardinal Way,' people like to pooh-pooh that or whatever. But call it history, an expectation for excellence—whether that comes from fans or the organization. It's just that commitment to winning and that you're going to make it to the playoffs and that you're going to compete for the World Series. I think it was something that I expected and was excited to be a part of."

Despite a palate sharpened from a Louisiana upbringing, Theriot couldn't identify the secret sauce. By this point he'd been part of the Chicago Cubs for a half-decade, privately fascinated by the rivals, much like Houston's Berkman had been. "I had admired St. Louis from afar for a long time. So playing against those guys, you always wanted to know what the secret sauce was," Theriot said. "What is it that's making these guys so good? I get it: Albert is the best player on the planet. But there's plenty of good players in the big leagues, you know? It just always seemed like St. Louis had an edge, no matter who they were playing. When I started that season, truthfully, I wanted to figure out what it was. What is it about this place that breeds so much success?"

Theriot was a spitfire, scrappy ballplayer, the kind that St. Louis disproportionately adored, except for he was playing this brand of baseball against St. Louis. Heading into 2010 the Louisiana State University legend was hoping for a long-term deal with the Cubs. That not only didn't come to fruition, but he also lost his arbitration case. So he made less salary than he thought he deserved. Then, in July of 2010, Chicago shipped Theriot to the Dodgers. He wore this new blue for 54 games. And in the offseason, St. Louis' Mozeliak scooped up the Dodgers' Theriot in exchange for pitcher Blake Hawksworth. Theriot promptly told the sportswriters that he was on the right side of the rivalry and spouted off to St. Louis radio about how the Cubs didn't prioritize winning a championship. Hell hath no fury like a Louisianan scorned.

The Chicago players were told of Theriot's comments and barked back. "There's probably a decent chance he's going to feel how hard the dirt is around the home-plate batters' box at least once, maybe once an at-bat," Cubs catcher Koyie Hill told the *Chicago Tribune*, a quote that has some a decade later trying to remember just who the heck was Koyie Hill. "I don't know how long it's going to take. I want to get an apology out of him."

As it was the Cubs didn't hit Theriot with a pitch in 2011, but Theriot sure hit Cubs pitching. He batted .325 with seven doubles and 10 RBIs against those guys.

Starting in spring training of 2011, Theriot became rejuvenated in Jupiter, Florida. He had infiltrated the St. Louis Cardinals. His gumption fit right into the gumbo. "Man, from the beginning, it was different," he said. "From the first day of spring training you could tell something was different…it was just a different feel. It wasn't like, 'Man, I hope we have a good year this year.' We were wondering whether or not we were going to win the World Series. It was never a question of making the playoffs or any of that stuff. It was almost like we were preparing ourselves to play in October in February. It was the first time I'd ever felt that. There was a sense of urgency about the spring training. It's so hard to explain, but when your superstar catcher—maybe the greatest catcher to ever put the gear on in the history of our game—is the first guy at practice every morning and the last guy to leave, you know at that moment that there's something different about this place."

Theriot was one of those ballplayers just bred to be a winner. He had this unmistakable and unshakable confidence you see in guys who come out of LSU. And in his first two seasons as an everyday player for the Cubs in 2007 and 2008, the club won the National League Central. But both times they were bounced in the National League Division Series. Finally, in 2011, he joined a franchise that had a history of winning—but needed guys just like him to get back to prominence.

So, did he figure out what the secret sauce was? "I did," Theriot said in 2020. "It was the guys at the top. Being in the business world now—and I have been for a while—I understand it even more. The success starts at the top dude. It starts with ownership. It starts with a general manager and starts with the manager obviously calling the shots. It spreads down. The way that the training room, physical therapy is handled. The chef. The clubhouse guys. The batboys. All of that stuff, man. I think people discount the importance of all of that put together. The powers that be in St. Louis with the Cardinals, who were making all of those decisions, just pushed all the right buttons for a long time…You've got a tough job as a general manager, and Mo did a great job. He is so underrated when it comes to putting together personalities. I can just say now in my second career and doing the things I do now, it's all about the people and how they communicate with one another and how they're pulling the rope in the same direction and blah blah blah, every cliche I could spit at you, but it's so true. What he did was assemble a group of guys that genuinely cared about one another.

"It was so rare on the professional side. You see it in college all the time. I played at LSU. There's a reason why we kicked everybody's ass. The team loved each other. Skip Bertman recruited personalities and he recruited the character as much as he recruited the talent. And because of that, we won five national championships in eight years and we were the most successful college program going, across all sports. Mo did the same thing. It seemed like in that clubhouse, Nick [Punto] and G-money [Laird] and all the guys, we really liked hanging out with each other. It's rare, bro. I played for a while. You just don't see that a whole lot. With what I do now with Traction Sports Performance, I see it at the youth standpoint, the high school standpoint, and the college standpoint. But one of my main messages is something I realized in St. Louis. It's that you have to genuinely care about your teammates more than you care about your own success. And once you can get that accomplished, the team can't be beat. We saw it in the playoff run. It was impossible to beat us. You couldn't because everybody was pulling the rope in the same direction."

In addition to the roster additions, there was this good vibe surrounding the Cards in the winter of 2010–11. The legendary Stan Musial, who had won seemingly everything in his life, won something new: the presidential medal of freedom. The Man was honored at the White House.

And the 2011 season was the year the Cardinals broadcasts returned to KMOX Radio 1120 AM. Since the 1920s the Cardinals games had been broadcast over the 50,000-watt station. Generations of fans fell for the Cardinals, while generations of little ones fell asleep to the lullaby broadcasts of Jack Buck. KMOX's reach touched people in the surrounding states, growing Cardinals fans on farms and in small towns dotted all over the midwest map like a spray chart.

There was just something fitting, something right, about the Cardinals games aired on KMOX. But beginning in 2006, the business of baseball disrupted even the most halcyon aspect of fandom: the club bought 50 percent of the radio station KTRS and moved the broadcasts down the dial. But KTRS couldn't reach all of Cardinal Country. For as much that's made about "Cardinal Nation," the figurative location of red-blooded Redbird fans all over America, Cardinal Country was an actual place—St. Louis' outstretched reach into regions of Illinois and Iowa and Indiana, as well as Kentucky, Kansas, and Arkansas. This was before MLB's online broadcasts became commonplace. So there was much trepidation from the most traditional of fans. Finally, after diligent efforts by KMOX boss John Sheehan, the Cardinals announced that KMOX once again would be the team's flagship station in 2011. "The Cardinals," KMOX sports director Tom Ackerman said, "were coming home."

Everything seemed to be falling in place that February for the '11 Cardinals. "And then," Holliday said, "you lose your co-ace."

It's interesting to think how this storybook season might've unfolded if Wainwright didn't need Tommy John surgery. If he pitched for the 2011 Cardinals, he probably would've won 20 games, maybe even the Cy Young. The Cards might've locked up the wild-card in mid-September. Heck, maybe even the division title. And they might've won the World Series still, which would've been super exciting, but there wouldn't have been the epic September comeback. And there probably wouldn't have been a Game 6. So not much storybook stuff. Or come to think of it, maybe not even book stuff. But here we are instead, on these very pages, reading the story of the amazing 2011 Cardinals in part because Wainwright missed a year in his prime.

Beginning with, well, Tommy John himself, numerous great pitchers had lost a year to Tommy John. But a case can be made that few, if any, were as good as Wainwright when he was injured. It's as simple as this: in 2009 Wainwright finished third in the Cy Young voting and in 2010 he finished second. Oh, and after missing 2011 and rediscovering his stuff in 2012, he finished second again in the Cy Young voting in 2013. And third in 2014. "I remember it being a real difficult story [to report] because you feel for Wainwright," Ackerman said. "And there are then serious questions over how the Cardinals would be able to recover from that. You really felt for him. He's such a great, positive force. A leader. I felt like the Cardinals had enough to be able to compete. But you wondered how they were going to do this without a great pitcher like Wainwright. Now, the Cardinals are supposed to be built to withstand hits to their roster and bounce back. But it's Adam Wainwright."

And as the season began, it turned out the Cardinals' pitching issues weren't only with the rotation. The 2011 season began at home, a sun-splashed Thursday afternoon at Busch Stadium. Carpenter started the first game of 2011 for the Cardinals—he would also start the last game of 2011—and pitched with precision against the San Diego Padres, allowing just two runs and two hits in seven innings. Holliday broke a 2–2 tie with a homer in the eighth inning. The fans in the stands happily watched, and the fans in their homes and cars listened on KMOX, as Ryan Franklin pitched the ninth for the save. But Franklin blew the save. Cameron Maybin uncorked a pitch over the center-field wall and onto that green batter's eye lawn, the first homer to land out there in the year 2011—but of course not the last. The Cards lost.

Franklin proceeded to blow three more saves before losing the cherished job as Cardinals closer. Since 1981 when Bruce Sutter first put on that baby blue V-neck, the Cards have almost annually employed a reliable closer. Todd Worrell, Lee Smith, Tom Henke, Dennis Eckersley, Dave Veres, Jason Isringhausen, and Franklin each were All-Stars except for Veres. But Franklin's demise in early 2011 was a hard-luck harbinger for what was to come—a year in which the Cardinals had eight different guys pick up saves along the way.

Game 6 Story No. 2

In St. Louis a red No. 6 references reverence for Stan Musial, the legendary man who wore that uniform number. No Cardinal ever wore it after he did, though to this day, thousands of Cardinals fans wear red 6s on jerseys and T-Shirts. But one Cardinals fan wears a scarlet 6.

Tim Baker wears the Scarlet Number figuratively in reference to the heinous and humiliating decision that haunts him. He's the guy who left Game 6 early. "To this day for most of Cardinal Nation, it's the David Freese game," said Baker's close friend, Jake Lampert. "For us it's the Tim Baker game."

Lampert and Baker grew up one house apart in suburban St. Louis. They went to preschool together, then Old Bonhomme Elementary, then Ladue Junior High, Ladue High, and the University of Missouri. "Plus," Lampert said, "our grandmas—my mom's mom and Timmy's dad's mom—were sisters. So whatever cousins that makes us, that's what we are. His dad and my mom are first cousins."

And on the night of October 27, 2011, Lampert and Baker joined six other friends in the Busch Stadium bleachers for Game 6 of the World Series. "We were sitting in 501, row 9, seats 5–12," Lampert said in the manner someone would say their children's birthdays.

For Lampert, a schoolteacher like Baker, the past couple months had been the craziest of his life even if the Cardinals had stayed 10½ out all September. Jake and Heather Lampert had their first child, Naomi, on October 13. "Heather and I had loaded up at the end of the season. We'd gone to the last six regular-season games," said Jake, who was 34 in October of 2011. "We went to the two games against the Phillies. Then we had the baby over the NLCS. My daughter's second night at home, she's laying on my belly watching the Cardinals win the pennant with me. Now, I did get into a lot of trouble going to Game 6 of the World Series. Heather developed mastitis, which is a breast infection related to breastfeeding. And whether I really didn't understand or I didn't want to understand, she went by herself with our newborn to the doctor that afternoon, while I went down to Mike Shannon's before the game. It did not go over very well. It took about five or six years for her to finally want to talk about Game 6, which is weird because that's all I ever want to talk about. She finally did forgive me. And I did bring Heather to Game 7 the next night, although we—and I put 'we' in quotes—decided to go home right after the game instead of partying like in 2006."

Baker, 35, was also a pretty new dad. His son, Louie, was 14 months old. But this was the World Series, so he drove downtown to Busch, parked in a nearby garage, and joined his bundled buddies in the bleachers. In the top of the seventh, with the score 4–4, Adrian Beltre hit a solo homer. The next batter, Nelson Cruz, hit a solo homer. And then, Ian Kinsler—of all Texas Rangers, the guy who played ball at their alma mater of Missouri—singled in a seventh run in the seventh. Now, admittedly, Tim was a snakebitten soul. Being a lifelong Missouri sports fan will do that to a man. The Mizzou Tigers had lost huge games over the years in historically bizarre ways, such as a touchdown pass kicked from one opposing player to another in the end zone…or on a 4.8-second full-court drive and layup in the NCAA Tournament…and, inexplicably, on a touchdown scored on fifth down. More recently, Tim himself made the two-hour drive for the 2009 Nebraska-Missouri game. The stadium lights went out before kickoff. Then during the game, a huge rainstorm swept through mid-Missouri. The Tigers lost the game, their quarterback got hurt, and a slowly drying Tim didn't get home until 3:30 AM.

Clearly, Tim was not the only Mizzou fan who was also a Cardinals fan. But this part of his identity played into the Game 6 decision that will live in infamy. "My dad would always turn off a Cardinal game or a Mizzou game or a Rams game," Tim recalled of his father, Lary, a popular history teacher at St. Louis' Clayton High. "He'd say, 'Oh, they're going to lose it, they blew it.' That same genetic quality that my dad had is something that circulates through my DNA. So it was a combination of thinking like him in the eighth inning and the fact that I was a man who at that point was craving sleep. Our son was our first born. And right out of the womb, sleep was hard for him. So I was thinking I would rather get a good night's sleep and wake up relatively speaking in a better mood after the Cardinals lost—rather than staying out late until the game was over, where I'd get no sleep and just be crabby the next day. And I was standing by Rangers fans, too, who kept letting me have it…All I could think about was sitting on Highway 40 [in postgame traffic]."

In the bottom of the eighth, Allen Craig hit a solo homer for St. Louis. But the Cards stranded the bases loaded. "I think I'm going to hit the road, guys," Tim said.

Tim left Game 6 of the 2011 World Series after the eighth inning. "I own it," he said. "I own that I made a mistake."

As Cruz led off the ninth with a groundout, Tim walked toward his car. "I was trying to figure out how to get out of this parking garage and onto the highway, which was a nightmare…The signage was terrible. It's pitch black. And you're literally right below the highway and trying to figure out how to get onto it."

The visitors didn't score, but they led 7–5 entering the bottom of the ninth. The Rangers were three outs from winning their first ever championship. With one out Albert Pujols doubled. In the bleachers Jake told a friend that was likely the last time they'd ever see Pujols in Cardinals red. Lance Berkman walked. Craig struck out. "The season on any pitch could be over," Jake recalled of the David Freese at-bat. "I had my flask of rum. I remember with two strikes, Evan Glass looks at me and says, 'You might as well finish it off.' And I did. The pitch comes in. But the angle from where we were seated, when the ball comes off Freese's bat, you couldn't see into the right-field corner. You couldn't see where the ball was going. So it's one of those things where you are kind of jockeying and craning your neck to get a look."

Cruz extended his arm…and the ball sailed over it. "There are only a few times where I can remember being in a stadium or an arena," Jake said, "where the place is shaking up and down. And people were just willing Berkman around the bases."

Pujols scored. Berkman scored. 7–7. "It's like a 30-minute ride home, and I had the game on," Tim said. "And pretty much every step of the way, I was thinking maybe I need to turn around and go back to the game. Then I thought I just needed to keep going west. I was feeling a bit superstitious—as if it must have been because of my departure."

And then Josh Hamilton hit a two-run homer in the top of the 10th. But the Cards cobbled together two runs in the bottom of the 10th, including another hit with two outs and two strikes—this time by Berkman. "I was just smiling," Jake said. "All you could do was laugh. At that point you're just thinking this is amazing. It's absurd. The top of the 11th, I remember Jake Westbrook coming out of the bullpen. Everyone was kind of laughing. This is what we've come to?"

Freese led off the bottom of the 11th. "I remember the ball coming toward us," Jake said. "And there's that moment that you realize it's going over the wall. Hamilton looks up at us, looks down, and just starts jogging back. After that it was pandemonium. People, who you know from your life who aren't even baseball fans, they're calling and texting me. And nobody wanted to leave the place. I remember seeing the 'We will see you tomorrow night' on the board. We obviously didn't know that that was the call. And after everyone was sick of yelling and screaming as much as they could, we went to Shannon's. The guy who ended up getting the home-run ball, he and his buddy had been a row in front of us and a little closer to the aisle. I bet they were row 8, seats 3 and 4. We were that close to the ball."

On the phone in the summer of 2020, Tim then revealed a painful addendum to his story. "I was on the very end of our group of seats," he said. "I probably would have been the closest one. Had I been there, I might have had a chance at getting it."

If Tim hadn't left Game 6 early, he might've been the guy who got the Freese home run ball. "Timmy," Jake said, "was not allowed back for Game 7."

"I've gotten hell from everybody," Tim said. "I think my own wife even piled on. I had a hard time showing my face for a while… Over the years I know I told some people I was at Game 6. But by and large, unless somebody said it on my behalf, I really have kept it close to the vest. It's one of those things like a middle school photo. The fewer people that see it, the better."

CHAPTER 3

ALBERT'S LAST RIDE

Albert Pujols' 40th birthday cake was as big as Daniel Descalso. "It was just under 6' tall," Mike Elder said. "It probably weighed 200 pounds, probably a bit more."

The cake was larger than life—or, if anything, as large as a life—and Elder was the baker who made it. Baker probably undersells what Elder does for a living. He's a cake artist, a confection craftsman, who is flown all over the continent to design a cake that looks so amazing that you don't want to touch it, let alone eat it. Elder has made cakes for George Lucas, Paul Rudd, Dale Earnhardt Jr., Danica Patrick. He even made the birthday cake for the famous and famously judgy chef Gordon Ramsay. "It was a British flag with a huge beef Wellington with an enormous knife coming down into the top of it. It was pretty rad," Elder said. "He thanked me."

But Pujols? This was a particularly special cake for Elder, who is a huge sports fan and based in Kansas City, where Pujols grew up. Elder even became friends with Pujols' wife, Dee Dee, for whom Elder made a large Wonder Woman birthday cake. For Albert Pujols' 40th birthday on January 16, 2020, Dee Dee pulled off a legendary surprise party for her legendary husband. For three nights she rented out rooms at Montage Los Cabos, which was the Albert Pujols of resorts. This 39-acre span of paradise is on the shore of the Santa Maria Bay in Cabo San Lucas. At the resort you can eat breakfast while watching whales breach, lunch poolside at an infinity pool, and order dinner at Mezcal off the seven-course tasting menu.

And before Pujols began his 20th season in the year 2020, he celebrated turning 40 with family and friends, including Adam Wainwright, Jim Edmonds, and Placido Polanco. And his five children were there, too, including Isabella, who is from one of Dee Dee's previous relationships and has Down syndrome. "The last night, we had this party on the beach and a sit-down dinner," said Joe Mazzola, Pujols' friend from St. Louis. "Then there was a fireworks show. Me and Waino, our jaws were on the ground. Across the bay was a mountain. They projected highlights of Albert on this 20-story mountain. You wouldn't believe how clear and perfect this picture was on a mountain. It was unbelievable."

A larger-than-life legend, seen larger than life.

Dee Dee had also flown Elder down to Cabo for the party. (Imagine trying to go through customs with 120 pounds of Satin Ice fondant.) For three days he worked in a spacious studio to build the birthday cake from scratch. The cake itself was tres leches with a vanilla bean buttercream, but the design was of a piñata—a donkey with thick and frilly horizontal stripes of red, orange, yellow, green, and blue. A cake like this generally goes for about $12,000. Every inch of the cake was detailed just so. The saddle bag on the piñata's side said "AP 40" and inside was an oversized taco, a baseball bat, an Angels hat, and limes and lemons—when Albert was a kid in the Dominican he used limes and lemons to play catch because he couldn't afford a baseball. "To me," Elder said, "the more you learn about a person, the more you can find little things from their history. Things that you know when they see it, you know they're going to understand what it is and why you chose that. It takes a while to put together, but it's worth it."

The original plan was to have the piñata stand on the ground. "But we didn't think that was fun," Elder said. "They decided they wanted it hanging like a real piñata. So then we had to pay another engineering company to come in and build a structure strong enough to hold it. And then it's a matter of me building my part. I used to own a hot rod shop and I've always been a fabricator of mechanical things. So it's really not completely out of line with what I used to do. I went to school for aviation and all this stuff. I just kind of built it really strong and then threw cake on it."

At the site of the party, the piñata cake hung gracefully in the beachside hut. People posed for photos with the edible artwork. "And when it was time to cut the cake, Albert didn't even know what they were talking about," Elder said. "He's asking, 'Where's the cake?' He didn't realize that was the cake. He complimented me so many times and told me, 'Oh my God, that's the most amazing thing I've ever seen!' I think one of the sweetest parts of the night was that he was so gracious and so happy that this party had been done for him. He literally had no idea it was happening. He spent most of the night dancing with his kids and carrying his daughter around. It's so nice to see a family and to see a father. I'm a dad, too. But I've never taken my daughters to the beach in Cabo. But it was really a neat experience. He spent so much time with his family, so much time dancing with his kids, making sure they were having a good time—and man, they did. There was a dance circle. One kid was in the middle and he'd do something cool and then another would. And then at one point, Albert got in there and did some dancing. It was pretty freaking awesome."

It was a celebration suited for a larger-than-life legend and a down-to-earth man, whose time in St. Louis was rivaled only by the legendary "Stan The Man." And someday at Busch Stadium, Pujols' No. 5 will be on display next to Stan Musial's retired No. 6. "Albert's slumps were 1–3 with a walk. That was a bad game for him," Matt Holliday said of Pujols, his teammate on the 2011 World Series champions. "You watch in awe. He continuously came up with big hits in big situations. He put the barrel on the ball. I got traded over there in '09. So 2010 and 2011, time after time you watched him come up big, hit huge home runs. It was almost like you *expected* every at-bat to be something special. You just can't say that about many players in the history of the game."

Pujols played 11 seasons in St. Louis, capping off his 11th with the Cards' 11th World Series title in '11. There are so many different ways to try to explain his St. Louis greatness. Perhaps this puts it in perspective best: in 10 of his 11 seasons with the Cardinals, Pujols finished in the top five of the MVP voting. That's a decade of seasons in the top five. In that 11th year, he finished ninth in the MVP voting. For most hitters in history, one ninth-place finish in the MVP voting would be a career highlight. For Pulojs it was his "worst" season. And in that 2007 campaign, he hit 32 homers with 103 RBIs. He batted .327 with a .429 on-base percentage. He slugged .568 and finished with a .997 OPS. "The stuff he would do, it was kind of a joke, honestly," said Jason Motte, the postseason closer of the 2011 champs. "There was one time we were in Chicago, and he'd been struggling. He's like, 'Fellas, I've been struggling. Don't worry. Today I'm going to hit a couple out.' We're all like okay, sure? Who says that?"

And Pujols actually hit three that day. "Even if the wind is howling out, to be able to say that and then go do it? He had a confidence he put out there," Motte said. "I'm glad I didn't have to face him. I've faced him a couple of times out in spring training out in Arizona. It didn't go well. He may be 2–2 with two homers off me. I'm glad that I got to be on the same team with a guy with that caliber of play. It was just unbelievable. He went out there and, even though he was the best, he still worked his butt off. He always wanted to get better. He always wanted to figure out what he could do to get better. Oh, he won MVP last year? Sweet. This guy is still here early, hitting. He was never satisfied. You know the saying: if you're not getting better, you're getting worse? There's other people around you getting better. So if you're just staying the same, you're actually getting worse. The gap between you and that other guy is getting smaller. He kept fighting, and it was crazy fun to watch. He had that ability to do things that not a lot of people could do."

There's something surely celestial about the fact that Pujols and Holliday, who so often hit back-to-back, were born on back-to-back days. In Stillwater, Oklahoma, Matt Holliday was born on January 15, 1980. Down in the Dominican, Albert Pujols was born on January 16, 1980. Also interesting, if not surreal, was that the greatest hitter of his generation was born the very day perhaps the greatest entertainer of his generation was born. Lin-Manuel Miranda, the man who wrote and starred in *Hamilton*, was also born January 16, 1980. He's won the Tony, the Emmy, the Grammy, and the Pulitzer Prize. He even won best musical for another show he created—*In The Heights*—before his masterpiece *Hamilton*, which is the tale of a resilient immigrant who rose to American fame by working hard and perpetually believing in himself. Sounds like the story of Pujols.

Pujols' grandmother was even named America Pujols.

She had 11 children of her own but helped raise her grandson, too, in an impoverished section of the Dominican Republic. But in the 1990s, America immigrated to her namesake. In 1996, the year Tony La Russa became the manager of the Cardinals, Albert Pujols and his dad moved to the United States, too. First to New York City—it's cool to think about Albert and Lin-Manuel, both 16 and precocious, finding themselves in New York at the very same time they were finding themselves.

And then, Albert came to Missouri. America—his grandmother and his next opportunity—was in Independence.

He reunited with grandma, enrolled in high school, and joined the baseball team. There was just something about his swing. It took him to a Kansas City junior college. Scouts percolated. The first pick of the 1999 Major League Baseball Draft was another Hamilton—a North Carolina kid named Josh. With the 402nd pick, the Cardinals took Pujols. In the 2011 World Series, Pujols would hit third for the Cardinals, and Hamilton would hit third for the Texas Rangers.

In 2000 at age 20, Pujols played the majority of the year in A ball with the Peoria Chiefs. "And then he got called up to Triple A for the playoffs," said Polanco, ultimately a two-time Major League Baseball All-Star who was in his third big league season in 2000 with the Cards. "That's how good this guy was."

In the best-of-five series for the Pacific Coast League championship, the home Memphis Redbirds were up 2–1 on Salt Lake in Game 4. Packed house. Bottom of the 13th. Pujols drilled a pitch to the opposite field for a walk-off, series-winning home run. So the greatest home run in Cardinals' minor league history was hit by Pujols...on a Triple A team for which he would only play three regular-season games. "After that he came to visit us in St. Louis [in 2000] because we were still playing our season," Polanco said. "I remember shaking hands with him. 'Oh, this is the Dominican kid that plays for us.' And I'm thinking this kid must be pretty good.

"So next year, he shows up to spring training. Back then he had to share a room with somebody else because he wasn't on the roster. Well, Albert was married and had a kid, and I remember him talking to the travel secretary. I told Albert, 'Why don't you just tell him you're going to stay on your own and then just stay with me? You don't have to pay me anything. Stay here for spring training and save your money.' That's what we did. He stayed with me for that spring training. I had my wife, but this is Jupiter, which is an hour and a half from Miami where my home is. So my wife would come on the weekends because the kids were in school. And I still had an extra bedroom. It worked out for everybody. They were great company, and I talked to him every afternoon about things to expect on the team and this and that. He was a really good student. We were always doing stuff together, whether it was working out or having breakfast, playing golf in the afternoon when we were off. Albert made that team that year. He won Rookie of the Year, and the rest is history. We've been best friends ever since."

The Roger Dean Stadium program sold to fans at the 2001 spring training games featured photos of all the Cardinals—even the non-roster guys. On page 21 there were baseball card shaped rectangles featuring the players such as No. 77 Kevin Polcovich, No. 76 Luis Saturria, and No. 68 Albert Pujols.

La Russa loves to tell the story of Pujols' 2001 spring training. It was this surreal time—this prospect was so young, with so little experience, and yet was so good. "We tested him so much at spring training once he started going well," La Russa recalled of the prodigious prospect. "Normally, a young player will expose where he's not ready. I would set up a lineup against a certain pitcher, and the coaches would say, 'You're trying to get him to go 0-for-4 so we can send him out.' During that process there was one really wonderful example to make the point. We shared the camp with Montreal, and they had this outstanding pitcher, Javier Vasquez. He was a veteran and had four or five ways to get you out. And I hit Albert fourth. I was thinking: *this guy's going to be a test for Albert, making the ball do tricks.* First time up, sure enough, fastball in, breaking ball away, and he strikes out. I'm thinking—*Yeah, maybe he's not quite ready.* Next time up? Fastball in, slider away, hits a line drive one-hopper off the right-center field wall."

Opposite field. The righty Pujols just had this tree-trunk base that was so stupidly strong that he could drive a ball to right with the power of a lefty slugger. Pujols made the club. He got a hit in his first big league game and then homered in his fourth. "And then," La Russa said, "it was nonstop greatness for 11 years."

Polanco was there for his best friend's rookie season but was traded the next year to the Philadelphia Phillies along with pitchers Mike Timlin and Bud Smith. In return the Cardinals got Scott Rolen, who would join Pujols and Edmonds to make up "MV3," one of the fiercest trios in baseball history. Fresh off winning MVP of the 2006

American League Championship Series, Polanco and the Detroit Tigers faced "MV3" and his old club in the 2006 World Series. He watched as his best friend won his first World Series championship. And Polanco was there in October again in 2011, facing Pujols and the Cardinals in the National League Division Series. Again, Pujols's team ended Polanco's season. "I knew the kid was good but not that good. Pujols has just been amazing," said Polanco, who also won three Gold Gloves in his 16-year career. "His hand-eye coordination and his ability to remember the pitcher's sequences—that's what amazes me the most. He remembers every count where he hits a home run: what game, what inning, what the score was. To me that's another talent. It's amazing to have that type of memory and that alone—with that work ethic and desire—is just scary."

Naturally, Pujols' greatest highlight came in October. Houston. October 17, 2005. National League Championship Series Game 5. A win would send the Astros to their franchise's first World Series. But Chris Carpenter was cruising. He was in his Cy Young season. For six innings the Astros could only piece together a lone run. They were down 2–1. Until the seventh. Future Cardinals hitter and present Cardinals killer Lance Berkman swatted a three-run homer. Houston led 4–2. Closer Brad Lidge tallied two quick outs in the ninth. David Eckstein and Edmonds got on base. "Well, here's Albert Pujols at the plate right now," Mike Shannon said on the KMOX call. "He's 0-for-4. And that doesn't happen very often either. He hit 41 homers during the regular season. Good speed on the bases. Eckstein at second, Edmonds at first. Two on, two out, Houston leads 4–2. Ninth-inning action. The pitch to Albert—swing and a miss! He went after the curve and he was fooled. Albert digs back in. Open stance, deep in the box, bends at the knees. Lidge is ready. With two on and two out, here's the 0-1 pitch… Swing and a long one! There it is, baby! The Cardinals take the lead as Albert Pujols comes through in the pinch, and the Redbirds lead this baby 5–4! What did I tell ya folks? David Eckstein, The Man. This could be a *crushing blow, a crushing blow* to this Houston club! Albert Pujols, you talk about a Most Valuable Player. How is that, baby? Woooo! That thing left the ballpark in a hurry. A three-run home run and the Cardinals lead 5–4!"

Pujols walked toward first base with his bat in his left hand while gazing at his Houston launch. The FOX cameraperson lost track of the ball and jerked the camera, trying to spot the ricochet. In the Astros dugout, Houston's Andy Pettitte mouthed: "Oh my gawsh."

Exit velocity of batted balls has become commonplace in the game, but it wasn't an available measurement in 2005. But an engineer named Greg Rybarczyk parlayed his expertise into sports, licensing his technology to ESPN. His Home Run Tracker analyzes homers in real time as well as numerous famous home runs from yesteryear. Rybarczyk estimated that the exit velocity of the ball off Albert's bat was 116.9 miles per hour. In the entire 2019 season—the whole dang season for every single team—only 11 batted balls had a faster exit velocity than Pujols' on the 2005 Lidge homer.

Yes, yes, it should be pointed out that the Astros won Game 6, thanks to Roy Oswalt, who also was on the mound again against St. Louis in the 2011 NLDS. This time he was throwing for the Phillies. Things would get squirrely that day. Berkman wouldn't return to the World Series again until 2011 with the Cardinals. But the 2005 NLCS won by Houston is forever remembered for Pujols' crushing blow.

Known as "the Mayor," Sean Casey played a dozen years in the bigs and has seen the best sluggers, including Pujols. "He's probably one of the greatest players I've ever seen. For me it's probably him and Barry Bonds," Casey said. "I remember the '04 All-Star Game. Before the game we're in the food room, I'm sitting at a table with Scott Rolen. It was 2004, and Pujols was dominating the league. I remember asking Rolen, 'Why is this guy so good?' He turns to me and says, 'Case, I've never seen him take a pitch off. That guy never takes a pitch off.' It could be 10–0 in the ninth or 2–1 or nobody on in the first inning, he never takes a pitch off. He's always focused. He has a killer instinct of being able to live in the moment and in the present. I look back at Pujols. He just consistently hit the ball so hard. He hits it to right center, left center. He's just in it, man. He's one guy I played against you just knew could always hit a rocket somewhere."

Pujols is a legend in St. Louis, but his legacy is in the Dominican. Calling what he does *charitable efforts* undersells it. He ignites lives. He's there at least once a year, if not more, in the startlingly poor neighborhoods. He and the Pujols Family Foundation have delivered food and clean water and mattresses and hope. They've repaired homes. They've flown down doctors and dentists. Again and again, Pujols comes through. "He's like a God down there," said his friend Mazzola, who has made dozens of Dominican trips with the Pujols Family Foundation over the decades. "I just saw what he did and how he inspired the people. He inspired me so much. This guy is the real deal. And it's not about him patting his chest or saying 'look at me.' It just struck me. The very first trip we took in a selfish way, I'm thinking, *Oh my God, I'm going down there with Albert Pujols. This is going to be really cool and neat.* Once I got there I was wondering, *What was I thinking?* None of it was about Albert. It was about the people he cared about. I was really selfish in what I was thinking. Our relationship, I always told him, 'You're my adopted son.'…Dee Dee, we talk a lot. I call her the 'Modern Day Mother Theresa.' She always laughs. She says, 'Mother Theresa doesn't have hot showers or gets her nails done.' I tell her that's not the point. The point is that you have resources, and you use them to help people."

Thirteen years after it happened, Mazzola still gets choked up talking about it. There was a trip to the Dominican in 2007. Mazzola was a videographer, so he was capturing footage of the service work done by the foundation. On the phone in 2020, Mazzola recalled a story first documented in an *ESPN The Magazine* article by Tim Keown. "What happened was this lady comes running down the street with this package wrapped, and she's screaming," Mazzola said. "It was a baby that had died. The baby died of dehydration. Albert came and prayed with them. Look at what this guy's doing. He's on his knees praying in a hut. I swear, this holy spirit came. My whole life changed from that moment on…Albert is so much beyond baseball. Then the next day, there was a funeral, and the whole village is walking with a casket the size of a shoe box. They're holding it in the air."

Pujols has won a lot of awards in baseball. None mean more to him than the Roberto Clemente Award, an annual recognition of a MLB player, as the league states that: "best represents the game through extraordinary character, community involvement, philanthropy, and positive contributions, both on and off the field."

The Clemente Award was for both his work in the Dominican and in the United States, where Pujols has influenced the lives of so many Americans with Down syndrome. He hosts an annual prom, a buddy walk, and Albert's All-Stars, a basketball extravaganza. "I love everything that the Pujols Family Foundation does, but the basketball game is by far my favorite event of the year," said former Cardinals pitcher Brad Thompson, who won a ring with Pujols in 2006. "The event is a two-hour-long smile." Former Cardinals and Rams players team up with St. Louisans with Down Syndrome for an unforgettable basketball game that occasionally breaks into a dance-off.

• • •

As the Cardinals headed into the 2011 spring training, Albert Pujols' contract status loomed over the club as ominously as Pujols loomed over the rest of the National League. He would play the season at age 31. He just accumulated one of the greatest individual decades in baseball history (shoot, in sports history). But he wanted a contract for massive money to extend over the next decade. Pujols set a deadline for February 15, but when he found out that was the day Stan Musial would get the presidential medal of freedom, he feared any spotlight shifting away from The Man, and the deadline was pushed to February 16.

That week the *St. Louis Post-Dispatch* featured headlines such as "TICK. TICK. TICK." and "TIME'S UP: DEAL OR NO DEAL?" The two sides couldn't come to an agreement. After the 2011 season, the three-time MVP would be a free agent. The new headline read: "NOW WHAT?"

But there were still 162 games for Pujols to wear the birds on the bat. And he would scintillate in his final season in St. Louis. "That stretch that I was on the team with him from 2008 to '11, I got a front-row seat for something I don't know if we'll ever see again," Cardinals pitcher and St. Louis native Kyle McClellan said. "It was at a point where if he came up to bat, you weren't going to the bathroom. It could be a May game against the worst-place team, you wanted to make sure you were there because he was going to do something crazy almost every single at-bat. He knew his swing so well and he knew his body so well. He had it perfected. There's a lot of people at that level who are extremely talented. There's a very short list of people that rise to the occasion when a game is on the line. He was just lurking. He couldn't wait. He could see it develop and he couldn't wait to be the one that came up with the game on the line. Yadier Molina is like that. Go back and find a game that ends with Yadier Molina getting out. If you do, it's a very short list. He always finds a way to pass it to the next guy. Albert, he usually just ended it. He would go up there and say, 'I'm going to hit a home run here,' and you know he was going to do it. He would say these crazy things, and you knew it would happen."

Perhaps the contract stuff loomed under that helmet of his, or perhaps the pain he so often played through was affecting his body, but Albert Pujols didn't start 2011 looking like Albert Pujols. He had just a .758 OPS in March and April. Then, a .752 OPS in May. At one point he went 105 at-bats without a homer. But his teammates carried him for a change. The Cards finished May with a 33–23 record overall.

Not many coaches could truly relate to Pujols the hitter. Sure, many coaches over the years were former ballplayers. But Pujols' existence, Pujols' experiences, were just in a different stratosphere of pressure and prowess. But Mark McGwire could relate. He was 47 that summer of 2011. Once an aging slugger, he was now a middle-aged hitting coach—a hitter's coach. Pujols gravitated to him. And the Cardinals coach was unafraid to share suggestions with the Cardinals' latest first-base slugger. Big Mac pointed out that he was expanding his zone, trying to break out of his slump. He suggested to Pujols to take more pitches, work the count, and earn some walks. That would at least get him on base—and, soon enough, he'd get better pitches at which to thwack. Pujols walked 10 times in March and April and 12 times in May, but by June 17, he already had 10 walks. And, sure enough, his June OPS was a preposterous 1.135.

June 4, 2011 was one of those Saturdays that made St. Louis St. Louis—Chicago Cubs in town, sunny day, cold Busch at Busch, extra innings, and a 12th inning Pujols walk-off. After the celebration at home plate, Pujols spotted McGwire and the two sluggers hugged. The next day he hit a walk-off homer again—this time in the 10th. As he came down the third-base line, Pujols did his memorable celebration with the quick feet, high knees, and pumping arms. "I just vividly remember it," said Cardinals fan Alec Baris, who was 13 during the 2011 season. "It was just Pujols deciding: 'I'm not letting this team lose this game.' Like he had for his whole career, he put the city on his back. That was one of his last, big regular-season moments that I remember him in a Cardinals uniform."

However, 14 days later, Pujols' left hand was fractured on a fluke play. He'd miss the next 14 games. But the Cards stayed afloat in Pujols' absence, and by the All-Star break, St. Louis was tied for first place with the Milwaukee Brewers with each team at 49–43. Actually, 2011 was just one of two St. Louis seasons that Pujols didn't make the National League All-Star team. (2002 was the other.) St. Louis' Lance

Berkman and Matt Holliday started for the National League, while Yadier Molina was a reserve.

From 1997 to 2019, the National League only won *three* All-Star Games. Sure enough, 2011 was one of the three. The American League lost 5–1 in part because Texas Rangers pitcher C.J. Wilson allowed a three-run homer to Milwaukee's Prince Fielder, who won MVP of the game, and the National League won home-field advantage for the 2011 World Series. At the time it was potentially bad news for Wilson's own team since the Rangers led the AL West. And maybe Fielder's team in Milwaukee would benefit from his homer and the World Series home-field advantage. Or would it be another National League team, hosting Games 1 and 2…and also potentially hosting Game 6 and 7 of the 2011 World Series?

Game 6 Story No. 3

She escaped the gleeful grasp of her teammates' dogpile and began to run—through the infield, through the dugout, through the maze of lawn chairs, and into the arms of her father. As she squeezed him and pressed the side of her face into his chest, the enlarged facemask from her softball helmet jutted into her left arm, and she did not care. She held on tight like she never wanted to let go. "It's something I'll never forget," said St. Louis native Dani Wexelman, who at the time was 14 and just crushed a walk-off hit at a national tournament in North Carolina. "He was the one battling cancer but showed up to support me."

Softball was her sport, baseball was their favorite sport, and Larry Wexelman taught his daughter how to play the game and love the game. "He was an absolute saint," Dani said. "He was in Vietnam. He was drafted right out of Mizzou. He was drafted by the Marines and fought. He got sick with cancer in 2000. He was infected with Agent Orange. He was my biggest fan. He passed in 2005. My biggest fan. He would come to my games with compressions on his legs and crutches and sit in the stands and watch me play. My dad is my world. He's the reason I don't complain—my dad did not complain once during his five-year battle. He's the reason that I don't take one second of my life for granted. I try to live for him and make good for him…And I know that he was on my mind a lot that October."

During the Cardinals' 2011 postseason, Dani was 22 at Mizzou. She studied journalism with hopes of becoming a television sports reporter, and each long night in the newsroom was one caffeine-fueled step closer to making her dream a goal. While still a student, she was credentialed that October for the National League Division Series. So she drove two hours to St. Louis for a story. The Cardinals' third baseman was interesting to her. Just like she was, he was from Wildwood, Missouri. "My favorite thing to tell people is that David Freese went to my rival high school, Lafayette High School," said Dani, a graduate of Eureka High. "And his mom was one of my language arts teachers in middle school. Mrs. Freese had a giant personality, so vivacious. You kind of just wanted to hug her, but also you knew that you were going to learn a lot from her, and you didn't want to disappoint her. At Busch that day, it was pregame, and I was nervously excited. I had to get the interviews myself behind a rope on the field. I'm fresh, doe-eyed, standing there at Busch Stadium, trying to get David Freese over. Can you imagine that? I had no idea what he'd do a few weeks later. I call him over. He's the kindest person. I tell him that I knew his mom, and he gives me a great one-minute interview…I felt unstoppable in that moment."

Looking back, 2011 was the final season of Dani's unbridled, unfettered fandom. Once she left college to become a professional journalist, she stowed away her Cardinals fandom in the attic of her soul. That's hard for some St. Louisans to do. But professionally, it had to be done. In a way that made the 2011 run even that much more special. It was a final season of innocence in Dani's final year of innocence. "I was still able to be in this fan-type stage where I wasn't quite in the real world yet," she recalled. "That team was special. The 2006 team was special, but this 2011 team felt different. Watching them claw their way to that championship series and how everything had unfolded, I bought into the team in a way I never had before…We felt a part of it. And that's probably the last time I felt I would ever use 'we' for the rest of my life."

Mrs. Freese's son emerged in the division series and won the MVP of the championship series. And five games into the World Series, the Cardinals trailed 3–2. On October 27, 2011, Dani and two friends from journalism school went to the bar called Big 12. Well, it's actually called Campus Bar & Grill, but it used to be called Big 12 Bar & Grill back when Mizzou was in the Big 12 Conference. But even after the name change—and even after Mizzou's conference change to the SEC—students continued to call the bar "Big 12" and might do so for eternity. "The night was unexpectedly outstanding," Dani said. "I wanted this more than I wanted anything. It was obviously a long night and a long game. There were some drinks consumed. My memory recalls, and I know these are facts: that they win the game, we get up on tables, and I'm basically throwing beer and spraying beer as if we had just won the World Series. Down to the last strike and you're just barely breathing. You're hanging on pitch by pitch. So to experience that in my lifetime, I'm grateful. I don't think every sports fan can say that they've had a moment like that where you truly are living and dying second by second. We had that. I wouldn't have wanted to be anywhere else for Game 6…Sports can change a life. I believe that a lot of people who were watching that season probably felt something out of body. I think that you feel this surge of happiness. It's just strictly from watching something so magical and so superhuman happen in front of you. I know the reason I appreciate that—and cherish it—is because of my dad."

Dani also remembers the feeling at age eight as she walked toward the field at Babler Elementary. She was confused and uncomfortable. Exactly why did her dad sign her up for a sport she didn't know how to play? But Larry encouraged his daughter and made her feel proud for trying this softball thing. And it was after all a lot like the game the Cardinals played.

She would play the sport for a decade. Her dad coached her team for a few seasons— "the highlight of my softball career," Dani said—and even on days there weren't games or practices, Larry proudly wore the team's teal jersey and his "swishy tearaway pants."

His daughter became a gritty ballplayer, hustling and stealing bases, unafraid to put down a bunt. She cherished her sports talks with dad—whether it was in the postgame car rides or dinners at Culpeppers, where they'd eat hot wings with the house salad. "My dad taught me the most valuable life lessons through the game," she said. "He armed me with the tools to overcome obstacles and adversity through softball—and without us knowing it, preparing me for life without him. I always wanted to rise to the occasion for him. I still do to this day. I can't remember him missing a game. Even when he was diagnosed in 2000—unless he was too sick or in the hospital—my dad would show up. With crutches, with leg compressions, post-chemo, post-radiation, post-surgery, bald, sick, exhausted, he always showed up. Can you imagine that kind of big love? I was the luckiest kid in the world."

And Larry loved Mary. Dani's parents had a beautiful relationship. And Mary was "literally superwoman," Dani explained of the woman who was there for her husband, the woman who was the family's breadwinner and also the woman who made sure dinner was cooked every night. "She made life as normal as possible for me," Dani said, "while hers was often unsteady."

One softball season when Larry felt that Dani wasn't getting a fair shake on her travel team, he wrote the coach a long, impassioned letter. Dani still has a copy of it to this day. It's one of her two prized possessions—along with a photo of her dad as a young boy with Stan Musial.

At Eureka High, Dani's hard work earned her a spot on the varsity team as a freshman. Then-Eureka coach Brad Wallach looked back fondly on those years. "No one has made a bigger impact on my life in such a short amount of time than Larry Wexelman," Wallach said. "At our games I'd see him sitting quietly behind the fence in a lawn chair with his feet and legs wrapped up. After one of the games in her first year on varsity, he managed to get up and walk out onto the field to me. I was wondering what he wanted to talk about. He only wanted to thank me for giving her the opportunity to play, nothing more. It was the truest example of grace under adversity I'd ever experienced. From time to time, we would talk after a game. It was always brief and it was always the same. He only wanted to tell me how grateful he was and to thank me. It always amazed me how selfless he was."

Dani was 16 in the summer of 2005. She struggled with going to the hospital. She wanted to see her father, but she didn't want to see her father that way.

On the 4th of July, Dani's mom brought her to his hospital room. Dani kissed her dad on the forehead. On the 5th, Dani and Larry spoke on the phone. "A call probably spent with me babbling about myself, and my dad just happily listening, like he always did," Dani said. "I know I told him 'I love you' and hung up the phone."

Her father died the next day.

"He's on my mind all the time," Dani said in July of 2020, a week after the 15th anniversary of his death. "I have him as my phone background. I attribute the reason I am the way I am—and who I am—to him. My dad is the reason that I know about sports, the reason I'm outgoing enough to be a sports reporter. I'm curious and love to tell stories. So I thought a lot about him that October of 2011, and getting to come home and tell the story of David Freese, I think he would have been really proud of me."

She returned home again for Game 7 of the World Series. "I knew I had to be back in St. Louis," she said. "There's no way that I can't be. So my friends were going to Paddy O's Bar [next to Busch Stadium]. I got a late start and I remember driving in and I was so nervous I was going to miss the first pitch. I'm driving down the highway as fast and responsibly as I can but probably over the limit. If I get stopped, no one [in Missouri] is going to be mad at me for what I'm driving to go do. So I ran to Paddy O's to get a spot. I sat with my friends, and we watched the game unfold. And the second that they won, we ran to the stadium. The stadium opened their doors to everyone outside. We're running in as fast as we can, we're not making any sense, I can't even think in a coherent thought because I couldn't believe what I had seen. I was so shocked and just rushed over by emotion that I, in my lifetime, was witnessing something so remarkable. I relished and cherished this moment. We're navigating throughout the concourse and decided that we wanted to hop down as far as we could go. We were going to push the limits and squeeze into rows with everyone else. We didn't have tickets and we just squeezed in with people who were welcoming us into their section, so we could watch the ceremony and be a part of the confetti. The air—that was the happiest air that I've ever been a part of…And my dad had this beautiful seat to this moment. He watched me run into that stadium and was celebrating upstairs. I just know that he was there for sure."

While at the stadium that night, Dani also thought about the journalists on the field, documenting history, asking the questions that elicited the most genuine and revealing quotes from the heroes themselves. She wanted to be down there as soon as possible. The next summer, she earned an internship for the Washington Nationals' Double A affiliate in Harrisburg, Pennsylvania. During the coming decade, she worked numerous journalism jobs, covering everything from baseball to rugby. By 2018 Dani was at MLB.com and MLB Network, doing work both behind the camera and in front. "My first national broadcast was the Perfect Game All-American Classic [for high school players]," she said. "In that moment I tried to calm myself, just thinking of my dad and realizing that, *Wow, I'm actually doing this. It's been a really long, hard road at this point with a lot of people who told me I should just stick to producing and not try and do the on-air thing.* My dad taught me that if you tried your best 100 percent, then that was enough. At that time when I got that gig, that was enough.

"We have a lot of fun with that broadcast. We did some in-game interviews. And then I got the postgame interview. I avoided the Gatorade bath. When the day was over, I had no thoughts left in my mind. I had used all the fuel in my brain to get through that game. But I called my mom, and she always tells me Dad is watching over me. It was definitely a special moment. I just did play-by-play a few weeks ago and I thought of him the whole time. It's just something that not a lot of women are doing. I did it for high school baseball, again for Perfect Game. I'm just trying to make the most out of this life and give it my all, knowing it's going to be good enough for him, so it's good enough for me."

CHAPTER 4

CARP AND CARDINALS CHEMISTRY

Late in the game, on a 2011 road trip in Milwaukee, it came down to Skip Schumaker. "My heart," Schumaker revealed, "was racing."

The Cardinals hitter had faced pressurized situations before, but this one was just different. "We called it the credit card game," Schumaker said. "We had team dinners quite often, and everyone would put their credit card in a pile. Someone starts picking them out, and the last card left pays."

That night the guys were at the steakhouse in Milwaukee's famous Pfister Hotel. "Usually our first night into each city, we'd have a pretty good size group come to dinner," Schumaker said. "Everyone was invited, and most guys came. You just don't see that in today's game or with any of the other teams I've been on. You get four or five guys sometimes. But this was everybody, coaches included...And the credit card game comes down to me and Kyle Lohse. Kyle Lohse just signed a $40 million deal, and I just got out of first-year arbitration. I was in complete panic. I'm not sure how to explain this to my wife. We're talking like a $15,000 bill. And thank God, my card got pulled, and Kyle had to pay.

"But that's just the kind of camaraderie we had. You learn the most stuff and decompress over a beer, a dinner, a card game. After games is really when you get to know people and learn to trust them. So when something bad does happen on the field or outside of the field, you're able to have some hard talks with some people. Some of these were just priceless times, and they're a big reason why we came out of the bottom in September and made the run we did…Even if we didn't win, that would have been my favorite team of all time. We had such fun off the field, but we went to war and we trusted each other on the field. We knew that nobody would mess up the most important part of tomorrow, which was our game, with anything. We always had fun whether it was with our families or playing *Mario Kart* or whatever it was. We'd play cards. When guys were with each other, it was never just groups or two or three. It would be big groups. That's what made it so much fun. Whether it was the Latin side [or other corners of a clubhouse], sometimes you get teams that are kind of cliquey. It was a combination of everybody together and it made it so much fun. Adding Octavio Dotel and some other high-character guys even at the deadline just made it where not only do we have lifelong friendships, but it was guys I'd go to war with, so to speak. I wanted to go into war with those dudes more than anyone I ever played with."

John Mozeliak, the bespectacled general manager who dressed with a bespoke style, brilliantly put together a 2011 team that thrived together on and off the field. Executives in every sport talk about chemistry. But regardless of the sport, the same two issues linger. First, sometimes the salary makeup of your club prevents you from acquiring just any player or personality you desire. And second, having superstars is imperative, but sometimes the superstars don't have super personalities. But the 2011 Cardinals were the perfect blend. "There are teams that you're on that you show up and, whether you're winning or losing, you're just not excited to be there," Kyle McClellan said. "There's a lull in the season. That 2011 team had so many personalities, you couldn't wait to get to the field every day. Winning or losing, we had the guys. Nick Punto, Gerald Laird, Ryan Theriot, Skip Schumaker, these were all guys that had roles on that team. Didn't matter whether they were the starting second baseman or shortstop, what they did in the clubhouse kept guys loose and having fun. Then you add the big personalities of a Lance Berkman, of Adam

Wainwright, Chris Carpenter. You couldn't walk by Jake Westbrook without cracking up. It was a team full of characters that was so much fun to be around. That allowed us, even when we were struggling and down, to still come to the field, have fun, want to be there, and try to put a great product on the field. And then we start rolling—then you're really talking about fun. That's a different kind of fun. It just goes to a whole different level. You can't manufacture that or fake it. It's either there or it's not, and that team had it like no other I've ever been on."

Jared Michael Schumaker became a beloved Cardinals figure by playing baseball with scrappiness and happiness. They called him Skip, which meant that his uniform number of 55 resembled his initials. It was a number the club happened to give him in his debut year of 2005, but it also had some personal meaning beyond the initial initials. Growing up in California, he rooted for the Los Angeles Dodgers. As the often-told story goes, a four-year-old Schumaker waited to get autographs from Dodgers players. Some of the guys wouldn't sign, when an unheralded young pitcher spotted the sobbing kid. He told the kid he was on the Dodgers. He posed for a photo and signed the kid's glove: "To Skip—a future big-leaguer."

It was Orel Hershiser, who became Schumaker's favorite player. And when Schumaker was eight in 1988, Hershiser won the Cy Young and the World Series MVP. Hershiser wore No. 55. Sure enough, after the 2012 season, the Cardinals traded Schumaker to the Dodgers. In the 2013 National League Division Series, Hershiser was asked to throw out the first pitch. So he asked for the current No. 55 to be his ceremonial catcher. And Hershiser arrived with a blown-up copy of the picture of himself and four-year-old Schumaker. Hershiser autographed it: "From one big leaguer to another."

As a St. Louis Cardinals player, Schumaker endeared himself to fans with his selflessness. In 2009 La Russa asked the outfielder to help out the club by trying to play second base. Schumaker worked diligently with coach Jose Oquendo and played 133 games at second base for that playoff-bound team (which, sure enough, lost to the Dodgers in the NLDS).

Schumaker was a doppelganger for the actor Freddie Prinze Jr., who starred as baseball player a decade prior in the film *Summer Catch* ("figuratively and literally a minor league movie" per *The New York Times*). Schumaker was 31 in the 2011 season. He played in 117 games for the Cardinals that year, hitting .283. At 5'10", 185 pounds, Schumaker wasn't known for hitting homers, but his power ascended on an important afternoon in June.

It was June 19th at home against the Kansas City Royals, the same day Albert Pujols suffered the scary hand fracture. And then in the top of the ninth, Fernando Salas blew the save, as the lowly Royals from across Interstate 70 tied the game 4–4 with a home run from an unlikely source—Alcides Escobar. But in the bottom of the ninth, the Cardinals won the game on a home run from a similarly unlikely source. On the mound was the Kansas City southpaw Tim Collins, one of the few big leaguers actually smaller than Schumaker. Collins stood 5'7" and twirled a curveball and other tantalizing pitches from a slow, rocking delivery. But he accidentally grooved one to the lefty Schumaker, whose compact swooping swing violently unfurled. Gone. Schumaker had given himself a Father's Day gift. As the Cardinals celebrated at home plate, Dan McLaughlin said on the television broadcast: "There is not a more well-liked guy on this team than No. 55."

Schumaker also provided some levity at one of the lowest times in 2011. On August 23, just before Carpenter's famous speech, the Cardinals trailed the under-.500 Dodgers 11–0. In the ninth inning, La Russa sent Schumaker out there to pitch against his childhood team. First batter? Struck him out. Schumaker walked the next guy. That brought up, of all people, Aaron Miles. While playing for Cardinals in previous years, Miles was generally the second base/emergency pitcher in blowouts. Now he was facing the Cards' second base/emergency pitcher in a blowout. And Miles drilled a Schumaker pitch for a two-run homer. But Schumaker got out of his inning with a fly out and then another strikeout—this one of the Dodgers pitcher Blake Hawksworth, the fellow the Cardinals traded to get 2011 sparkplug Theriot. Two strikeouts in an inning for pitcher Skip Schumaker—that's something a Cards pitcher hadn't done since the first inning that night.

"When you're going through some highs and lows and peaks and valleys, it's important to have some high-end character guys like Lance Berkman, Ryan Theriot, Gerald Laird, Nick Punto," said Schumaker, who, too, was known for his character—and being a character. "Those were some high-end character guys who really changed the dynamic."

Schumaker's wife, Lindsey, actually went to high school with Punto. (They were Mustangs at Trabuco Hills High in Mission Viejo, California.) "He's in my area, still lives in my area," Schumaker said in 2020. "His son is actually in the same class as my daughter. So I've known Nick since 1994. I've known him a very long time. So in 2010 I called Nick and called John Mozeliak and told him that I thought Nick would be a really good fit. I knew he was a good clubhouse guy, obviously a good defensive bench guy. I knew he was coming off an injury-riddled season in Minnesota. I just thought this would be a perfect fit. So I called Nick—I think he was on the ski slopes—I asked him if he would be interested in coming over here. He was obviously very interested and wanted to join this team with some guys he knew—and a team he knew could contend."

Punto was a 21st-round pick and the second most notable player to ever come out of California's Saddleback College (former Cardinals killer Mark Grace played there). Punto was a 5'9" infielder in the majors, making his debut two days before 9/11 and playing his final regular-season game on September 27, 2014. On that day Punto was with the Oakland A's on the road in Texas, playing in the same stadium where he started Games 4 and 5 of his only World Series. In his final at-bat, Punto singled. The pitcher? The Rangers' Neftali Feliz, who allowed the ninth-inning triple to David Freese in Game 6.

Punto played admirably in his lone year in St. Louis; he was sure a good glove guy at second base. He led all 2011 St. Louis second basemen, shortstops, and third basemen with four defensive runs saved per Fangraphs.com. (Pujols led the whole team with 10.) And while Punto only had 166 plate appearances, he made the most of the matchups, hitting .278 with a .388 OBP and .421 slugging percentage (.809 OPS).

And his biggest at-bat and moment of the season came on September 9, 2011—the 10-year anniversary of his Major League Baseball debut. The Cards were in a huge September series. Really, in 2011, all September series were huge, but this one was against the Atlanta Braves, the team leading the wild-card race. Down 3–1 Schumaker led off the ninth with a single off Braves closer Craig Kimbrel. With two outs Kimbrel walked two, including Theriot. Pujols came to the plate. Bases loaded, bottom of the ninth. Two outs, down two. It was an epic matchup—the 2011 National League Rookie of the Year vs. the guy who came in fifth in the NL MVP voting. Kimbrel hadn't allowed a run since June 11. Pujols perfectly placed an inside pitch the opposite way. It swooshed parallel to the first-base line into right field. Two runs scored. "I suffered a bit of hearing loss from the noise," La Russa wrote of that at-bat in *One Last Strike* while describing "the sensation coming up from the bottom of your feet through the cement floor into your head, while the sound waves vibrate and the roar echoes around our cave."

Alas, Theriot was thrown out trying to score. But with the score 3–3, the ballgame went to extras. Bases loaded, bottom of the 10th inning. Punto kept battling. Nine pitch at-bat. And he ripped a line drive to center—deep enough for a game-winning sacrifice fly. "Nick was not only a clubhouse guy," Schumaker said, "but also a gamer—a no-nonsense player who you could trust in the biggest situations."

Punto's teammates mobbed him at first base, as they ripped off his white jersey. They shredded "The Shredder."

For many kids born in the late '70s such as Punto, *Teenage Mutant Ninja Turtles* was an important part of their childhood and not just because it enhanced their knowledge of Italian Renaissance artists. Be it a cartoon, comic books, or movies, the *Teenage Mutant Ninja Turtles* were staples during the late 1980s and early 1990s. The Shredder was the ubiquitous bad guy. Well, Punto thought it would be funny to sneak up on unsuspecting teammates and rip their shirts off—generally by pulling from the collar. He became The Shredder. "Nick didn't just do jerseys," Schumaker said. "You'd walk into the lobby after dinner; he'd just get on a wild hair and rip your $100 shirt."

Punto was 33 in the 2011 season, so early on the veteran would only shred the shirts of the younger players. But as the season went on, "he didn't discriminate," McClellan said. "There were some older veterans who got it. There were many times where people got shredded on bus trips, on plane trips. Some guys' buttoned-down shirts would end up losing all their buttons on the trip. You always had to be careful wherever Punto was at…What we started doing—we got clever—is we got snap shirts. Then he got really mad when he went to get somebody in kind of a Western style shirt that had the snaps all the way down, and it wasn't effective. It was pretty deflating for him."

About two weeks after the September 9 shredding of The Shredder, Punto pulled off an on-field shredding of rookie Adron Chambers, who scored the winning run of a crucial game on a wild pitch. "Walk-off wins are so important for teams because you see that celebration," McClellan said. "They're jumping around, having a good time. That carries over into the locker room after the game. When you bring up Punto and that shredding, it was just a thing where you get in that situation: if we get a walk-off, be looking out for Punto because he's going to do his thing. It kind of took on a name and an animal of itself. That stuff carries over. The next day, you're still talking about it.

When you play 162 games, the monotony of that wears on you. And when you have moments like that throughout the year and excitement and energy, it just brings out a new kind of fresh feel to it. That was a big part of his thing that he created."

Famously, Punto shredded Carpenter after the Game 5 National League Division Series win and David Freese after Game 6 of the World Series. But nearly a decade later, another shredding remains in the minds of the 2011 Cardinals—and it didn't happen after a game. "He wanted to feel the wrath of our bullpen catcher Jeff Murphy," Schumaker recalled. "He was a big, redneck, Nebraska guy. He had forearms that were like 20 inches. Nick wanted to see how strong he was. So one time on the bus, Nick took his belt off and hit him across the neck and just went back to his seat. He wanted to find out how strong Murph was. So Murph walked all the way to the back of the bus calmly. He didn't even react to the belt across his neck. He goes up to Nick and says, 'You want to see The Shredder? Here's The Shredder,' and Murph shredded his jeans. That was one of the most impressive things I've ever seen was Murph shredding Nick's jeans. I'm pretty sure that was in Atlanta. It was that long bus ride at the beginning of a road trip…Nick brought a different dynamic. But he's also one of the best friends you could possibly imagine. He was fun-loving, kept guys light, he was playoff-tested already. It was the perfect fit and just what we needed at that time."

• • •

Back when he wore the purple pinstripes, Matt Holliday occasionally faced Chris Carpenter, which meant he had to face Chris Carpenter's face. "If he left it over the middle of the plate, and you popped it and got frustrated…he would stare at you," recalled Holliday, once a Colorado Rockies star. "He didn't like you to even think that you could've put the barrel on the ball when he pitched it to you…When you face Chris Carpenter, you felt that this guy is one of the best pitchers in the league. He had such an intensity. He was mean."

The meaner the demeanor the better. That's how Carpenter approached pitching, channeling his overbearing forebearer, St. Louis legend Bob Gibson. It's as if attitude was a skill. It helped Gibson dominate the Detroit Tigers in his first start of the 1968 World Series and it helped Carpenter dominate Detroit in his first start of the 2006 World Series.

But being mean means you have the means. A bad pitcher who acts mean is a farce. A good pitcher who is mean is a force. "Carp's a gamer," reliever Jason Motte said. "He reminds me of the movie *Major League*, when Bob Uecker said, 'This guy threw at his own son in a father-son game!' Carp was one of those guys from a pitching standpoint, where I'm pretty sure Carp would throw at his own son at a father-son game, if it meant intimidating someone. He was out there to win. We're not out there just getting participation trophies. So Carp went out there with one thing in mind—I'm going to do everything I can do to win this ballgame. And I think that rubbed off on a lot of us."

Back in 2009 it was Carpenter who impressed his teammates by making an impression on his new teammate. Mark DeRosa had played and played well for the Cubs in 2007 and 2008, and both years Chicago topped St. Louis for the division title. Sure, DeRosa spent 2009 with the Cleveland Indians. But when the Cardinals traded for him in June, DeRosa was, for all intents and purposes, a Cub upon arrival to the clubhouse. "Chris Carpenter met me at the door and was very hesitant to let me come in," DeRosa shared. "He said, 'I need to know your head's right and you're a Cardinal. And you're going to walk in this door as a Cardinal or else you're not allowed in.'"

That was Carp—unabashedly loyal, unwaveringly competitive, unquestionably Gibson-esque. "I played in St. Louis long enough that I had other guys come over like a Lance Berkman, Carlos Beltran, who had played against him for years," said Motte, who spoke about Carp for a little more than three minutes and used the word "compete" or "competitor" nine times. "And once they got there, they're like—'Man, I hated you.' And he's like, 'Good! I'm not there for you to like me.' He was out there to compete."

When the Cardinals got him, though, some wondered if he'd even be the best "Chris Carpenter" that Cards ever had. Cris Carpenter had pitched for St. Louis from 1988 to 1992 and posted a 3.66 ERA. Chris Carpenter arrived in December of 2002 with a high 4.83 ERA in a substantial number of starts (135). Oh, and he was recovering from elbow surgery. Oh, and after he recovered and made some minor league starts in 2003, he injured his shoulder.

So he didn't make his St. Louis debut until 2004, the year he won the National League Comeback Player of the Year (an award Berkman would win for his 2011 campaign for the Cards). Carpenter worked diligently with pitching coach Dave Duncan and logged a 3.46 ERA with a 15–5 record. The next season he won the dang Cy Young Award. He almost pulled off the unprecedented two-fer yet again—this time in the same season. Carp missed most of 2007 and 2008 due to elbow injuries and, ultimately and somberly, Tommy John surgery. But in 2009 (17–4, 2.24), he won the Comeback Player of the Year honors... and came in second in the Cy Young voting to Tim Lincecum.

Besieged by injuries over his career, the 6'6" Carp still completed six full seasons with the Cards. Five times he finished in the NL's top 10 in win-loss percentage, five times in strikeout-to-walk ratio, four times in innings pitched and WHIP, three times in ERA. "When you get the chance to play with him," Holliday said, "you see his work ethic and everything that goes into it—and what a Teddy Bear he is on days he's not pitching. Just really getting to know him, I was so impressed with his leadership. I got over there and [witnessed] all the things that he had taught Adam [Wainwright]—from watching your teammates throw bullpens to starting pitchers staying in the dugout and cheering teammates during games instead of going into the clubhouse and getting snacks or going into the training room and getting their arm exercises in. A lot of teams or guys will use the game to do some of their stuff up in the clubhouse, and Carp, whether he learned that from the guys before him like Darryl Kile or Woody Williams, he held that you're going to be in the dugout, rooting for your teammates the whole game. He held pitchers accountable with their work ethic and thought that everybody should watch everybody throw a bullpen.

"Everybody watched how hard he worked with all of his injuries just to be on the field, what it took for him just in between starts to be able to make those starts and go out there and gut it out. He just demanded respect. Guys felt like if you weren't putting the effort in that he was that you were letting him down. I think that he was the kind of leader and teammate where you just didn't want to let him down. He was a competitor. Him and Adam—we were lucky to have two guys who, while they're different personalities, when it comes time to pitch, they're just absolute gamers. Those were two of my favorite pitchers to ever get to see do their thing."

But by late June, the 2011 season—a season that would define his legacy and solidify his red jacket status—wasn't really going too well for Carp. Entering his June 29 start, Carp was 2–7 with a 4.26 ERA. But that day at Camden Yards, Carpenter pitched a complete game. He just kept battling on the mound for 132 pitches, a pitch count that would make a fan in 2021 wince. On the Fourth of July in 2011, Carpenter made his next start—a day game at Busch Stadium. There was naturally a bunch of red in the ballpark but also white and blue, too. Hot dogs—and this is science—taste better at a ballpark anyways, but then consider the Americana scrumptiousness of a ballpark hotdog *on* the Fourth of July?

The Independence Day broadcast from Fox Sports Midwest was dually aired on the American Forces Network and watched not only by United States military in 175 different countries, but also ships at sea. And Carp pitched his ass off. Against the division-rival Cincinnati Reds, he threw eight shutout innings. In the second inning, Carpenter faced his old teammate Edgar Renteria. "The Barranquilla Baby" was by then in his final year, in which he would turn 35, the same age as Carpenter. With two strikes and two outs, the righty Carp whisked a frisbee in front of the righty-hitting Renteria. The breaking ball was called for strike three.

By the eighth inning, though, neither team had scored. Pitching for Cincinnati was Johnny Cueto. Oh, they hated him. Across the state he'd later became a World Series hero with Kansas City, but in St. Louis, Cueto is eternally loathed for his role in the brawl the season before. Some Cardinals fans are surely getting angry right now just reading about Johnny Cueto. He was the guy in 2010, who was pinned against the backstop during the infamous Reds–Cards brawl. So to break free, he abruptly began kicking his metal cleats into the head of St. Louis catcher Jason LaRue. A face full of soulless sole. Insanity in real time. LaRue had to retire from baseball because of concussion repercussions.

So, yeah, on July 4, 2011, St. Louis was hoping to beat Cueto. But he pitched masterfully, and the game was 0–0 in the bottom of the eighth. The Cardinals' Colby Rasmus, a top prospect who clashed with La Russa and never blossomed, was on third base when Mark Hamilton pinch hit for Carpenter. A former Tulane standout, Hamilton would later in life become a doctor. But he tallied 66 plate appearances for St. Louis in 2010 and 2011.

As Hamilton came to bat, a rainbow appeared behind the Arch.

And Cueto fired an inside fastball to the lefty Hamilton, whose inside-out swing grounded a ball to third. Next to Renteria on the left side of the Cincinnati infield was another Carp teammate from the Cards' glory days—third baseman Scott Rolen. The perennial Gold Glove winner tracked down the grounder, as it spun away from him nearing foul territory. Rolen unleashed an incredible throw—even by

Rolen standards—but Hamilton beat it out, sliding headfirst into first. Rasmus scored. Nick Punto jumped to the top step of the dugout and gleefully smacked the padding on the rail. Carpenter hopped up from his spot on the bench and smiled. Mark Freakin' Hamilton. And in the ninth, Fernando Salas came in for his 15th save for St. Louis. At that point in the season, the Cardinals were 46–40 and in first place, a game ahead of the Milwaukee Brewers.

And Carp was looking like Carp, once again. "He checks all the boxes," La Russa said of his longtime hurler. "A true No. 1 who's going to take the game and want to be out there. And if it isn't good enough, 'I screwed it up, and it wasn't about my teammates.' And if it is good enough, 'It's about my team that got the runs.' He works. And he cheerleads in the dugout. 'Hey you guys bullshittin'? Come on, if you're a pitcher, you'd want us to pay attention, so get your ass on the top step.' And he had a code of ethics about respect...I saw one guy say, 'I'm sorry Mr. Carpenter, I won't do it again.'"

In 2017 the Cardinals Hall of Famers, wearing their red Brooks Brothers jackets, united in a room at Busch Stadium before a game. La Russa was in a conversation, actually speaking about Carpenter's greatness, when Carp must've heard his own name. "He just gave me a dirty look!" La Russa playfully said aloud.

Then La Russa jokingly yelled across the room: "We're talking about you! Don't give me a dirty look!"

"I did?" Carpenter replied. "I think it's just my face."

• • •

Behind the plate for so many Chris Carpenter masterpieces was the best defensive catcher of his generation—and maybe any generation. It was the man Carp, using a football term, called his left tackle and blind-side protector. "I say this," Tony La Russa shared, "with all due respect to guys who are famous and in the Hall of Fame—Fisk and Berra and Bench—there aren't any of them better than No. 4. The way his brain works, the adjustments he makes, the feel he has for what the pitcher and hitter can do, he checks every box in excellence."

Yadier Benjamin Molina, the son of a factory technician who built catchers as a side job, is forever simply Yadi, a St. Louis four-letter luminary a la Pele or Cher (even Carp has to share his nickname with Matt Carpenter). So popular in St. Louis, Yadi could show up in the public library and they'd give him a loud ovation. He began catching for the Cardinals in 2004 at age 21. And by 2020 and nine Gold Gloves later, he was still back there, inspiring the St. Louis Cardinals and St. Louis.

Molina was 38 as the Cards made yet another push to the playoffs, though this 2020 season was different since he had endured COVID-19 and missed some of the already shortened season. In a September game against the Milwaukee Brewers, who just like 2011 were in a race with St. Louis, Milwaukee led by double digits. It was just one of those nights. And then a Ryan Braun swing hit Molina's wrist as Molina tried to catch the pitch. Imagine the pain. But Molina stayed in the game. "He's a Hall of Famer and a guy that has the most physical and mental toughness I've ever managed—and may ever manage," Cardinals skipper Mike Shildt said after the game. "Clearly he was compromised. How he continued to play? I will always marvel at this guy's desire to compete. This is a guy in a 12–2 game at the time, takes a bat to his hand that we're still evaluating [with X-rays], and plays two more innings. You talk about tough? You about being dedicated? You talk about competitive? He's the most competitive, toughest player, and smartest player I may ever manage. My respect level for him is through the roof…Let me capture my words appropriately here: it's what makes him great. And it's hard to capture unless you've been on a field, and I'm not minimizing that. I'm not saying you can't capture it if you haven't been privy to it. But I've been privy to being on the field, and Yadi's a gladiator. He's an absolute gladiator.

"And there's an instinct, a competitive spirit, a will that is almost indescribable unless you experience it on a field. And look we're not doing battle in a sense of a war, and I don't like to use those analogies because we play a game, but the fact of the matter is: the guy is competing. I said, 'Hey man, 'We don't need this. Let's get you off the field.' And that's what makes him so damn special. Regardless of circumstance, he's got the heart of an absolute lion. And that's why he's such a winner, and there's no mistake why this guy's been a part of such a winning franchise for so long. And you talk about value. We talk about WAR [Wins Above Replacment]. You can't quantify a person of that will and in that strong of desire to compete in a win. You can't quantify that in a WAR. He wanted no part in coming out of that game."

Molina once posted on social media that "I train to play 174 games because that's what it takes to be Champion, I'm not tired and the day I feel tired I'll express it myself." The 174 meant 162 regular-season games in addition to winning 11 playoff games...and playing in the All-Star Game. He's the toughest of dudes with a piercing glare, but his most-memorable moments have him grinning that boyish grin—say, flying into the arms of Adam Wainwright and Jason Motte or floating around the bases at Shea Stadium in 2006. And he is fiercely loyal to his club. Just ask Brandon Phillips, Kris Bryant, or even Arizona Diamondbacks manager Torey Lovullo.

The 2011 season was Molina's third as an All-Star—by the end of the decade, he had made nine career Midsummer Classics—and he hit .305 for the eventual world champs. The old line about Molina was he could hit .000 and still be important to the Cards because of his prowess as a defensive catcher. But in 2011 he could've just been an okay defensive catcher and still would've been important because of his hitting. But, of course, he wasn't just okay as a catcher; he was the standard. "Him and Albert both, neither one is a vocal leader. They're not going to stand up and 'rah rah,' but they were guys who led because you knew they put the work in," teammate Kyle McClellan said. "You knew that they were prepared—and you knew that if you didn't give everything you had, you were going to let them down, and that wasn't going to fly. That wasn't going to be acceptable. You know going into a game that Yadi's going to be your catcher, that he's prepared, and that he's watched all the film. He knows the gameplan and you're going to follow his lead. And if you don't execute, you're going to let him down. It gives you that extra motivation. It's like as a kid you don't want to let your parents down. You didn't want to fail Yadi. And when you did, you tucked your tail down and you didn't want to see him the next day because you'd failed him.

"That's just tremendous leadership. He commands that respect because he puts the work in. Albert was the same way. You couldn't outwork those two guys. On top of that, they had tremendous talent. There's plenty of guys who have great talent, and you respect that. But it's a different category of people who have the talent and the work ethic. [Molina] definitely has a big personality. He's a big kid. He knows what it means to have fun when you're playing. Now, you might not see it on the field where he's intense and he might not be showing he's having a lot of fun, but he's a sneaky behind-the-scenes guy. He likes to laugh, he likes to have a good time. But when he's on the field, it's all business."

Molina has tattoos of his Gold Gloves on his left bicep and the trophy given to the World Series winner on his right. He has earned every honor with honorable hard work. A constant over his multiple Cardinals eras has been lowering ERAs. The Molina intangibles are talked about in the St. Louis bullpen and on St. Louis barstools. "He's the best defender I've ever seen," Cardinals Hall of Fame catcher Ted Simmons said. "Complete and total awareness."

Game 6 Story No. 4

It's a 15-hour drive from Albuquerque, New Mexico, to Jackson, Mississippi, so R.L. Nave decided to split his trip into two days. And, of course, there was a ballgame to watch that first night. He did some planning and figured out to avoid paying for a hotel that he could stay with his cousin and her boyfriend in Arlington, Texas.

There are approximately 19,500 cities in the United States of America, and the St. Louis native watched Game 6 at a bar in the home city of the Texas Rangers. "It was right next door to Cowboys Stadium in Arlington and it's packed with Rangers fans," said Nave, who was 33 that night of October 27, 2011. "And they're having a great time because by the time we showed up the game was almost over, and the Rangers were up by two to three runs. But there's no place to sit. These women have a booth and they invited us to sit with them. I said, 'I've got to warn you. I'm a Cardinals fan.' They were fine with it. I think they were feeling good because they're about to win the game. I'm going to be their little mascot right now—like, let's take pity on the poor Cardinals fan. So we sit down and we're talking, and I could see the TV screen over the shoulder of one of the women. There's a double. Interesting. They're not going down without a fight. Then a walk. And so, when Freese gets up to bat and hits the triple, I'm like: 'Oh my fucking God.'"

Back home in St. Louis, Nave was raised in University City, home of Nelly and Tennessee Williams and Dave Garroway and Bradley Beal. Asked about finding the Cardinals as a young boy, he chuckled and explained that in St. Louis: "You're born a Cardinals fan. At some point someone gives you a St. Louis Cardinals onesie, and that's what you are."

He has childhood memories of his mid-1980s Topps cards and he'd keep the Cardinals players in a separate pile away from the riffraff from the other teams. During the 1985 postseason—the one when St. Louis was introduced to Tom Niedenfuer and Don Denkinger—young R.L. would place his Cards cards out in front of him in the TV room. His childhood memories were illuminated with memories of cardboard Cards, televised Cards, and crossing paths with actual, real-life Cards. "I got Ozzie Smith's autograph at fucking Woofie's, the hot dog place in Overland," Nave said. "It was just wild. Ozzie Smith goes to Woofie's for a chili dog, and you can get his autograph as a kid. They didn't seem like apart from us as St. Louisans. Those guys we looked up to, but it was not out of the realm of possibility that you might just see Vince Coleman at the mall…It was just a magical time."

And that 2011 night at the Arlington bar, Nave watched as the underdog Cardinals deeply wounded Texas hearts deep in the heart of Texas. "At this point it's quiet as fuck in the bar. You could hear a pin drop," he said. "I'm also doing this thing where I don't want to seem too excited. One, I'm the only Cardinals fan in there. And two, we're like the only three Black people in this bar. So then everybody is just glued to the screen for the next two innings. I'm just sitting there acting like, *This game sure has gotten good!* And what was once a friendly conversation turned cold. They were giving me the side eye. So by the time Freese hits the home run, I'm standing. Everybody is standing at this point watching the TV. He knocks it into center field, and I'm not wearing Cardinals gear. So nobody really knows that I'm a Cardinals fan. I kept it under control. But I felt those ladies kind of leering at me, and my cousin goes: 'Yeah, we need to get him the fuck out of here.' They grabbed me by the arm and said, 'We have to go.' You never know what's going to happen with drunk sports fans. I've gotten into shouting matches with people in Chicago just for wearing a Cardinals T-shirt in broad daylight. So we weren't taking any chances…We walked out into the parking lot and we were celebrating: 'Yeah! Yeah!'

"We had just watched one of the best playoff baseball games in our lifetime. I could just imagine the similar scene playing out in St. Louis, and it just made me so happy to think about that…It's obviously the best baseball city in the world, right? The Cardinals and Cardinals baseball are the things that unite St. Louis more than anything. We can be divided on politics and race and county vs. the city or north side vs. south side, but everybody just has so much love for the Cardinals—and everybody loves on each other when the Cardinals win."

Nave adores St. Louis because it's home and because it's the home of the Cardinals. But he also appreciates St. Louis the way he does Jackson and Birmingham, Alabama—two other places he's lived the past decade. "St. Louis, it's kind of an underdog city," Nave said. "As a journalist I've always been a bit attracted to underdog places. I lived in Seattle, I lived in Boulder. I was never really interested in any of those places. They weren't scrappy. I like scrappy places. I like places where tension exists in many different ways. Growing up, St. Louis always had this Chicago inferiority complex except when it came to baseball. If you grow up a Cardinals fan, the rest of the country can think the Midwest is just full of backward, toothless, cousin-marrying hicks, but we've always had that baseball tradition to be proud of—no matter where we went in the world. It's cool to have those two sides: being an underdog city in the eyes of a lot of Amercians but to also be known as having this incredible baseball team and rich tradition. Those [are] seemingly diametrically opposing things. And then also when Nelly became a thing, it became a little cooler to be from St. Louis. But the Ferguson stuff…I tell people all the time that I think St. Louis looms large or much larger in the American imagination than people give it credit for."

To get a true understanding of the Cardinals' fanbase—which Nave was raised a part of, as was David Freese—you have to also acknowledge the complicated contradiction that is St. Louis. The city is known for its amazing baseball fanbase, so strong and proud, as Nave described. Yet when the hats are off and the jerseys are off, the fanbase itself is divided by race and racial tension, sometimes subtly, other times conspicuously.

Ferguson was terrible in many ways—a young man was killed, and many businesses were burned and looted in riots—but it also shined a searing spotlight on issues. It led to an awareness of divisiveness. And it inspired tough conversations about those tough issues. Many of these issues—about race, fairness, and economics and about racism, respect, and the police—St. Louis had been sweeping under their Cardinals-themed rug for years. "I was very proud during Ferguson," Nave said of the political activism in 2014 after a white police officer shot and killed an unarmed black teenager. "My grandmother lives in Ferguson and has for about 25 years. And then people all the way in Palestine are holding up Ferguson signs? I guess I didn't think St. Louisans had it in them to come together in such an organized way and to really launch one of the most important civil rights movements in my lifetime. That was just cool, as a St. Louisan, as a journalist. I went back a little bit to write."

In Mississippi, Nave worked for the *Jackson Free Press*, an alternative newsweekly. He drove home that summer of 2014. He wrote a particularly powerful piece with the headline: "If They Gunned Me Down." In the piece Nave shared that his mom worked for a police chief in a nearby municipality. In the summer as a kid, he'd go with his mom to work. The police officers would order lunch from Northland Chop Suey in Ferguson and they'd give young RL a ride in the squad car to pick up the food.

But as Nave grew older, he encountered police in more harrowing ways. He talked about an officer summoning him to a squad car because Nave's shirt matched the color of a fight instigator at a party. "I wasn't scared at the time," he wrote. "But in light of recent events, it occurs to me that one wrong, sudden move could have been the end of me."

And in a piece called "Ferguson: An American Moment," Nave wrote that "the Declaration of Independence, which codified all the grievances of the Founding Fathers against the British empire and provided the foundation for the American Revolution, itself sounds like it could have been penned by St. Louis activists. Just replace all the instances of 'British soldiers' with 'Ferguson Police Department' and be crushed by the weight of what is happening in Ferguson. It is that realization that Ferguson is in that way a uniquely American creation that has us terrified."

After the 2020 police killing of George Floyd in Minneapolis, America became Ferguson. The protests were potent and poignant and in all 50 states. Looking back at Ferguson through the lens of 2020, Nave said, "I was happy about some of the reforms that came out of Ferguson. But this trend started before Ferguson. In some ways the city of St. Louis is as much, if not more, divided now than it has ever been. The state, too. I just feel like people have become more entrenched. Missouri used to be a purple, bellwether state. That said that Missourians were reasonable and open to compromise, and it was more about state over any sort of partisan ideology. Now, I feel like people are pretty entrenched. And Missouri is just a deep red state."

But that red is also a Cardinals red. The influential Cardinals bring so much positivity to St. Louis and the surrounding areas. With heroes both Black and white, the team has inspired generations of fans, some who even learned some little lessons of racial harmony by simply watching a 6–4–3 double play. And even though the Cardinals had been dominant in many seasons, St. Louis was and is, as Nave pointed out, an underdog town. It's yet another reason why the resiliency of the against-all-odds 2011 team resonated with St. Louis citizens. What a fight. What an autumn. Fans of all races were swept up in the magic. "Aside from just family stuff, being a Cardinals fan and going to Cardinals games was probably the biggest part of my childhood," Nave said. "When I tune in to a game, all of those home feelings rush back. Especially in October."

CHAPTER 5

Uniting Joplin

As a boy in Florissant, Missouri, he threw in the yard to his father while pretending to be a Cardinals starting pitcher. In the St. Louis area, it's what kids did. But this kid was the kid who actually pulled it off. And on April 5, 2011, he threw in a different yard to Yadier Molina, while making his first start as a Cardinals pitcher.

Of course, most people remember that David Freese of the 2011 team was from St. Louis, but so was Kyle McClellan, who went to Hazelwood West High School (class of 2002). He threw 141⅔ innings for the 2011 champs. It was a dream come true but also a dream made true. McClellan's mental resilience and pitching brilliance took him from the 25th round of the Major League Baseball draft to the St. Louis Cardinals' starting rotation after 202 appearances as a Cardinals reliever. McClellan came to 2011 spring training around Groundhog Day, expecting to relive *Groundhog Day*. It happened, after all, in 2008, 2009, and 2010. McClellan arrived to Jupiter, Florida, and prepared all camp to be a starting pitcher...only to be then told he'd be a reliever. But each season he was indeed sturdy and stellar out of Tony La Russa's bullpen.

Finally, heading into the 2011 camp, the Cardinals told McClellan just to come to camp as a reliever. "Then after Wainwright's first bullpen session, news comes down that his elbow is hurt," McClellan said. "So they ask me: 'How quick can you get ramped up?' This is the one year where I didn't prep...It didn't take me long though. I was able to get back into that mode. And honestly I always wanted to be a starting pitcher at the major league level. I felt like I was built for that. I was a low-90s, high-80s guy with four pitches, not typically what you see in the back end of the bullpen, although I enjoyed the back end of the bullpen and using what I had to do the job."

He would replace his good friend Adam Wainwright in the Cardinals' rotation. On April 5 McClellan made that first MLB start—a home game, too. McClellan was so excited that he finished his warm-up tosses early. He was ready to get the game going, so the umpire walked toward McClellan and explained they had to wait a couple minutes until the 7:15 start time.

He allowed two runs in the first inning. But none for the next five innings. The game was tied after he finished in the sixth, so he didn't get a decision, but the Cardinals did win 3–2. And while no one could replace Wainwright, a Cy Young contender, McClellan sure pitched like one in his first four games. After his April 22 start, he was 3–0 with a 2.16 ERA.

McClellan struggled in some starts after that. But even by May 29, he was 6–1 with a 3.11 ERA. Then his hip started bothering him. He went on the DL. "And then the first time I came back, I felt my shoulder," McClellan recalled. "So the shoulder became a slow deterioration over time. We were trying to figure out what was going on. I had a start in Washington; it was a struggle for me. It was nothing like the first half of the season. I wasn't as effective as I was. So they made the move to get Edwin Jackson [at the trade deadline] and they put me in the bullpen. At that point I'd been stretched out, so a lot of those wins I got in the bullpen were coming from starters who weren't going deep. Someone would get pulled early, I'd come in for a few innings in the middle of that. I just happened to be in the right place at the right time and got some of those wins. I had said my whole career: 'Wins are for starters.' As a reliever if you're 8–1, it's not like you had a great year. You just happened to pitch in the right roles and the teams scored runs at the right time. Starting pitchers, that's what they're out to do."

Sure enough, McClellan finished with 12 wins and a 12–7 record. Only Kyle Lohse (14–8) and Jaime Garcia (13–7) had more wins than McClellan did. As for the other St. Louis starters, Jake Westbrook finished 12–9, and Chris Carpenter was 11–9. "But to know that if I win 11 games and not 12 that year, we don't get into the postseason?" McClellan said. "You can go back to a hit or an RBI or a run scored or a play in the field or a win. If all of those don't add up just the way they did, we never get that chance to go into the postseason and create the drama that we did. So for me, not being on the playoff roster—I was coming off my shoulder [injury]. At the end of the year, between the innings I took and just the physical side of things, it was not good. So I wasn't able to be on the roster for the NLDS or the World Series. But to look back, I'm able to say I literally left everything on the field that season. I gave the team and the organization and the city everything I had so that we could have this opportunity and I'm thankful we had great people in that place for us to get there. I'm proud of the contribution I had to give us the opportunity to have that great postseason."

He's one of the life lottery winners. Consider how few American kids even make it to the majors—let alone onto the team they rooted for as a child. There were some added pressures. He had to change his phone number a couple times because of all the ticket and appearance requests. "If I was pitching for the Mariners and I blew a game, nobody would know. But if I blew a game in St. Louis, everybody knew, and I would hear about it. So that was kind of the negative," he said. "Everybody was able to see the ups and downs. But I wouldn't trade it. To be able to drive home and sleep in my bed? My parents got to come to every game I pitched at home. My family and my friends. The benefit post-career has been even better, when I think about the things my wife and I do from a charity standpoint. If I would have had a career in Chicago or San Diego, my platform wouldn't have been nearly the same. It's been something that we've tried to use to improve the lives of other people and use our platform for good. Not a selfish use of it. So few get to play here and even fewer win a World Series. It's a very small category that I've been placed in. In the city of St. Louis, the way they treat their athletes, the way they show their appreciation, it's just a cool connection with the city to be associated with that 2011 team. I hope the Cardinals win a World Series this year and they win it again next year, but I don't think that 2011 team is ever going to lose its luster because of the way we won it."

He wears his World Series ring proudly—especially when he's trying to raise money—he said with a chuckle. Upon retirement McClellan devoted his energy to his charitable works in North St. Louis, as well as Haiti. No. 46 for the Cardinals created Brace for IMPACT 46. The organization has helped build hospitals and schools in some of the poorest regions of Haiti. Kyle and Bridget McClellan have made numerous trips there to personally interact and care for the citizens. It's extraordinary work and extraordinarily selfless work. He's a caring soul, and it was on display in the summer of 2011, when McClellan and some other Cardinals visited a Missouri town called Joplin.

• • •

It was almost astounding, the ease at which they blew the lead. Up 7–1 in the fifth inning against a team that had lost eight of its past 12, the Cardinals were tied 7–7 by the seventh. The Kansas City Royals had battled back against numerous Cards relievers—many with the common denominator that by fall they would no longer be Cards relievers. "We were playing in Kansas City. It was extremely humid. You could tell it was just a very active atmosphere," said John Mozeliak, the Cardinals' general manager, of the May 22, 2011, matchup. "And it was more of a slugfest game."

But these Cards, who would become famous for resilience, dabbled in some of it in the extra innings. Yadier Molina already had two singles, a double, and a triple, but his biggest at-bat was his 10th-inning walk. The bases were loaded, and it produced the game-winning run. "There are always moments in a season where you say, 'Huh, it might work,' and that was sort of the first sign of that," Mozeliak said. "You could tell they enjoyed winning that game. And that was a tough game to win. It was an important game in the sense of how I felt like it brought us together…It all of a sudden felt like a team. After that game we flew to San Diego, and it was just a very jovial, fun flight… As we landed though, it was a bit melancholy as we were learning of what happened in Joplin."

In the southwest corner of Missouri, Joplin is a two-and-a-half-hour drive from Kansas City and a four-and-a-half-hour drive from St. Louis. And although it had its share of Royals fans, Joplin was a passionate part of Cardinals Country, which spread across the state and other states. And one of the great Cardinals of all time was from the Joplin area. Ken Boyer, whose No. 14 is retired by St. Louis, won the National League MVP in 1964, the year the Cardinals won the World Series. He grew up just 16 miles from Joplin in Alba. "Joplin is a small town in the sense that there's only about 50,000 residents here or so," said Joplin native Danielle Campbell, "but we are kind of the hub for the surrounding area. So since we are in the four-state area, a lot of trucking comes through here. A lot of small rural communities come to Joplin. For their shopping, for their hospital care, for work, for pretty much anything they may need, they come to Joplin. Our population goes from about 50,000 to around 200,000 during the day."

Campbell loved the Cardinals because her grandpa loved the Cardinals and she loved her grandpa. His name was Tom Smart. "I can remember my grandpa getting out a glove one day and saying, 'Hey, let's go play catch,'" she said. "So we played catch, and he taught me how to throw and he taught me how to hit, and I signed up for Little League. It went from there. So I think it was more of a love for it because of how much my grandpa loved baseball and loved softball. The time spent was we'd go out and play catch, or he'd make me go run drills. We'd practice hitting, too…Oh gosh, I loved the game."

Campbell played softball for the Joplin High Eagles. She was a junior in 2010–11. She also sang in the choir. And on the afternoon of May 22, 2011, when the Cards played at Kansas City, Joplin High School held its graduation ceremony. The choir performed, so Campbell saw her teammate, senior Mikaila Craig, graduate from high school. Mikaila also adored playing softball, and her senior season was particularly fun. Her sister, Leanne, a freshman who made the varsity, was also on the team. But for all the big moments that spring, this was perhaps the biggest.

Following Mikaila's high school graduation, her proud parents threw her a celebration. Twenty-six family members and friends arrived at the Craig home to celebrate Mikaila. "During the party I remember standing in the garage with my dad, watching the storm," Mikaila said. "And then like everybody says happens, the sky turned orange. It sounded like there was a huge train coming right at us. The trees in our front yard started falling over, which is when we decided to go inside. We didn't have a basement or anything, so we had I think nine little kids in the bathroom in the bathtub with pillows over their heads. Everybody else was just in the bathroom and the hallway. It was pretty intense. I remember hearing distinctly everything from outside—all of the debris breaking the windows everywhere and holes through the walls. The half of the house that we were in was not hit by the tornado. But if you cut a line down the middle of the two-story house, the other half of the house, which is where the bedrooms and the garages are, was completely destroyed. Our half was safe, and nobody was hurt or injured. The other half of the house was gone."

Because school was still in session for underclassmen, Campbell had some math homework to do that night. After she got home from the graduation, she logged online, but wouldn't you know, the electricity went out. She joked to her mom and sister, as if she was crestfallen: "Oh man, this sucks, now I can't do my math homework!"

Her mom was making dinner, and her 13-year-old sister was playing with Tinker, their dog. Tinker was a mutt who showed up on their doorstep four years prior. "The power went out, and the tornado sirens went on," Campbell said. "Joplin's sirens went off for high winds. They went off for multiple reasons. It never seemed to be for tornadoes. So we ignored it and just continued doing what we're doing. About that time I heard what they call the train sound. Basically, they say when a tornado is approaching it sounds like a train is coming at you. The wind picked up, and the branches broke around us and I said, 'Mom, I hear that train sound.' And we had a basement, but we couldn't get to it, so my mom said, 'Girls, go to my closet.' Her closet is in the center of the house, which they say: if you don't have a basement, go to the center of the house."

Glass started breaking. And then our house started shaking. We were directly hit by the tornado. The roof was ripped off of our house. Half of our roof caved in. We wound up getting trapped inside the closet. My mom held the door closed. It was just shaking the whole time. There were bricks flying. In that moment it was one of those things where you know you're thinking: *Holy crap, this is it. We're going to die.* We're sitting there, and I was praying to God. My mom did say, 'Girls, we're getting hit by a tornado, I think we need to start praying.' We started praying, and in my head, as we're praying, I'm thinking: *God please protect us. Please make sure everything is okay. Keep us safe.* I'm praying in my head, *God, if someone has to go, my sister is too young. And my sister needs my mom. So let it be me.* It was definitely a very surreal moment for a 17 year old who was about to do math homework just minutes prior."

The Joplin tornado of 2011 was categorized as an EF5—the worst a tornado can be. For 38 minutes the tornado ripped through Joplin with winds exceeding 200 miles per hour. One-hundred and fifty-eight people died. It was the deadliest tornado in the United States since 1947. More than 1,100 were injured. And there was $2.8 billion in damage. "Time kind of stopped," Mikaila said of the graduation party. "We walked outside and realized every single car—there were nine families there, so nine cars in the driveway—was completely totaled. Our neighbors' houses were completely flat on the ground. So then you go into rescue mode. You go out and try to find your neighbors and make sure that they're okay. They had cuts and gashes and were bleeding from all different places. We brought them over to our house and just tried to walk through the neighborhood. We were pulling people out of their storm cellars and walking past dead cows in the middle of the street. We saw signs of restaurants and businesses that we knew were from like 10 miles on the other side of town, but here they are in our neighborhood…I was still in my graduation dress covered in water for several hours. You don't think about being comfortable or everything. Everybody is just soaking wet from the rain and being outside pulling people out. Everybody is covered in mud and blood and dirt and water and all this stuff. You're not thinking about that, right? You're thinking about the neighbor across the street. We knew that they're old and have a lot of issues. Are they okay? Are they safe? Are they alive?"

Meanwhile, Craig's teammate was still trapped in the closet with her mom, sister, and dog. "We couldn't get out. The A-frame of the roof caved in and was against our door," Campbell said. "Our neighbor came over and was yelling for us, and my mom said, 'We're here. We're okay. But we can't get out.' All of a sudden, it was like he was standing on top of our house looking down into the closet, and he said he'd get us out. He completely—by himself with adrenaline—lifted that A-frame off of the closet door so we could open it."

Danielle's mom was able to make a call to Danielle's grandparents to tell them they had survived. In the closet they grabbed what they could. Danielle put on two different shoes. They used a belt as a leash on Tinker. They went to a neighbor's house with a basement. It was chaos down there. At one point Danielle remembered being passed an infant to hold temporarily. Danielle's grandparents—Tom and Linda Smart—lived in a different part of town. They drove as close as they could—about six blocks away—and continued on foot, hoping, praying, to connect with their daughter and her girls. "My grandma talks about how unrecognizable the place was," Danielle said. "My grandma looks over at him and says, 'Tom, that's their house.' He said, 'No way.' She said, 'That's their house. That's their stained glass window. And there's Susan's car smashed under the trees.'...So they came into the house and were yelling our names. Someone told them that we were okay and that we were over at another house in the basement. That's how they were able to find us. They walked up and hugged us. Then, of course, my grandma was crying. We were a mess...I remember walking out on our front porch and just looking around and seeing everything completely flattened...And then as we turned, we weren't too far away from a private Christian school, and the only thing standing was the cross and all of the debris."

The enormous iron cross at St. Mary's was a stunning image amid the wreckage. Four miles away was Craig on Meadow Lane. "We slept at home that night," Craig said. "I remember we had everybody in the living room just sleeping on the floor and couch cushions and blankets and whatever we could. But everybody stayed in the house that night. My dad has several things that he brought down as safety precautions in case anybody were to come into the house. We were trying to keep everyone close that first night."

One of the last nights in the house, it was the first night of the rest of Craig's new life. The tornado affected essentially every aspect of her world. They couldn't rebuild her childhood home because it was too totaled. "I did go back one time by myself just to go back to the house and kind of sit in and realize everything that happened and realize that my home is gone and that I'll never be there again," she said. "It was really, really difficult going back. I think it was a way of keeping looters out of our abandoned house, but my dad had put up a picture of me and my sisters. They were big pictures of us and it said, 'This was their home.' He was trying to play the empathy card to keep people out of there. But, oh man, that was difficult. That was really hard."

What do you do when a city is destroyed? Where do you start?

In the coming days and weeks, Joplin began to put the pieces back together, but so many pieces didn't fit anymore. The damage was overwhelming. Nearly 7,000 homes were destroyed. The high school, churches, and businesses were all piles of memories in the aftermath.

Then the Cardinals came to town to help. David Freese, Adam Wainwright, Kyle McClellan. They wore their gleaming white home jerseys with shorts and tennis shoes. "I'd been watching on the news and just thought, *we're going to go down there and do our thing,*" McClellan recalled. "And when I got back, I was telling my wife about it. She said, 'Yeah, I've been watching on the news,' and I said, 'No, it's so much different. You have to be there to see it to understand what these people are going through, how devastating that tornado was, and how massive it was.' I remember driving down roads and seeing houses that were leveled. And then the next house you go by, you could see clothes hanging up in the closet, but the whole front of the house was pretty much removed by the tornado. I remember going to a park, and we were signing autographs, and a kid came up and said, 'Can you sign my jersey?' And his parents said that was all he had left from the tornado—the Cardinals jersey and the clothes he was wearing…It's hard to explain to somebody that hasn't been there how big that tornado was. So it's just crazy to think about us going down there, bringing a little bit of joy, and taking their minds off of what was happening for just a split-second."

On June 17, 2011, the Cardinals hosted the Royals at Busch. That evening was dedicated to Joplin. Both teams wore the same patch. It had an outline of Missouri, a smaller logo of the Royals and Cardinals and MLB, and the words: TEAMS UNITE FOR JOPLIN. That evening the KMOX and Fox Sports Midwest broadcast doubled as a fundraiser for Joplin. There were broadcast auctions of once-in-a-lifetime Cardinals experiences from pitching lessons with McClellan to dinner with Lou Brock. They raised $100,000 for Joplin.

And for that game, the Cardinals invited two girls from the Joplin High softball team to throw out the first pitch. "Back in Joplin we had gone out and my grandpa and I measured out the distance for the pitch," Campbell said. "I had never thrown a baseball, and a baseball was so different than a softball. He taught me the way to hold the baseball. He was down at the other end catching the ball as we're laughing at how different it moves and how ridiculous my throws were. We practiced multiple times."

Campbell remembered finding her cherished softball glove in the wreckage of her home. She brought it to Busch Stadium that night. Campbell, Craig, and their families were treated with VIP access that night at Busch Stadium. They got a private, behind-the-scenes tour. They met the Cardinals players in the clubhouse. "And Fredbird," Campbell pointed out.

The girls each received a baseball autographed by the eventual World Series champions. And they each got a personalized Cardinals jersey with their last names and uniform numbers from the Joplin High Eagles. They were even interviewed on the broadcast with Dan McLaughlin. "It was because something horrible happened, but the Cardinals day was just a really incredible experience," Craig said.

And, of course, they threw out the first pitch. "We had thrown the pitch, and they were taking us up to one of the boxes," Campbell said. "And my grandpa looked at my mom and said, 'Security is going to have to pull me off this field!'"

Two years later, McClellan was no longer a Cardinals pitcher. He threw seven games in 2013 with, of all teams, the Texas Rangers. His last big league game was in June of that season. "I remember driving back to St. Louis from when I was with the Rangers," McClellan said. "I wanted to purposely go through Joplin and drive down that stretch again. You could still see that path [of the tornado] and you could see that they were rebuilding, but all the trees were pretty much snapped off, and you can clearly see where that tornado had gone. So it was a pretty wild experience. But I was glad I was able to be a part of it and hopefully bring some sort of distraction to what those families were going through."

Game 6 Story No. 5

Twenty-five seconds into the YouTube video, it gets you. Every time. Sometimes, it'll be via a chill shooting through your arms. Other times, tears will climb to the edge of your eyelids and hold on for dear life. But it gets you, somehow, every time you watch the damn thing. The video is called "Some Nights you win the World Series…." It's a compilation of fan videos from Game 6 and Game 7. You'd be surprised with how many people record themselves watching a live sporting event.

So for the first 24 seconds, you see snippets of nervous fans in the ninth inning. Two on, two outs, two strikes. A guy in a red hoodie and black jacket presses his hands together in front of his face, as if he's gently praying. The guy next to him slaps his own thigh five times. Another video shows a guy biting his nails with Halloween decorations on the wall. There are two girls in a college dorm room: one with a hoodie over her head, the other girl on the floor, pleading with a television screen.

The music playing is by the group called fun. It's the song "Some Nights," and it's enrapturing. And then at the 25-second mark, there's this beautiful confluence of moments and emotions. You see a clip of the David Freese at-bat. The ball sails as Nelson Cruz flails, and at that moment in sync, the drumbeat begins and picks up. It's this glorious, rapid beat, something out of Paul Simon's *Graceland* album. The video shows two guys step on top of a coffee table and a fellow jumping up and down—hopping really—as if his feet are creating the drumbeat. As the video continues, you experience the same emotions from fans—before and after—Freese's walk-off homer. And then there's the final out of Game 7 captured in a packed St. Louis sports bar with the camera shaking, bodies bobbing, beer spraying and soaking the masses.

After the Allen Craig catch, the video continues to show clips of celebrating fans, including this one older woman at 1:46 who seems to be doing some sort of dance move. The clips keep changing on the screen with more shrieking and hugging, but the woman returns at 1:58, sliding back and forth this time while chanting: "Yes! Yes! Yes! Yes!" She's back at 2:21, unveiling a hand-twirling, fist pump while screaming. And finally one last time she's on screen at 2:29. She takes a deep breath and then, suddenly, musters all the remaining energy in her body and shouts: "We're No. 1!"

She was delightful and genuine and sweet and silly. Just who was this dancing granny? "That's my mom," said Cari Bruewer Strachan in 2020. "It's Game 6 when Freese hit the walk-off. We won, and she lost her ever-loving mind. She just turned 75 and she's still a nut. She's kind of like June Cleaver with a margarita."

Judy Bruewer raised her St. Louis family in Berkeley but moved to St. Charles, Missouri, in the 1980s. She's a divorcee and lives with Cari's son, who recently returned from the military. All these years later, she relishes being the dancing lady in the famous YouTube video. "I had no idea that doing that dance that one night here in my living room would make such a big commotion," Bruewer said. "It really did, I'll tell you. I've had nothing but rave reviews and people calling me after that. You'd think I'm famous, all these people calling me…It was something so unbelievable that it really is hard to put into words. I guess that's the reason that I just exploded into a dance. I've always loved the Cardinals. When I was a little girl, Mom and Dad used to take me down to Sportsman's Park. So I've been to the original park. Then, as I got older, I went to Busch Stadium and, of course, now I've been to all three. The stories just go on and on. And all the memorabilia that I have? I think what it is: you just want it so bad for the team. You just can't stand it. And then when they do it, oh my gosh, you just explode. Other people let go in other ways, but I had to do the dance."

Bruewer lives life the way others say they want to live life, but then life gets in the way. She is a free spirit who seizes the minute. At the wax museum in Branson, Missouri, she hopped into the bed with the wax Hugh Hefner and promiscuously posed. At a Harley Davidson store in Kentucky, she posed on a bike in a black leather jacket and a bandana. At Busch Stadium she asks fans in opposing jerseys if she can playfully choke them for a photo. One time she got an officer to handcuff her—for a photo opp.

And her masterpiece—besides her supporting role in the "Some Nights you win the World Series...." video—was her fake Busch beer commercial, which she and Cari playfully filmed at a stream in Colorado. With Judy's gray hair and glasses, she looked like she was innocently fishing from upon a large stone in the sunshine. She said: "Oh, I got a big one!" She rocked her body back and forth and pulled her fishing line out of the water. But on the end of her line were three cans of Busch beer connected by the plastic rings for a six pack. "This is the way to go fishin', I tell you!" Judy said to the camera. She popped the top of one can and chugged the beer.

"She doesn't believe in catch and release," Cari deadpanned from behind the camera.

For her day job, Judy was a preschool teacher. "It's funny. The dads would always come back into the room after they dropped off their kids," Judy said. "And they'd be more interested in talking baseball than about what their kids were doing. I had to laugh about that."

She loves the Cardinals so. She has a different Cardinals shirt for every day of the week. Her house is decorated in Cardinals everything. She has so many Cardinals flags on her car that her daughter said it looks like a parade float. When Judy turned 75 during the 2020 pandemic, her friends and family made their own cars into floats for a driving parade in front of Judy's home. "It doesn't matter if it's a regular game that doesn't mean anything or if it's a World Series game," Cari said, "she acts like a damn nut."

At home Judy will watch the game with the TV on and the radio on. Not with the TV sound off though. Both broadcasts will blare. She said she doesn't want to miss a thing. "My younger grandson always calls me and asks if I'm watching the game," Judy said. "I say, 'You bet!' They have to check with me. I love the Cardinals and the games. It's family. It's family-oriented. Anybody can go in and be yourself and enjoy it. And if you're crazy, so what? Everybody else is hooting and hollering. You can just let go."

By 2011 Judy was divorced. And both Cari and Cari's husband, Bob, had battled overwhelming health issues in recent years. "I've had four different cancers now," Cari said. "It's a whole other book. We've really gone through a lot—our family—in the last 15 years."

In the mid 2000s, Bob had been diagnosed with stage 4 colorectal cancer. After several months of treatment and after a frightening surgery, he was told he'd be lucky to live another six months. "By the 2011 World Series, we were celebrating his five-year mark of being cured," Cari said. "I, too, had been battling several cancers throughout the years and had just received my first clean bill of health. Knowing and appreciating how precious and short life is, we were going to partake in the World Series celebrations from tailgates and pep rallies."

Not that the games weren't stressful and intense, but the wins injected them with hope and happiness, which brought them to the night of Game 6, the night Judy danced. For the first of her moves, Judy had her hands out, and each time she squeezed the air, she said: "Whoo! Whoo! Whoo!"

Asked to describe said dance moves, Cari exclaimed: "Oh my, how can I say this without her being mad? We were calling it 'her crazy squirrel dance' because we had the rally squirrel, and she had her hands like the squirrel when she was dancing around."

Judy was indeed wearing a red rally squirrel T-shirt the night of Game 6. She was also wearing her Cardinals socks—but not shoes. "I got so excited. I just took off out the front door," Judy said, "and started running around. People heard me yelling and screaming all around. I was so excited. My daughter said she wished she'd gotten that on video."

The next night they all decided to go downtown. They didn't have tickets. They just wanted to be in the vicinity of Game 7 on the fringe of the fervor. They first spent some time at Mike Shannon's and then, as the final inning neared, went outside Busch Stadium. There was a sea of people, hoping to catch a peek or hear a shriek. "And then after the seventh inning," Cari said, "we broke into the stadium."

Wait, what? "Yeah, some big, tall guy nudged the gate, and it popped open, so he opened the gate, and everybody started running in," Cari explained. "I grabbed my mom because she's older. She's not real fast, but she gets around good."

At first this all sounded a little far-fetched, but sure enough on YouTube, there's a video called: "BREAKING DOWN THE GATE AT BUSCH STADIUM | GAME 7| 2011." "It was so crowded," Judy said. "My whole family, we were out there, and they said, 'Hold on, Mom! We're going to go through!' I thought, *Oh my gosh!* My arm went one way, and my purse went the other. My son yelled and said, 'I've got you. Don't worry.' Somebody grabbed me, and I didn't know who, but I knew I was going through."

Cari and Judy scurried into a bathroom to hide and regroup. There was a beer near a trash can. Cari had Judy take it, so it looked like she'd already been inside the stadium long enough to buy a beer. "So we got to see the last two innings of Game 7," Cari said. "I have a video of her crying, catching confetti in her purse. She was sitting there shouting my name, 'Oh Cari, isn't this wonderful?' She's just crying. It was really wonderful."

All these years later, Judy can still see the confetti in her mind. She said it looked like snowflakes and diamonds in the sky. "After that," Judy said, "I was dancing."

CHAPTER 6

La Russa and the Wild Cards

The confines of the visiting manager's office at Wrigley Field aren't too friendly. It's small and drab and tight in there. But during John Mozeliak's visit with Tony La Russa on August 19, 2011, it may have felt like the walls were actually closing in on him. "He told me," Mo recalled, "that he thought it might be time."

La Russa would retire at season's end. He had only told his family at this point and hadn't even told Dave Duncan. "We talked, quite a bit," Mozeliak recalled of that day, "on sort of the relevance of what was happening. At the time our club [66–59, seven-and-a-half games out of first place] was still directionally not sure where it would end up in terms of the success we ended up having. There was still some frustration. But I think for him, he just wanted me to know, and I appreciated that because it was allowing us to at least start planning… My head was obviously spinning. I went back to the hotel. I had reached out to Bill [DeWitt Jr.] to let him know. I kind of took a deep breath and in earnest started making a list. It was probably 30 or 35 names of potential replacements."

La Russa was born in October and he was born for October. But in August of 2011, he knew he was only guaranteed one more September. But his last regular-season month was maybe his best month. And it earned him one final October with the Cards. "I knew how bad he wanted to win and I wanted to win even more because of that," said Brad Thompson, who pitched for La Russa's 2006 World Series champion Cardinals. "He hated to lose. He hated to lose much more than he liked to win. There is no way around that. You've got to respect that, man. It sounds like it could be a grind through a whole season to have a manager like that. But when you have a manager like that, you tend to win more…I'm still scared of Tony! I'm still scared he's going to pull me out of a game. I never wanted to let Tony down…There's just the reverence around Tony. He's done special things. But when you're around it every day, you see the conviction that he manages with, the care he brings."

When La Russa arrived in St. Louis, he had already lived a lifetime of baseball. And had worn so many labels: bonus baby, bust, lawyer, prodigy, genius, innovator, champion. As a player he petered out in 203 career plate appearances, maddeningly finishing his short career with a career average of .199, a tick under the infamous Mendoza Line. He toiled in the minor leagues all the while growing a major league mind for the game. As the story goes, he retired as a player in '77 and became a minor league manager in '78 (while picking up a law degree on the side). He was promoted to the Chicago White Sox's Triple A dugout in '79. And on August 2, 1979, Tony La Russa became manager of the actual White Sox. He was 35.

It started his legendary managerial career and also led to a fun little trivia question: how many decades did La Russa manage in the big leagues? Since he retired in 2011, the answer was five. But in the fall of 2020, when he shocked baseball and announced he'd return to the Sox at the age of 76 as skipper for 2021, that would make six decades. He won the division with the Sox in 1983, was fired by 1986, and hired in that same season to take over the Oakland A's. With the Bash Brothers and Cy Young winners and seemingly a Rookie of the Year every year, La Russa and the A's won three consecutive pennants from 1988 to 1990—and won it all in 1989.

He left for St. Louis after the 1995 season and from 1996 to 2011 La Russa directed the proud National League franchise back to relevance, back to October, back to glory. In his 16 St. Louis seasons, the Cardinals made the playoffs nine times. He won a pennant in 2004, won a ring in 2006, and, of course, nabbed a second ring in 2011. He became a legend behind those transition lenses. Even in a city with a five-star restaurant called Tony's, "Tony" in St. Louis means La Russa. "I'd run through a brick wall for him," said Lance Berkman, who admitted that when he played for the Houston Astros, La Russa was someone "you just couldn't stand…But when you're on his team, he's totally different. He's nothing like the persona that you think from the other side. He's very personable. He really cares about his players. And the thing that I respect the most about Tony is he'll do whatever he thinks is necessary to win the game that day. In other words, he doesn't manage to save his job. He doesn't appease the fans. He doesn't even manage to appease the players. He's there to win that night's game. And I just love that about him.

"There's a reason that his teams were as successful as they were in multiple organizations. It's because he's got this unique charisma that makes guys want to please him. I have an uncle that's the same way. You can't really explain it. He's a little bit stern, he's a little bit aloof, but for some reason, there's something about the guy—you just want to earn his approval. Because of that he just gets the most out of his players. And one of the toughest things to do at the major league level is to get a bunch of millionaires to buy into playing every single night with an edge."

And La Russa was an innovator—developing bullpen roles that never existed or sometimes batting the pitcher eighth—all while balancing intuition and integers. He was creative, daring even. In the 2011 season, he wedged Allen Craig at second base for eight starts just to maximize the outfielder's bat. And in an important September 1 game against the Milwaukee Brewers, he rested Chris Carpenter, believing the extra day would benefit Carp in the long run. And so, La Russa started Brandon Dickson in his Major League Baseball debut.

Dickson allowed three runs in three-and-one-third innings, but the Cards' bats bailed him out in a 8–4 victory.

Dickson would never start a big league game again. "La Russa is kind of like a mad scientist," said Jason Motte, the young hurler who La Russa used as closer for October of 2011 similar to October of 2006 when La Russa utilized the rookie Adam Wainwright. "I feel like the more I get away playing for him, the more I kind of see some of the other things he was doing...Tony was out there playing a chess match. He was playing this chess match with people, and sometimes they were aware of it and sometimes they weren't. To be able to play for a guy like that—and then to be able to throw the last out in his final game—that's pretty cool. Every time I get to see him, I always give him a hug. And he says, 'You're like the son I never had!' And I say, 'You say that to everybody!' Playing for him I went from someone who was a rookie and really young and not really understanding as much about the game. He had gameplans, he knew matchups. It may not always be what someone else had in mind, but he had his gameplan and stuck with it. And the guy was a Hall of Famer, so he obviously knew what he was doing. It was an honor and a privilege to be able to play for a guy like that."

A personality trait that made La Russa great was his unabashed desire to learn from other leaders. He was wildly confident in his own abilities, but he still soaked up philosophies—whether it was from reading books by Bill Walsh or hanging out at Pebble Beach before the 2011 season with Bill Belichick. He'd quote John Madden, saying that in spring training, you're "starting from zero." Bob Knight visited Busch Stadium during the 2011 season. Fresh off winning the 2011 NBA Finals against LeBron James' first Miami Heat team, Dallas Mavericks coach Rick Carlisle spent time with La Russa both at home and on the road during the early autumn. Carlisle even attended the famous Game 5 in Philly.

A Cardinals infielder in 2011, Ryan Theriot previously battled La Russa's clubs while playing for the Chicago Cubs. "He was prepared for every situation," Theriot said. "His communication skills are off the charts. He didn't deal with everybody the same way. He would talk to certain people one way and other people another. He knew how to push the right buttons. I'll give you an example: we were going into Milwaukee in 2011. I had a ton of success off of Milwaukee in my career and always did well there. We played there a ton in the Central. I get to the yard around noon and I wasn't in the lineup. And so I was pretty pissed because of my numbers off the guy who was pitching. I was hitting like .400. And so I got into Tony's office. He always had an open-door policy. Anybody could go in whenever they wanted to. We all had that type of relationship with him where we didn't feel bad about doing that. I go in and I'm like, 'Skip, what the hell, dude? Here's my numbers in this stadium and off this guy. I see the ball really well off him.' He's got his reading glasses on and he kind of takes them off and he breaks out like five sticky notes that he had scribbled stats on the day before. He goes, 'Well, if it's June 30th or later and the temperature is 75 degrees or higher and barometric pressure is X.' All this crazy crap. He tells me that 'if all of these factors are in play, you hit .130.' 'Really?' He nods his head. He was that prepared with everything.

"I played for some incredible managers, Hall of Famers. If Dusty [Baker] wins one, he's going in the Hall. He may go in anyway. Bruce Bochy is going. Joe Torre is. La Russa. Skip Bertman at LSU was a stud. But Tony gave us a certain calm. He was so prepared therefore we were so prepared. He used to always talk about our edge. What was our edge that day? It would almost make us feel like we had an advantage against the opposing team, when in reality we probably didn't. He would convince us that we did. It was a hell of a year getting to play for him. I think what I loved is that we all genuinely cared about each other and wanted everybody to succeed. That just kind of fed into that narrative. It's not a selfish me, me, me type deal. It's a we type deal. A lot of that comes from Tony. He's the greatest to ever do it. He's the greatest manager to ever write a lineup card."

La Russa was 66 during that 2011 season—he turned 67 on the day of Game 3 of the National League Division Series—and he poured so much energy in each inning and pored over each pitch. He made sure the umpire was being fair and the other team wasn't pitching inside on purpose. In his book *One Last Strike*, La Russa estimated that he watched 750,000 pitches over his career.

In 2011 La Russa infamously endured shingles. His face was engulfed with pain, and his right eye had swollen like a boxer's after 15 rounds. Cards traveling secretary CJ Cherre described the skipper skipping six games as a remarkable admission of brutal pain since La Russa detested missing work. But in a risky but rewarding homage, pitcher Kyle Lohse helped lighten the mood of the club with the skipper gone. On May 12 at Wrigley Field with La Russa away from the team, Lohse actually put on the manager's uniform. Lohse also donned La Russa-like dark glasses and pushed the hair out of the back of his hat just so. He took out the lineup card before the game, tried not to smile, and his teammates gave him a standing ovation when he returned to the dugout.

La Russa returned renewed. The Cards continued to win and went to the All-Star break tied for first place. But in July it finally became clear to him—this would be his last season with St. Louis. He didn't want the team or the public to know. He told his wife, Elaine. He told ownership. He told Mozeliak. And, of course, he finally told Dunc. David Edwin Duncan was Don Tony's consigliere. His former teammate and forever pitching coach, Duncan was "directly responsible for hundreds of wins if you look at my record," La Russa beamed.

Signed one year apart, they were roommates and teammates in the Kansas City A's organization in the 1960s. "When we were all 18; he was 28," La Russa said of Duncan's wisdom.

And in 1983 his old buddy came back in his baseball life for the '83 season because the Seattle Mariners wouldn't give Duncan a $5,000 raise. Late in 1982 La Russa's White Sox had eight games against the Mariners. Seattle's skipper was Rene Lachemann, who La Russa also knew from the old A's days. Lach's pitching coach was Duncan. "Lach told me, 'Dave wants a $5,000 raise, and the owner is not going to give it to him,'" La Russa recalled of the conversation that changed the course of baseball history. "And Dave said he wasn't coming back because Dave's a very principled guy. So Lach said, 'If Dave's going to go, I'd rather him go with you than go with somebody else.' And we had watched Dave grow. So he came with us for the '83 season. We had 99 wins and the Cy Young winner, LaMarr Hoyt. And Richard Dotson won 22 games when he was 24. One of the things that always pissed me off was when they would say, 'Dave doesn't work well with young pitchers. He always wants veterans.' And that's so much bullshit because he worked with whoever you brought him…As I came to find out—we were together from '83 to 2011—he was the complete pitching coach. Sometimes a guy might be strong in some areas but not others."

Sean Casey, the former Cincinnati Reds All-Star first baseman, observed them from their National League divisional matchups. "I always felt like Duncan was a genius," Casey said. "When I think of La Russa, I think of Duncan, too. Just two geniuses together, feeding off of each other…Those staffs were always tough. Dave Duncan always kept them good. We're all thinking: 'Here's another mediocre pitcher. Now Duncan teaches him a cutter, and he's a stud.'"

Duncan's staff in 2011 was not his best—in terms of dominance and names—but it was one of his greater coaching accomplishments, as he navigated a season without the Cy Young candidate Wainwright while rotating numerous guys into key bullpen roles. As for the rotation, Carpenter led the staff with 34 starts and finished with a 3.45 ERA. Jake Westbrook, a former All-Star with the Cleveland Indians, tallied a 4.66 ERA, while Lohse was lowest with a 3.39 ERA. Kyle McClellan gave way to Edwin Jackson at the trade deadline. And the final starter was Jaime Garcia, the Mexican-born, Texas-bred southpaw who finished third in the Rookie of the Year voting the season before.

Garcia finished the 2011 season with a 3.56 ERA, which isn't bad to begin with but is also a bit misleading. In his first start of 2011, Garcia hurled a harbinger: a shutout with nine strikeouts. He dominated April and was somehow even better in May. Maybe the Cardinals did have a Cy Young candidate on their staff after all? Entering his final May start at Colorado, Garcia was 5–0 with a 1.93 ERA. He'd allowed 14 earned runs all season.

Denver was a destination town for many 20-something St. Louisans, and without a baseball team until 1993 in the state, some Coloradans were Cardinals fans because they listened to the powerful watts of KMOX Radio. So the annual Cardinals–Rockies series made Coors Field seem like Busch Stadium. Thousands of Cardinals fans arrived on May 28 curious to see this young Garcia guy with the miniscule ERA. They got their own version of 11 in '11—11 Rockies hits and 11 Rockies earned runs against Garcia—in only three-and-one-third innings. Garcia's ERA catapulted from 1.93 to 3.28. "We had a lineup that could do damage against lefties," recalled Ryan Spilborghs, a Rockies outfielder who had three hits and four RBIs that game. "If you didn't have command that day or if you walked a couple guys, regardless of how good you were, you could get tagged. The game can snowball on guys, especially when good pitches drop in for hits in front of outfielders playing too deep. It's really amazing watching a guy lose confidence in a start like that. Our lineup could sense it and pour it on."

In August Garcia faced the dang Rockies again—this time at Busch. He allowed five earned runs in five innings. So for the 2011 season, Garcia finished with a 3.56 ERA. But take out those two Rockies starts, and Garcia's 2011 ERA would've been 2.95. So he was a 2.95 pitcher against every other team that season.

As for the Cards' 2011 bullpen, La Russa and Duncan had a lot of fascinating weapons, but some misfired during inopportune moments. "Playing in the big leagues, I know this is a fact: the roster you start with isn't the roster you're going to end with," said 2011 Cardinals bullpen coach Derek Lilliquist, who pitched for the Atlanta Braves and its famed pitching coach, Leo Mazzone. "There's a number of factors for that. There are injuries. There's non-production. There are guys that go backward. The guys that we had and were counting on in the bullpen—for instance a Ryan Franklin or a Brian Tallet or a Bryan Augenstein—those guys just...well, Ryan was at the end of his career. The other two just didn't produce. Bryan ultimately got hurt and was done for the year, I guess. We needed help in the bullpen. We needed better production...It just evolves, and you're constantly trying to put guys in the right spot to be successful."

When it mattered most, in the autumn of the season, the Cardinals figured the bullpen out. And the man who would put "-30-" on ballgames was No. 30, Jason Louis Motte, who joined St. Louis closer lore.

• • •

The symmetry was beautiful.

Jason Motte was born during the 1982 season. That fall the bearded Cardinals closer, Bruce Sutter, threw the final pitch of the postseason, earning the Cardinals their ninth championship. Motte grew up to become a bearded Cardinals closer. And in the fall of 2011, Motte threw the final pitch of the postseason, earning the Cardinals their 11th championship.

Sure enough, Sutter actually became Motte's mentor. Friend, really. "I got to know him a little bit better just through the World Series stuff," Motte said. "And really since then, he's been someone I've called to talk to, and we'll also text back and forth. A good friendship was born there in St. Louis."

So, when Motte's first son was born in 2016, Jason and Caitlin named the baby: Sutter Motte. "Baseball-wise, obviously he was a great player and stuff like that," Jason said of Bruce. "But just the person I got to know from all my years there—and the person everyone around said he was—was just a very kind individual. A good friend and a good friendship formed over the years, and we were just happy to do that. He was honored. He said, 'You know, you're going to make this old man cry!'"

From Sutter to Motte to—who knows, maybe Sutter Motte himself in the future—the Cardinals closer has always been a time-honored position in St. Louis. A college catcher turned into a pro pitcher, Motte could spot his fastball. But an encounter with Cards pitcher Russ Springer in 2008 spring training began another transformation. "Russ saw me throw my bullpen. He asked me to throw a slider," Motte recalled of the former LSU star who pitched 18 years in big league bullpens. "He watched it and goes, 'You need to throw a cutter. Hold it like this.' I was thinking, okay? I had no idea what I was doing, and it took me three or four years to get it to do what I actually wanted it to do. I figured out how to manipulate the ball, my hand, what felt good. Guys like Ryan Franklin, Dave Duncan, [former bullpen coach] Marty Mason, they were all down there in the bullpen, putting that confidence in me. 'Hey, relax. Don't overthink it.' I didn't really try to overthink much. I didn't have much, so I couldn't overthink too much…Yadi caught one cutter, and it actually did what it was supposed to. Sometimes it wouldn't really cut. I'd just yank it. Sometimes it'd just go straight. But this time it did what it was supposed to do, and I could see the surprised look on Yadi's face behind the mask. 'Hey, that was it!' Whatever I did there, that was good. Keep doing it. It took a lot of people to help get me what I needed to not just go up there and throw heaters all the time."

Pitching coach Dave Duncan was one of those helpers. "Dunc didn't talk a ton. But when he did call you in, when he did talk to you,

you felt like you needed to voice record it or get out a pen and paper and write it all down," Motte said. "When I came up for the first time [in 2008], I remember standing out in left field at Busch Stadium after we came back from Arizona. Dunc came up to me and asked how I was doing. We're just talking, shagging during BP, and he goes, 'Keep doing what you're doing. What you have is good enough to get outs… If you're not a 2–0 change-up guy, don't throw a 2–0 change-up. If you're a 2–0 heater guy, throw a 2–0 heater. What you have will play.' That was the message. I wasn't always successful, I had my bumps in the road. He would bring me in after a couple of rough outings, and as a young guy, you're thinking: *I'm getting sent down, I'm gone.* Instead, he'd say, 'Let's go look at this.' We'd work on location. When he would talk, you wanted to sit there and remember it all. It was that good. Dunc was awesome."

Overall, the 2011 team's 3.79 ERA was 12th best in baseball. Duncan's 2011 Cardinals pitchers led all of baseball with a 47.7 percent ground-ball rate. And the Cards allowed 2.76 walks per nine innings, the fifth lowest total in the game.

But on August 20, Derek Lilliquist was in his Chicago hotel room when he got a text from Duncan. "He told me he had to mind some things at home for a few weeks and he told me to take care of the guys," Lilliquist recalled. "At that point I didn't know what had happened or what was going on. Later that morning in Chicago, Mo and Tony told me that I was going to take over the staff while Dave is gone."

Duncan's wife, Jeanine, had brain cancer. He left the club to be with his wife. "Tony runs a tight ship and he's a master running a ballgame," Lilliquist said. "All I did was make sure the pitchers got their work and that they got all the information they were supposed to get. I just made sure everybody was on the same page…Our backs were against the wall, obviously. It was a point where I think everybody really, really focused on being a unit."

• • •

He came to the Cardinals to be the starting shortstop to try to make the playoffs. And on July 31, the Cardinals traded for another guy to be the starting shortstop to try to make the playoffs. "I'm the ultimate competitor when it comes to anything," Ryan Theriot said. "I want to win, I want to be the best. That's just how I've been wired. Physically, I'm not a very imposing guy, so I had to be that way in order to have success. So nothing would drive me more crazy than Rafael Furcal coming on board and playing shortstop, right? However, the scenario and the way it was delivered—and more importantly the way he was—made it okay. It actually made it good and exciting for me. I go from having consistent ABs and playing daily to being a backup [and playing some second base]. I'll tell you, bro, it didn't bother me a bit. That's nuts, right? My family is telling me how much this sucks and I'm like, 'Not really.' This is what we need. It's not what I need. Who cares about what I need? This is about what we need. This is how we're going to win. We've got to have this guy, and I know it may sound stupid and corny, but that's why the team did well."

Like so many of his new teammates, the former Atlanta Braves infielder had accomplished many things but didn't have a ring. Furcal was in his 12th season and he arrived in St. Louis with a singular goal. In his first four games he had four hits, four RBIs, and four runs scored. And like so many of his new veteran teammates, Furcal had a vivacious personality that infused the clubhouse.

The Braves drafted Adam Wainwright in 2000, and he played in their organization through 2003. "I got to hang out with Rafael a lot when we were in Atlanta in spring training together," Wainwright said. "And we knew each other from playing against each other. We always talked a little trash to each other in between games. He always called me 'Wisenwright.' He's funny because he's one of the only players I played with whose English got worse as the season went on...We always loved playing games with him because he was notoriously bad with names. We were on the team bus one night and we went around the team and said, 'Hey, what's his name? What's his name?' One after another. Of 24 or 25 guys, he got maybe like five guys right. Molina and Pujols, the big dogs. He knew people, but he knew them as the name he called them. Motte was Monty. He didn't know what else his name was besides Monty.

"You want to talk about a guy who changes the clubhouse atmosphere with their energy and their likability and their fun-ness? Man, I'm telling you, adding Rafael Furcal was one of the biggest trades we ever made since I've been a Cardinal. I know that's a big statement, but it's true—he changed the whole culture in there. He's so fun and he loves calling out media members and talking to guys like that. He is one of the all-time greats at loosening the atmosphere and making it fun-loving in the clubhouse. He's a complete stud, an underrated defensive player. He had big hits. Huge key plays. But one of the biggest things he brought was the energy level, and that changed when he came over. He was so great for that team."

"And his voice is great," Theriot said. "I swear he's the voiceover for that movie. The one with the little bitty monsters? *Gremlins!* He talked like a Gremlin, bro."

On July 26 the Cardinals (55–48) led the National League Central. They were a half-game up on the Milwaukee Brewers (55–49) and a full game up on the Pittsburgh Pirates (53–48). Meanwhile, the Braves (60–44) sat atop the NL wild-card standings (back in 2011, only one wild-card team from each league made the playoffs). So, John Mozeliak solidified the roster. He got Furcal from the Los Angeles Dodgers for a minor leaguer named Alex Castellanos on deadline day. And four days prior on July 27, Mozeliak had made one of those deals that's tied to your name forever. Sometimes that's a bad thing. But this was a good one, a risky, hungry move—because Colby Rasmus was still only 24 years old.

The prospects of prospects provide a sort of bone-tingling feeling because of the unknown. The known is boring. The unknown is captivating because it stirs the imagination. In 2005 team executive Jeff Luhnow had his first draft. He himself was the unconventional pick for the Cardinals' front office, a late-30s engineer and management consultant who never worked in baseball (or played the game past high school). But he was data-driven and just driven, so Cardinals chairman Bill DeWitt Jr. hired the guy. In Luhnow's first year as scouting director, he used the 28th pick in the 2005 draft to pluck a high schooler out of the map dot town of Seale, Alabama. Rasmus received a $1 million signing bonus and blossomed in the minors. When the Cardinals traded Jim Edmonds after 2007 to the San Diego Padres in exchange for a young third baseman, this seemingly opened up center field for Rasmus to roam. But the Cards kept Rasmus in Triple A for 2008, and that year in a thoroughly modern milieu, Cardinals online message boards became a place for Rasmus family members to vent frustrations. The kid's dad, Tony Rasmus, continued to coach and mentor his son, tinkering with Colby's swing.

Finally, in 2009, Colby became a Cardinal at 22 (with a .714 OPS). But his 2010 season? Scintillating. His OPS was .859. But his relationship with his other Tony became complicated. Tony La Russa and Rasmus had a huge argument in the dugout during July of 2010. Rasmus demanded a trade. But the Cards kept their prospect. One July later with Rasmus struggling in 2011, La Russa told reporters that Rasmus was listening "to somebody" for coaching instruction. Frank Cusumano, the beloved hometown sports guy for Channel 5, followed up by asking La Russa about the role of the actual team coaches in Rasmus' development. "No, he doesn't listen to the Cardinal coaches much now, and that's why he gets in these funks," La Russa said. "But I actually feel concern for him because he hears it from so many places. He's got to get confused."

Still, he was only 24. As recently as May 13, 2011, his batting average was .313. But by July 27, it was .246. As La Russa described in *One Last Strike*, Mozeliak asked La Russa a point-blank question: "Can we win if we trade Rasmus for the help we need?" Namely, a starting pitcher and a reliable lefty reliever. Remember from 2007 to 2010, the Cards made the playoffs just once and were swept in three games by the Dodgers. The 2011 season was an operation for October. "Yes, we can win," La Russa replied.

The trade was announced on July 27. Rasmus to the Toronto Blue Jays, who had just acquired starting pitcher Edwin Jackson. So Toronto traded Jackson, relievers Octavio Dotel and Marc Rzepczynski, and outfielder Corey Patterson to St. Louis for Rasmus and relievers Trever Miller, Brian Tallet, and P.J. Walters. In the *St. Louis Post-Dispatch*, the great columnist Bernie Miklasz wrote: "You may have heard that the Cardinals made a big trade Wednesday, shipping Colby Rasmus and Tony Rasmus to Canada. Why Toronto? Easy: because Siberia doesn't have a major league baseball franchise. And the Cardinals clearly wanted to get Colby and his daddy as far away as possible…It's unclear if the Cardinals will receive a father to be named later."

The Rasmus trade was debated across baseball. On the MLB Network, reporter Ken Rosenthal said: "Already you're hearing people in the industry raise their eyebrows about it. What people are questioning is: hey, how can you trade Colby Rasmus and not get young players back?"

But that was the point—the Cardinals made the trade primarily to beef up the 2011 team. In Jackson they got an innings-eater who had a 3.13 since the calendar turned to May. Rzepczynski (2.97 overall ERA) was the lefty reliever they coveted. They called Rzepczynski "Scrabble," which brought back memories of the old ballplayer Doug Gwosdz, whom they called "Eyechart." And Dotel, a righty joining his 12th MLB franchise, had a 1.86 ERA since a poor appearance on May 9.

And Dotel fit the 2011 Cardinals mold: an effervescent veteran looking for his first World Series title. "Dotel and Furcal, those guys set the mind-set of the team and the personality of the team," Theriot said. "Hats off to Mo for bringing the right dudes in. Dotel is such a dominant personality. He's always happy. Always has a smile on his face. Very encouraging. Veteran, been around for 100 years. Thank goodness he had some success because that brought even more of that stuff out. And he was the worst card player in the history of cards. He helped me buy some diapers that year. And the same thing with Furcal. I knew him better than I did Dotel. So I knew he was going to fit in great. What I didn't know was how it was going to work out, not only on the field but off. He was just wonderful for everybody. Anytime you can get the different backgrounds of guys meshing together like we had that year? We've got guys from all different countries that are just wanting to be around each other, and that's what we had. It was as unselfish a scenario that you could ask for in pro ball."

As for the demise of the Rasmus tenure with St. Louis, there was blame pointed in different directions, depending on who you ask—be it the Cardinals' front office, Rasmus himself, or one of the two Tonys. But there another less-explored culprit.

St. Louis radio host Tim McKernan was at a wedding, when an old college buddy made him an offer he couldn't refuse. McKernan hosted the popular morning radio show called *The Morning After*, which annually held a January event for listeners and always drew a nice crowd. McKernan's buddy was a lawyer and said he could get the rapper J-Kwon to perform at the radio show's event. J-Kwon is most-famous for—and really only famous for—the 2004 song "Tipsy," which climbed to No. 2 on the Billboard chart. "He says, 'I can get him to perform at your thing, but the deal is you've got to include Joshua.'" McKernan recalled. "So I said, 'Who the fuck is Joshua?'"

As it was, Joshua was a caucasian R&B singer. He had somehow connected with J-Kwon, and they collaborated on some music. "So he tells me that if I can make sure Joshua plays at the event, then I'll make sure J-Kwon is there," McKernan said. "And I said, 'Sure, I don't really give a damn.' This isn't the Oscars. It's at Lumiere on a Sunday afternoon. So J-Kwon does 'Tipsy,' and it's great. And then the deal was that Joshua had to perform, so Joshua is backstage. And apparently he's never performed in front of anybody before. Literally no one. So he's freaking out, saying he's not going on stage. That's fine. Nobody knows who you are anyway. I don't care. I just want to get this thing done with. But he's back there, and the girls are standing around him and are like, 'You can do this! They want you!' He's psyching himself up. He finally goes out there and performs."

It did not go well. "And so, once that happened, it became part of *TMA* lore—that we had this guy perform," McKernan said.

On YouTube in later years, a Joshua music video surfaced of his song "Love Circus." He was on a boat in the Lake of the Ozarks singing autotuned lyrics alongside dancing women with cans of Bud Light. "So we used to play his songs coming back from break on *TMA* as one of our many inside jokes," said McKernan, who hosted the radio show with Doug Vaughn and Cardinals sideline reporter Jim "The Cat" Hayes. "And so The Cat goes up to Colby Rasmus, and Colby Rasmus had never been on a hotter streak in his Cardinals career than what he was doing in June of 2011. And Colby agrees to play Joshua as his walk-up music. Colby Rasmus is on a heater and he strikes out in his first at-bat. And they play 'Love Circus.' They play it again. He goes back and strikes out again. And he calls up to the press box to tell them to stop playing the song. It was during the game. And so help me—he goes in the tank. He never turns it around. And the Cardinals trade him in exchange for Rzepczynski, Dotel, Corey Patterson, and Edwin Jackson. So, we always have said that we are unheralded for our part in the Cardinals' championship in 2011 because without Joshua and 'Love Circus' they never play that music and who knows? Maybe Colby continues on his heater, and the Cards never make that trade."

The trade indeed was pivotal for the Cardinals' 2011 season. But not right away. Actually, it was at that point entering August when the team began to unravel.

• • •

The Knights of the Cauliflower Ear, the time-honored legion of successful and eccentric St. Louisans, were founded in 1935. The most famous guest to ever attend their annual dinner was Harry Truman, who like the 2011 guests, was known for a surprising upset.

The Cardinals attended the dinner in 2011. Tony La Russa was there, along with John Mozeliak and numerous players. But this wasn't after the against-all-odds victory of the wild-card or the world championship. It was August 24, 2011. Hours earlier, a sub-.500 Los Angeles Dodgers team won their third straight game at Busch. "When you get beat in a series, especially when you get swept at home," La Russa told reporters postgame, "that's as bad as it can get."

Once in first place, the Cardinals dropped to 10 games back of the Milwaukee Brewers—and 10½ behind the Atlanta Braves in the wild-card. In retrospect, it was respectable that they even attended the dinner that night. August was awful. On July 26 the Cards were in first place. And entering August, the Cards sat two-and-a-half game back of the Brewers. But St. Louis went 10–12 in its next 22 games. This included two walk-off losses in two different cities within three days. And in that most recent Dodgers series, the Cardinals were outscored 24–7. Playoff probability websites had the Cards' 2011 postseason chances right around 1 percent. The offseason felt ominous. Would Albert Pujols re-sign? Would La Russa return? Would the Cards regret trading Colby Rasmus, especially since their win-now strategy appeared to backfire? And after winning the 2006 World Series, the Cards would've entered 2012 with just one postseason appearance since.

At the Knights of the Cauliflower Ear dinner, the broadcasters from KMOX radio would emcee the event and interview different Cardinals from their tables. "I remember looking at John Rooney and Mike Claiborne and thinking, *how are we going to get through this?*" said Tom Ackerman, the longtime KMOX sports director and on-air personality. "It was a hot day. They'd just gotten swept by the Dodgers. How do we make this into a positive night? The season is clearly slipping away from them. There wasn't a lot of hope or feeling like anything could happen. So players are getting interviewed and they're doing their best to put on a smile and talk about how appreciative they are of the fans. Then, it's Wainwright's turn. I go over to their table. He stands up with a smile on his face. I asked him how he was doing recovering from Tommy John surgery. He said, 'I'm doing well. I'm hoping these guys will hold on and play some great baseball so I can try to talk Tony into letting me pitch.' That kind of got people laughing."

The 6'7" Adam Wainwright looked out at the crowd of fans and teammates and Cardinals staff and just started preaching. "Right now it's not easy for anyone because we're not winning. This city deserves us to win, and we want to win," Wainwright spoke to the group. "The way I look at it, we play the Brewers six more times. Yeah, we're down 10 games now. But if we beat them all six times, we're down four games. I don't think anybody in their right mind would be comfortable ahead of us only up four games. So we've got a great chance because no one expects us to come back and win. We have a greater chance to do it because nobody is expecting it! We've proven it before that we can surprise people! And we have the people that can do it!"

The room erupted. There were cheers and cheers of beer bottles. Why not the Cardinals? And at Busch Stadium, a similar sentiment was shared in a now-famous players-only meeting by Wainwright's mentor. "I remember Chris Carpenter speaking because he really didn't do that too often," Skip Schumaker recalled. "He was more of a guy that would show what kind of work ethic he had, and his preparation was as good as I've ever seen anybody to this day. He was no-nonsense. He really didn't speak up too much, and when he did, people listened. So I just remember thinking, *Oh shit. Carp's speaking?*"

Carpenter's speech to the team after the Dodgers series was in reference to the coming weeks. He feared the Cardinals were going to be embarrassed if they kept playing that way. "He kind of just rallied the guys and said, 'Hey, forget about all the expectations of the front office and the coaching staff and the fans. We need to show each other that we're a championship team,'" Cardinals infielder Daniel Descalso said. "We decided we were going to go out and try to salvage things one series at a time. And before you knew it, we were playing much better. Obviously, the Braves had to do their part and collapse for us to catch them. I think they felt us coming though, and we really got hot at the right time. I think for some reason we were playing tight for all those months before that meeting. We kind of got everything out in the open. You could feel sort of a collective weight lift off of everyone's shoulders. We just decided we were going to go out and play like we knew we could play instead of trying to force the issue. There are high expectations being a part of that organization. The expectation is to win, and that's okay, but we were just playing too tight. We weren't out there playing loose and taking it to the other team."

Or, as Jason Motte described it, "He said that we pretty much just needed to play our butts off for the next month or so."

• • •

The Black man was from Pensacola, Florida, and the white man was from Jackson, Mississippi, but they had grown up in different Souths—and not because of their age or states.

Chris Maloney asked Adron Chambers to come into his office. Chambers was nervous. He normally could predict why the Memphis manager wanted to talk to him. Maloney asked him about his mother, if they had been in touch. Chambers remembered his tone wasn't bad. So it wasn't an emergency. "He told me: 'Adron, you're going up. Call your mom and let everyone know that you're going up to the major leagues,'" said the Triple A outfielder. "Being from the South, he's from Mississippi, so he saw segregation or heard about it. So I think when it comes to Maloney and me, he understood me and the fact that there weren't a lot of Black players on my team. He saw the significance of the opportunity for me—not only just to make it to the major leagues, but to help my family and things like that. He was looking at it more on a personal level, and I really appreciated him for that...And I think he saw how much I did to be able to receive that opportunity to be a part of the Cardinals."

A proud Maloney broke into tears upon delivering the new of Chambers' ascension to The Show. Chambers had improved immensely at Triple A Memphis and he relied on Maloney for tutelage. Chambers was a former college defensive back at Mississippi State, where Maloney played college baseball in the 1980s before he got a stomach virus and lost his starting job to...Will Clark. Chambers ultimately transferred to Pensacola Junior College and played baseball, and in the 2007 Major League Baseball Draft, the Cardinals selected Chambers in the 38th round. And in early September of 2011, he was promoted to the actual St. Louis Cardinals. Soon the 1,153rd overall draft pick would leave his fingerprints—and footprints—on franchise history.

Inspired by the speeches of Chris Carpenter and Adam Wainwright, the Cardinals immediately took three of four from the Pittsburgh Pirates. Oh, and then St. Louis went up to Milwaukee and swept the Brewers in a three-game statement series. In the September 1 finale, the game Brandon Dickson started to give Carpenter extra rest, the kid only lasted three-and-one-third innings, allowing three runs. But Albert Pujols picked him up, as Pujols would do, by pulverizing two homers, including a grand slam. The Cards won big. Something in Milwaukee was brewing.

Wainwright was right that night with the Knights. The Cardinals sure could make it interesting if they kept beating Milwaukee. The Brewers were having a historic season, considering they'd only made the playoffs once (2008) since losing to the Cardinals in the 1982 World Series. And three days after the series in Milwaukee, the Brewers came to Busch for three in September of 2011. They split the first two. So on September 7, St. Louis was nine-and-a-half games back of Milwaukee, heading into a weighty rubber game, and Carp would toe the rubber.

"We had a never-say-die mentality, and the team refused to lose," Ryan Theriot said of the September Cardinals. "Chris Carpenter wouldn't let it happen."

On that night a sharp Carp allowed only four hits and nary a run in a showdown against Zack Greinke, a fellow former Cy Young winner. The Cards only pieced together a pair of runs off him—the second when Rafael Furcal ambushed the fifth inning's first pitch for a solo shot—and led 2–0 in the ninth. The swift game, a throwback to the days of Bob Gibson, had only just cracked the two-hour mark. The leadoff hitter was Nyjer Morgan, an irrelevant pest for so many prior years—but now a relevant one since he was hitting .300 for a rival in a pennant race.

Nyjer Morgan. The name still makes St. Louisans scoff. Maybe Morgan would've fit in better in baseball's more-expressive era of 2020. But in 2011 old-school baseball traditionalists—elitists, if you will—disapproved of Morgan's exuberance. Sometimes, he went over the line. He'd say he was just drawing a new line. When Morgan arrived in Milwaukee before the 2011 season, superstars Prince Fielder and Ryan Braun told him to just be himself. This freed Morgan the player—he had the best year of his career—and Morgan the personality. He was confident and creative and cuckoo. He had a fast-talking alter-ego he named Tony Plush, who would show up in interviews, tweets, and nightclubs, sometimes wearing a fedora and sunglasses per a *Sports Illustrated* cover story on Morgan. Writer Lee Jenkins described the Brewers outfielder as "a man of many names and voices, poses and expressions, some explicit but every one of them entertaining…The team has even taken on some of Morgan's identity: it's a high-stepping, head-bobbing, shoulder-shimmying juggernaut with an affection for baby oil, naked golf, and on-field choreography that stretches baseball's rules of decorum. 'We're coming at you like a SWAT team!' Morgan hollers, raising his hands and curling his fingers into claws. 'Aaaah!'"

And there Morgan was at the plate on September 7 down two runs in the top of the ninth, facing Carpenter. The first swing of the left-handed Morgan was a swat (lowercase), which drilled the ball home-run distance but just to the right of the right-field foul pole. As the at-bat continued, broadcaster Al Hrabosky broke the news to viewers that the Atlanta Braves had just lost a heartbreaker in the ninth inning to the Philadelphia Phillies. With a win the Cardinals would be just six-and-a-half games back of the wild-card—with the Braves coming to town that weekend for a series.

In the batter's box, Morgan battled. Ten pitches. And on the 10th, he swung and missed at strike three. Morgan would tell reporters that famously fiery Carpenter cursed right then. Morgan stared at the pitcher while walking toward the dugout, shouted something his way, and then took the chewing tobacco out of his mouth and whipped it in Carpenter's direction. All along, Carpenter wasn't watching, instead pacing behind the mound.

But Pujols was. From first base he started to come toward Morgan's direction. Cameras caught Morgan mouthing two curse words at Pujols. Umpire Derryl Cousins quickly intervened, a few Brewers grabbed Morgan, and both benches cleared. Morgan was ejected. "He wants to know why," Hrabosky said, as the camera showed Morgan in the dugout. "Maybe it was T. Plush that did it."

An unfazed Carpenter returned to the mound and promptly got out both Braun and Fielder to win the game. It was his first shutout since 2009. "He's a good player, he's a serious talent, he just plays the game a different way," Carpenter told reporters of Morgan after the win, which put the Cards eight-and-a-half games back of Milwaukee. "I didn't know anything was going on until I heard Albert screaming. I'm not concerned about it, to be honest with you. I'm not going to play his game. There's a certain way to compete. There's a certain way not to compete. He competes hard, but he does it in a different manner. It's unfortunate because it takes away from the player he is, and he's a really good player. I was focused on what I was doing and executing pitches. I'm not going to allow him to take me out of my game. He's yelling at me from second base. He's yelling at me when he hit the double. He's yelling at me the whole game screaming and yelling the whole time. I'm not going to allow it to happen. I don't know if that's the way he plays—trying to get guys out of their game or what, but I've been around too long to let that happen."

Later that night the Brew Crew's Morgan tweeted twice about the Cardinals. "We're still in 1st and I hope those crying birds injoy watching tha Crew in tha Playoffs!!! Aaaaahhhhh!!!" And as for Pujols, Morgan tweeted, "Alberta couldn't see Plush if she had her gloves on!!! Wat was she thinking running afta Plush!!! She never been n tha ring!!!"

The season series was over between Milwaukee and St. Louis. It was hard to believe then, but the very next month, they'd meet in another series. Another foe, the Braves, were connected to the Cardinals through the autumns. Take 1982. Heading into that season, the Braves hadn't been to the postseason since 1969, while the Cards hadn't been since 1968. But they met in the 1982 National League Championship Series. Joe Torre, a former MVP player with the Cardinals, was the Braves manager. St. Louis won that series and the World Series.

When the Cards met up with Atlanta again in the 1996 NLCS, St. Louis hadn't won a title since '82. It was Tony La Russa's first year as manager. The Cards hadn't even been to the playoffs since 1987. And La Russa's Redbirds jumped to a 3–1 lead, thanks in part to a Game 4 pinch-hit triple by rookie Dmitri Young, who drove in two. It would be the most famous triple in Cardinals history until the 2011 one by David Freese, who just happened to be a 13-year-old boy in the stands on the day of Young's triple. But the Braves won the next three games to win the 1996 pennant.

La Russa's Cards wouldn't make the playoffs again until 2000. Sure enough, they met Atlanta (and Rookie of the Year Furcal) in the first round. And they swept Atlanta in that first round. By

Acquired in the 2011 offseason, Lance Berkman would prove to be an integral part of the St. Louis Cardinals' lineup during both the regular season and postseason.

Through the ups and downs of the 2011 season, the Cardinals could lean on their two Gold Glovers, Albert Pujols and Yadier Molina, who received their awards before a game in April of 2011.

St. Louis Cardinals manager Tony La Russa jogs out to deliver his lineup card before the start of the game against the Philadelphia Phillies on May 16, 2011, in his first game back after missing six games due to shingles.

David Freese (left) and Adam Wainwright (right) sign autographs for 11-year-old Casey Sade of Joplin, Missouri, at the Joplin Athletic Complex on June 8, 2011, as part of the St. Louis Cardinals' initiative to help those impacted by the tornado that devastated Joplin.

Turnabout is fair play, as Nick Punto, "The Shredder," gets his jersey ripped open, following his walk-off sacrifice fly in the 10th inning of a key victory against the Atlanta Braves on September 9, 2011.

A former football star, Adron Chambers hits a three-run triple in the seventh inning of a September 20, 2011, game to help the St. Louis Cardinals defeat the New York Mets 11–6.

Teammates drench pitcher Chris Carpenter on September 28, 2011, after Carp's complete-game shutout against the Houston Astros helped clinch a wild-card berth, something that seemed unthinkable just a month prior.

A squirrel runs past the leg of Skip Schumaker during his at-bat in the the fifth inning of Game 4 of the National League Division Series against the Philadelphia Phillies, leading the St. Louis Cardinals and their fans to embrace the notion of the "rally squirrel."

Chris Carpenter throws during his masterful performance in Game 5 of the National League Division Series when he outdueled Philadelphia Phillies ace Roy Halladay.

After struggling in the previous contest, Albert Pujols celebrates after hitting a three-run home run during the sixth inning of Game 3 of the 2011 World Series. It was the first of his three home runs that game.

With the St. Louis Cardinals down to their last out in the World Series, David Freese watches his two-run triple tie Game 6 of the World Series.

David Freese hits a walk-off home run during the 11th inning of Game 6 to win the game 10–9 and send the World Series to a Game 7.

Teammates swarm St. Louis native David Freese after his epic walk-off home run wins Game 6 of the 2011 World Series.

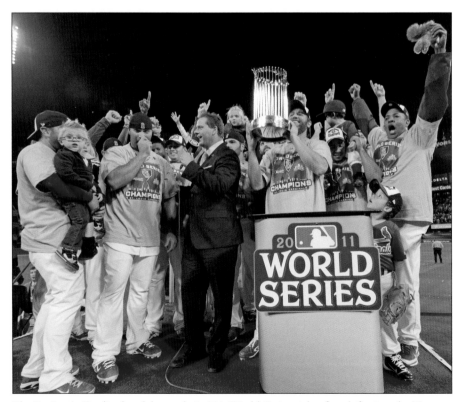

The St. Louis Cardinals celebrate their 11th World Series title after defeating the Texas Rangers 6–2 in Game 7 of the 2011 World Series.

2011 the Cardinals were again in a heated battle with Atlanta—but not necessarily against Atlanta. The Cardinals fought the Braves all September for the wild-card. The Braves' lead was sizable, but the team was vulnerable. They were playing weird baseball. They lost five of their first seven in this slippery September. Atlanta was a wild-card in and of itself.

So every night, it wasn't just about if the Cardinals won—it was also about if the Braves lost. The Cards and Braves did actually face each other three times in September, and St. Louis swept those guys. The games from September 9th to 11th at Busch featured the Nick Punto walk-off sacrifice fly, which led to the shredding of "The Shredder" himself. There were three strong starts from Edwin Jackson, Jaime Garcia, and Jake Westbrook. And Lance Berkman went 7-for-10 in the three-game sweep.

And so, when Atlanta humbly flew back to Atlanta, the Braves only led the wild-card by four-and-a-half games. For the first time all year, the Cardinals were 12 games better than .500. "Everybody in that clubhouse just really pulled for each other," Ryan Theriot said. "Waino had a lot to do with that. Matt Holliday had a lot to do with that. Berkman was important. These are guys that had been around for a while, but they understood what needed to happen for us to win…Hell, you look at the way Lance Berkman does his thing, and the dude he is his entire career. This dude is special, bro. Yeah, he can hit. Ain't no doubt about it. But he's a special human being."

In St. Louis Berkman's 2011 is often overshadowed by so many other storylines. But the guy finished the season seventh in the MVP voting. He hit .301 with 31 homers. His OBP was .412, and his slugging was .547 (for an OPS of .959). And during that amazing run in September, Berkman hit .374. "He destroyed the ball," Theriot recalled.

The Cards won their next series at the Pittsburgh Pirates and celebrated in rare fashion. La Russa seldom allowed the vets to do this, but they persuaded the skipper to have the young players dress up in costumes. On the flight from Pittsburgh to Philadelphia, all Cards with three or fewer years of service time wore some form of lacy, racy outfit. And there was Chambers draped in a frilly red outfit with a red cowboy hat—and a red mask over his eyes.

In the first matchup of that Philadelphia Phillies series on September 16, Chambers made it into the game. He pinch ran for Berkman in the top of the ninth with the Birds up 2–1. In the bottom of the ninth, the Phillies were down to their last strike. Carlos Ruiz batted with a runner on second in the ninth, and Philadelphia still down 2–1. Ruiz drilled a ball to right. It tailed toward the foul line. Acquired in the Colby Rasmus trade, defensive replacement Corey Patterson tracked it down on the run, and the ball landed in Patterson's glove...and popped out. Tie game. La Russa kicked a trash can in the dugout.

After a scoreless 10th inning, Furcal again made a September impact—this time with a leadoff double. La Russa had some decisions to make with Patterson at the plate and Pujols on-deck. La Russa had Patterson sacrifice bunt Furcal to third, knowing Philly would walk Pujols. Philly, of course, did walk Pujols. So with one out and a runner on third, the guy after Pujols was, yep, Chambers, who had replaced Berkman. Even though a double play would end the inning, the Phillies had to consider Chambers' speed and possibly being safe at first. And, who knew? Maybe La Russa would have the speedy kid squeeze? So the Phillies had their infield in.

No. 56 for St. Louis worked the count like a veteran would. With two strikes he fouled off everything the hurler had. And on the eighth pitch, the lefty Chambers ripped a ball into right field. Chambers' first MLB hit was an 11th inning go-ahead RBI single against the team with the league's best record. Chambers reached first and clapped twice. Then he briefly pointed to the sky. Theriot leaned forward on the padded dugout railing with his pointer finger in the air. "My very first hit, I think that's what kind of ignited us," Chambers said. "That kind of elevated us…That was something that boosted me, too. That, to me, was the moment where everything kind of switched. It was like a difference right there."

The Cards held on to win. And the Braves lost to the New York Mets. St. Louis was just three-and-a-half game back of the wild-card with 12 games to play. Remember the 1 percent chance of making the playoffs? This was just an improbable run…so far anyway.

The Cards proceeded to take three of four from the Phillies. The win on the fourth night—September 19—was courtesy of Kyle Lohse's outstanding outing. "After the game I'm standing right outside of Tony's office, and he's doing interviews with the media," recalled CJ Cherre, the Cardinals' traveling secretary. "The Braves and Marlins are on the TV. The Braves were winning. And I would never go in there—*never go in there*—and interrupt his meeting. But all of a sudden, I'm standing there, and the clubhouse just erupts. You would have thought there were 200 guys in there. The players go absolutely crazy. And Tony looks up and he's got this bewilderment on his face. So I walked in and I told him, 'Tony, you're not going to believe this, but Chipper Jones lost a *ground ball* in the lights, couldn't make a play. And Omar Infante just hit a home run to win the game for the Marlins.' His mouth was agape. The media are all looking over. That was kind of funny. That was the one time I caught Tony speechless."

Groundball in the lights? The game was played in Miami's old ballpark, which was the Dolphins' stadium, too. The light structures were lower there than in baseball-specific parks. And on this night in the wildest month baseball had seen in quite some time, a chopper to Chipper had him blinded by the lights.

The Cards were two-and-a-half games back of the Braves and the wild-card with nine games to play. Heck, the Cards were only five-and-a-half games back of the Brewers at this point, but Milwaukee was still mashing. The Cardinals continued to cheer in the clubhouse, and the cheers turned into chants: "Happy flight! Happy flight!" In his

Gremlin voice, Furcal was the vocal leader of the celebratory mantra, which the guys cheered on their way to the next city. "That was a raucous bus ride just to the airport that night," Cherre said. "The guys were excited, and there was so much chatter going on. Everybody was laughing. It was just really fun. Once stuff like that happens, you go, *maybe this is our year.* This team just kept coming back. You had the veteran leadership. Berkman helped out immensely. It was a really good group and fun group."

"During the season in the clubhouse," pitcher Kyle McClellan recalled, "everyone was enjoying each other, giving each other trouble. I think athletes do that better than anybody, and you see that when you get to the real world [after retiring]. Our work environment is way different than anybody else's in that there's a lot of guys giving each other trouble. And that's what brings your team together...Here's an example: you've got Adron Chambers who comes up. He's a young guy. Adron always talked about his college football, how he was a good college football player. He claimed he shut down [NFL receiver] Sidney Rice. So Gerald and Punto and Theriot, all big football guys, they say, 'Hold on a second.' They start grilling him. So he's in the middle of the locker room telling a story about Sidney Rice, and they had our video guy pull up the game. So they come in, and we're analyzing Adron while he's claiming to shut down Sidney Rice. It was just stuff like that. It was fun-loving."

The night after the happy flight, the Cards hosted the Mets. Yet again, the Cards trailed late. This time they were down 6–5 in the bottom of the seventh inning. With the bases loaded and two outs, Theriot came up and thwacked a ground-rule double. The Cards took the lead 7–6. After an intentional walk to Yadier Molina to load the bases yet again, La Russa went to his bench.

Adron.

The gritty 5'10" Chambers worked the count for eight pitches, the exact amount he faced in the Philadelphia at-bat for his first hit.

And then some more September magic. Chambers whisked a liner to right, far past the unsuspecting outfielder. All three runners scored. The third—Molina—touched home while gleaming a grin as wide as the plate itself. Down 6–5 to start the seventh inning, the Cards were up 10–6, and then The Shredder ripped a pitch for a hit to make it 11–6, the eventual final score. "If you go back and look at the YouTube after I hit it, I threw my hands into the air," Chambers said. "The camera goes to the dugout, and everybody was at the top step. Tony even smiled. For me, knowing Tony and the stories that I've heard, he was a straightforward dude, but he was serious. So to see him smiling?...We still had some things that needed to happen. But as we kept winning, you could see the attitudes starting to change. We knew we were doing better. We were getting guys out. We were winning games. But then it was like, 'Oh shit. We have a chance to make it.'"

The next day on September 21, the Marlins shut out the Braves. With a win against the Mets, the Cardinals would be one-and-a-half games out of the wild-card with seven to play. And while a lot of Cards were hot, one guy had been frighteningly frigid. La Russa even benched David Freese for some September games. But La Russa started him this day, and with the Cards down 4–3 in the seventh, Freese walloped a three-run homer. He had his first ever curtain call at Busch. After the win Freese told reporters: "As a kid in St. Louis growing up, you watch Big Mac do them and you watch Albert do them, but going out there and the fans wanting you? That was special, very special. Obviously the biggest hit of my career."

• • •

Nick Evans. You don't know the name, and that's a good thing. If the Cards somehow missed the 2011 playoffs, his name would be known and remembered in the St. Louis area—from Fenton to Festus, from O'Fallon, Missouri, across the river to O'Fallon, Illinois. Nick Evans was the guy who hit the ninth-inning grounder that Rafael Furcal botched.

The Cards blew the September 22 game to the New York Mets. If the Cards missed the playoffs by one game, this would be the game fans would point to for years. It was home at Busch. The Cards led 6–2 in the ninth. *6–2!* Jason Motte walked the first Mets hitter and then got Evans, who finished with 408 career at-bats, to hit a slow chopper to short. But Furcal messed up the shovel throw to second base. Instead of no one on and two outs, there were two on, no outs. It was the normally sure-handed Furcal's fifth error in six games, and New York scored six runs and won. The inning had unraveled. Perhaps the season had, too. "That game felt like it might have been it for us," Cardinals general manager John Mozeliak recalled. "We had a retirement party that night for Mike Bertani [the director of stadium operations who worked for the Cardinals for 55 years]. I remember walking there with Bill DeWitt and Craig Stapleton, one of our investors, and just feeling beside ourselves. Ugh. This season could be over. Then I got a call from Furcal's agent. He said Furcal was very distraught. I reached out to Tony and I said, 'Skip, I think he's not sure what he means to this team. Could you talk to him and let him know the importance?' Bill and I and Mr. Stapleton then proceeded to the Cardinal Club for this retirement party. But then we decided to go to dinner and drown our sorrows a little bit. We ate at Dominic's that night."

And that night Tony La Russa received another phone call. It was from Albert Pujols. As La Russa shared in *One Last Strike*, Pujols told him: "Rafael is in a bad way right now. He thinks he cost us a shot at the playoffs."

"How bad is bad?" La Russa said to Pujols.

"He's talking about hanging them up. He's planning to quit."

La Russa called Furcal. Voicemail. He called again. Voicemail again. He asked Furcal to meet him the next day before any final decision. And when Furcal came into his office, La Russa immediately noticed Furcal's face. He thought to himself it was like the difference in those theater masks—instead of smiling this one was frowning and forlorn. But La Russa navigated the situation well. The two talked candidly. The skipper explained that Furcal had helped get them to this point in the first place. La Russa gave Furcal September 23 off, and Furcal didn't quit. The Cards lost; the Atlanta Braves won. The loss eliminated the Cardinals from the division race. Nyjer Morgan and the Milwaukee Brewers were the National League Central champs.

The following day on September 24, La Russa put Furcal back in there at shortstop. It was a home day game against the Chicago Cubs. Chicago led in the ninth 1–0. This one would be brutal. But Matt Holliday singled. Pinch-runner Tyler Greene got to third, and when Yadier Molina walked, La Russa replaced him on the basepaths with the former cornerback, Adron Chambers. Skip Schumaker walked, and the bases were loaded. Ryan Theriot walked. Tie game.

Furcal came to bat with the bases loaded.

And in one of the most famous highlights of the September comeback, pitcher Carlos Marmol threw a wild pitch, and Chambers sprinted home with his hands in the air. The Cards won 2–1 on the rarest of walk-offs. The image was fitting of the Cardinals' September: frantic, lucky, opportunistic, thrilling, and hard to believe it actually happened.

Oh, and the Braves lost to the Washington Nationals. And the next day, the Braves lost to the Nationals, too. Furcal was in there again on September 25. And he hit a huge homer to propel the Birds to another comeback victory. After that there were just three games left in the season. The Cards were one game back of Atlanta, who had three games at Philadelphia. Normally, a clinched team takes their foot off the pedal, but the National League East champion Philadelphia Phillies had been on a losing streak, so they took these Braves games seriously. The Cards, meanwhile, wore Hawaiian shirts on their happy flight for three games in Houston.

• • •

The boy's birthday was the day of Game 162. "I remember my parents asking me what I wanted to happen on my birthday. Did I want to go out for dinner?" said Cardinals fan Alec Baris, who turned 14 on September 28, 2011. "I told my parents I didn't want to see friends or go out. I told them I wanted the Cardinals to win the wild-card."

In Game 160, both the Cards and the Atlanta Braves lost. St. Louis was still a game back. In Game 161, the Cards were down 5–0 in their second game against the Houston Astros. Jake Westbrook got tagged. But spearheaded by Nick Punto, Lance Berkman, and Allen Craig in the fourth, St. Louis furiously came back. Five-nothin' became 5–5. "Unleashed fury," John Mozeliak said. "That just showed that this team didn't quit."

St. Louis won 13–6. Atlanta lost again. And so, improbably, the Braves and Cards were tied for the wild-card heading into their final games—St. Louis at Houston, and Philadelphia at Atlanta. There were three possible scenarios:

- If the Cards lost and the Braves won, the Cardinals' 2011 season would end right then.
- If the Cards won and the Braves won, the teams would play a play-in game at Busch Stadium the next day.
- If the Cards won and the Braves lost, the Cards would win the wild-card, and the Braves' season would be over.

Naturally, there were nerves heading to the Cardinals' Game 162. Sure, Chris Carpenter was throwing. And sure, the Astros were 56–105. But this was the same Astros team that took a 5–0 lead the day before. And if there was one certainty about this crazy year it was simply that nothing was certain. But before Carpenter even threw a pitch, it was the Cardinals who took a 5–0 lead.

Jon Jay led off with a single followed by hits from Craig, Albert Pujols, Berkman, and David Freese. And after Yadier Molina grounded out, Skip Schumaker and Punto got hits, too. All along, the Cardinals followed the Braves score. In a meeting room to the right of the clubhouse, traveling secretary CJ Cherre watched both games with Chad Blair, the Cardinals' longtime video coordinator. "Even Albert came in between innings," Cherre said. "We were up big at the time. And he came in, had a bat in hand. He's getting ready to hit and he just wanted to check in on the game. He said, 'Don't worry about it. The Phillies are going to win this game and we're going to win the wild-card tonight.' Chad and I just looked at each other and thought, *I guess we don't have to worry!*"

Carpenter's first 15 starts of the season earned him a record of 1–7. His ERA was 4.47. From that point on, he made 19 more starts—and went 10–2 with a 2.73 ERA. And in his final five starts of 2011, he averaged eight innings pitched with an ERA of 1.13. "Carp went out there with that look in his eye," Jason Motte recalled of that last night in Houston. "Carp would probably have had to go 12 innings for one of the relievers to get in."

And there was a special guest—pitching coach Dave Duncan returned from his time with his ailing wife. He would be a part of any postseason action. The Cards beat the Astros 8–0. At the very least a Game 163 was guaranteed. "Nobody talks about the gem Chris Carpenter threw that day," the birthday-celebrating Baris said. "Complete game, shut down the Astros pre-trash cans. And then after that, I was never more into a baseball game that was not the Cardinals in my life than the one with the Braves and Phillies. It went to extras, of course. I remember there was a chance they almost walked off. It was getting late, my parents wanted me to go to bed. I said, 'No way.'"

The Cardinals nervously watched Atlanta from the visitors' clubhouse in Houston. Some players sat at their lockers; others filtered into the kitchen and dining area. All sat on pins and needles. "We're all thinking, *Holy crap, this can happen. How did we get here?*" recalled bullpen coach Derek Lilliquist. "You think back to August, and we're wondering how we were going to climb out. You're thinking this is going to be Mount Everest to try to do so."

The night was unique because in real time fans were living out the same emotions as the players; they had this bond or connection to the Cardinals in a very human and personal way. What unfolded was the most epic night of baseball since the 1882 Cincinnati Red Stockings first pulled up those stockings and played a ballgame. In addition to the Braves–Phillies game playing out, there were two American League games with playoff significance. The Boston Red Sox and Tampa Bay Rays were tied for the wild-card, entering the final day. Boston played the Orioles at Baltimore, and the Tampa Bay Rays hosted the New York Yankees, who had already clinched the American League East title. The night turned into a carnival. "It was a magical night. No one ever thought baseball could be like that," said Greg Amsinger, the St. Louis native who was live on MLB Network that night. "That's what it turned into. It was the greatest sports theater we've ever enjoyed. Fingers crossed, we get another night close to it."

6:53 PM CST: With his team already up 1–0, The Yankees' Mark Teixeira pulverized a pitch for a grand slam. It's only the second inning, and the home team Rays were down 5–0.

7:02 PM CST: Atlanta's stadium erupted as Dan Uggla's bat did. Two-run homer. Braves led 3–1 in the third.

7:12 PM CST: Pujols lasered an RBI single to start the Cards' five-run first.

7:35 PM CST: Boston's Dustin Pedroia uncorked a homer into the Camden Yards bleachers, and the Red Sox led 3–2 in the fifth.

7:56 PM CST: Uggla tried to score on a looped single to right, but Philadelphia's right fielder Hunter Pence threw a perfect strike home. Uggla was out, and the Braves couldn't add to their 3–1 lead in the sixth.

8:06 PM CST: Atlanta shortstop Jack Wilson booted a grounder, and the Phillies scored, cutting the lead to 3–2 in the eighth.

8:33 PM CST: Rain delay in Baltimore.

8:56 PM CST: The Phillies tied the game 3–3 with a Chase Utley sacrifice fly in the ninth.

8:59 PM CST: With the bases loaded and two outs, Atlanta closer Craig Kimbrel was pulled and replaced by Kris Medlen, who got Michael Martinez to pop out and send it to extras.

9:23 PM CST: In the bottom of the eighth, the Rays trailed 7–3, when Evan Longoria's long ball drove in three. New York still led 7–6, but the stadium was deafening.

9:25 PM CST: Carpenter recorded the final out of the 8–0 shutout, and the Cards guaranteed at least a play-in game if Atlanta also won.

9:33 PM CST: Chipper Jones, the aging Atlanta legend, drilled a deep ball into the gap in the bottom of the 10th inning. With two outs and a runner on first, the base runner took off. He would've scored, but center fielder Martinez tracked the ball in stride and made a game-saving catch.

9:47 PM CST: Tampa still trailed 7–6 with two outs in the bottom of the ninth. Dan Johnson, hitting .108, was summoned off the bench by Tampa manager Joe Maddon. Two strikes. And Johnson homered. The game was tied. It was a miracle in Tampa.

9:58 PM CST: Tarp pulled in Baltimore.

10:13 PM CST: In the bottom of the 12th inning with the potential winning run at third, Atlanta's Martin Prado grounded out to end the inning.

10:28 PM CST: Philadelphia's Pence, who threw out Uggla at home in the sixth, hit a grounder to drive in a go-ahead run in the top of the 13th inning.

10:40 PM CST: Down 4–3 in the bottom of the 13th inning, the Braves got a base runner when Uggla walked with one out. Freddie Freeman, who would finish second in the Rookie of the Year voting to his teammate Kimbrel, came to bat. The Phillies' first baseman was at the bag, holding on Uggla. Freeman ripped a grounder down the first base line…but the first baseman was right there. A 3–6–3 double play.

It was over for Atlanta. Freeman slammed his helmet into the grass. Up eight-and-a-half games in the wild-card to begin September, the Braves went 9–18 in the month. As *St. Louis Post-Dispatch* reporter Derrick Goold put it: "It was the first night since June 8 that the Braves didn't at least share in the lead for the NL wild-card. It was the only night that mattered."

The St. Louis Cardinals were in the playoffs. They were the 2011 National League wild-card team. They would play the Phillies in the National League Division Series, while the Milwaukee Brewers would play the Arizona Diamondbacks. "It was such an improbable rise to catch the Braves," said the Cardinals' Daniel Descalso, who hit .303 in September. "The guys went wild, as we should."

It led to an instant and unique celebration. "That was one of the cooler celebrations for me. It was so spontaneous," Jason Motte said. "On the field you win and you're celebrating, but there's the media, and you have to do this trophy ceremony on the field, and next thing you know it's 90 minutes and you go pop champagne. So we were sitting there in Houston, and champagne and beers and everything are sitting there. The final out happens, and it turned into instant euphoria. Super overwhelmed with so much emotion. Holy cow, we're in! This is crazy. It was just a free-for-all with champagne, beer, shit being sprayed all over the place."

And back in St. Louis, 14-year-old Baris thought to himself: *That was the best birthday present I could have asked for.*

But while the NL wild-card winning team celebrated, the American League winner hadn't yet been determined.

10:48 PM CST: Tampa third baseman Longoria couldn't make a play on a soft roller by New York's Greg Golson, who was given a hit. The Yankees were alive in the top of the 12th inning.

10:54 PM CST: With Golson on third base, teammate Jorge Posada hit a grounder to third. Longoria scooped it up, but instead of throwing to first, he intelligently spotted Golson stuck on the baseline and tagged him out. It was the first out of the inning—and the biggest of the Rays' season. They got out of the inning unscathed.

10:54 PM CST: In the Boston-Baltimore game at the very same moment of the Golson out, Red Sox closer Jonathan Papelbon had recorded two outs in the bottom of the ninth with Boston up 3–2, but Papelbon allowed a double to Chris Davis.

10:59 PM CST: Baltimore's Nolan Reimold doubled to tie the game 3–3.

11:02 PM CST: As Wednesday became Thursday on the East Coast, Baltimore's Robert Andino singled to left, and Reimold beat the throw home. The game was over. Boston lost 4–3. It was Papelbon's first loss of the entire season. And his final pitch for the Boston Red Sox.

11:05 PM CST: With the Boston score posted on the Tampa scoreboard, fans knew that if the Rays won, they were in the playoffs. Longoria came to the plate in the bottom of the 12th inning. Walk-off home run. Tampa Bay won 8–7 and made it into the playoffs after being down to their last strike in the ninth. "It ended up being just the perfect storm," said Amsinger of the MLB Network. "You'll never see what we saw that night because it was the first time that it happened. And I think the Cardinals players knew this was extraordinary. I could see it on their faces as they watched the Braves and the Phillies play— and when they celebrated."

Game 6 Story No. 6

They had just experienced it together and, as the spinning cyclone that was Game 6 spit them outside of Busch Stadium, they just knew it had to happen the next night. Howard Schlansky told Mike Vredenburgh that he should propose to Schlansky's daughter at Game 7 of the 2011 World Series.

Mike Vredenburgh first met Rebecca Rubin-Schlansky in April of 2010, shortly after Rebecca decided once and for all that she would move to California. They were introduced at a dinner party in St. Louis. "I had no idea she would be there," he said. "Even when I met her there, I thought she was into my roommate."

"I was kind of into his roommate," Rebecca said.

"We all hung out together as a group for a while," Mike said.

"And then I found out he had season tickets for the Cardinals," Rebecca said with a laugh, "And I was like: 'Hey, I'm maybe not so into the roommate.'"

Rebecca and Mike were raised in St. Louis. They went to rival high schools—she went to Clayton, and he went to Ladue. The night of the 2010 dinner party, Rebecca was 26; Mike was 29. Rebecca's plan was to live in St. Louis for the summer before she'd go get both her master's degree and doctorate at the University of California-Irvine. "We went to games that summer," Rebecca said. "I always went to games during the summer."

"My family splits season tickets," Mike said. "We get like 12 to 15 games a year, but they're really good seats. It's Section 156, Row 2 right behind the visitor's dugout. They're old Boatman's Bank seats from back in the day."

"When I was younger, I always liked calling for time and temperature," Rebecca said. "'Boatman's Bank time is...'"

They had a fun summer together—sort of a Sandy-and-Danny Zuko thing at Busch instead of the beach. In September of 2010, Rebecca moved to California. "We were kind of like—we'll see where this goes," Rebecca said. "Then basically we did every three weeks. I was coming home or he was going there. So we saw each other a lot. We were dating that year—2010 to 2011. And I came home on breaks. And that whole summer of 2011, I was home."

After Rebecca went back to California in August of 2011 and the Cards began their amazing playoff push, Mike sometimes attended Cardinal games with her father because his own father couldn't go. Jim Vredenburgh had both squamous cell oral cancer and rectal cancer. "He was in pretty rough shape," Mike said.

Mike and his dad had attended the 2006 World Series together five years earlier. They were at the clinching game. "We had tons of baseball memories for sure," Mike said.

Mike was a similar age of a certain generation of St. Louisans who were alive in 1982 but too young to remember it. So the 2006 World Series was really a lot of people's first World Series win. To share that with his dad was something he cherishes, sort of like a family heirloom. Jim was an ever-present influence in Mike's life and his baseball life. In 1987 they sat in the bleachers together during the contentious National League Championship Series against the San Francisco Giants. One San Francisco player had called St. Louis a "cow town," which didn't go over well with the million or so people who allegedly lived in a cow town.

Growing up, Mike played catch with his dad in their yard, and they watched Cards games on KPLR Channel 11. And Jim never missed one of Mike's own baseball games—from third grade through senior year. Mike cherished those drives home, as the ballplayer and his biggest fan recapped the game.

Earlier in the fall of 2011, Rebecca had booked a trip home for October 28, 2011. It was a Friday afternoon, so she wouldn't miss any class. But when the Cardinals made the World Series and the schedule came out, "I was devastated that I wasn't going to be in St. Louis for Game 7," she said.

Per the schedule, Game 6 (if necessary) would be Wednesday, October 26, 2011. And Game 7 (if necessary) would be Thursday, October 27, 2011. She was coming home on Friday. Sure enough, due to a threat of weather, MLB postponed Wednesday's Game 6 for one day. So…Game 6 was now Thursday. And Game 7 was Friday, the day Rebecca arrived in St. Louis. "And I've already asked her parents for their hand in marriage type-thing," Mike said, joking about the phrasing. "Wait, their blessing, her hand? There was a hand involved. So they'd given me their blessing."

And so it wasn't weird for Howard and Mike in the car ride home from Game 6 to discuss a possible proposal at Game 7. Originally, Mike was going to propose during Thanksgiving. Of course, they had to get Game 7 tickets (they did). And hope that Rebecca's Friday flight wasn't delayed (it wasn't). So, with Mother Nature's twist of fate, Rebecca was able to be in St. Louis for Game 7. And then to find out she was going to Game 7 with her dad and boyfriend? "When Mike told me we were going, I think I hit him," Rebecca said. "I channeled my inner Elaine Benes."

The night couldn't get any better, right? Mike, Rebecca, and Howard had tickets in the club suite on the third-base side of Busch Stadium. "It's the glassed-in area where they have the really delicious cinnamon pretzels," Rebecca said.

"It's all-inclusive," Mike said. "You get beer and stadium food as part of the ticket. This is all part of the story. I had a lot of beer that night. The nerves were going for various reasons."

That was the catch—he was going to only propose if the Cardinals won the World Series, so first, the Cardinals had to win the World Series. Oh, and there was another catch. "In the months leading up to this, when we were talking about getting married and thinking about engagement," Rebecca said, "I told him, 'I will say no to you if you propose to me in front of anybody else. Anybody!'...So, Game 7 of the World Series makes total sense given that directive, right?"

In the first inning, the Texas Rangers took a 2–0 lead. "At that point," Mike said, "I kept looking at her dad."

"I'm thinking we're done at that point," Rebecca recalled of her Cardinals.

But, of all people, David Freese doubled in the bottom of the first. He drove in Albert Pujols and Lance Berkman to tie the game just as he'd done with his triple in the ninth the night before. The Cards took the lead in the third and added on in the fifth and seventh. The score was 6–2. "And I'm getting texts left and right because I'd let a few friends and family in on the details by then," Mike said. "Her parents knew. Some of the guys knew."

"Really?" Rebecca said. "That's so cute."

"So the game's going on," Mike said. "Her sister almost blew it a couple of times with texts…I remember it was going into the eighth inning. Rebecca had gone to the bathroom. Her dad had the ring—her grandmother's ring. It was in a pullover coat that he had. I started to fish it out. I had a moment to get it on my person."

Before the ninth inning, Jason Motte took the mound to warm up while up four runs. "In hindsight, it was a little presumptive of me," Mike said of a Cardinals' win.

Outside of the suite, there was a short wall along the concourse behind the sections of seats. Fans could stand behind it and look out to the field. As Mike and Rebecca sauntered out there, Howard lingered in the distance—with a camera ready. And Mike got on one knee. "I opened the ring box upside down and asked her to marry me," Mike said.

"It's the end of the eighth so everybody is looking on the field," Rebecca said. "In my memory of it, it's all slow-mo. I'm standing to his left, and he turns to me and gets on one knee. And my first thought in my head, I didn't say this out loud, was: 'Don't do it. Everybody is here.' There were like 40,000 people there. But it was really, really lovely. And the Cardinals were about to win the World Series, so no one says no to anything at that point. I distinctly remember it. There was no one to the right. I'm looking around, and there was no one looking at us. So it was actually pretty cool. We were surrounded by 40,000 people, and nobody saw us."

"We watched the ninth inning arm-in-arm, and then the fireworks went off," Mike said, "and it was for us."

Rebecca wouldn't be the only person getting a ring. Asked to describe the moment when Allen Craig caught the ball and Rebecca felt the simultaneous experience of being engaged and her team winning a championship, she said: "There's a lot riding on this quote! But this is how I was thinking of it at the time and kind of the way I still think of it: I really, really love that baseball is a part of our story this way. Part of my affinity for baseball is the way that it is intricately woven into the fabric of the American story. So all of these moments, all these peak moments and these pit moments in United States history, it's often reflected in baseball. That's one of the things I love about it. At the time what also struck me was that baseball and particularly this incredible ride of the postseason was stitched into our story in a similar fashion."

"I mean, prior to Rebecca," Mike said, "my true love was the Cardinals."

After watching the celebration on the field, the future newlyweds and the future father of the bride headed out of the stadium. Mike called his own father. "It was pretty special. Everything kind of came together," Mike said. "To be able to share it with him was amazing."

At age 60, Jim Vredenburgh died on March 8, 2012, knowing his son had fallen in love and would be married.

The next year, before the ceremony, the bridal party went to Busch Stadium. Mike and Rebecca took wedding photos at home plate, in the Cardinals' dugout, and near a pennant that celebrated the 2011 World Series champs. They pointed up to the stands to show friends the spot where Mike proposed.

And now they're a family. Mike and Rebecca have two daughters.

CHAPTER 7

THE 2011 NLDS

A couple weeks before the Cardinals–Phillies series was a Cardinals–Phillies series. The Birds were in Philadelphia for four—St. Louis won three games in that series, too—and before one of the September games, Nick Punto ran into his old boss from his old team. "Nick knew Ruben Amaro Jr., the GM at the time because Nick was a Phillie," said Skip Schumaker, who hit .283 for the 2011 Cards. "So they went and chatted, and Nick asks Ruben what he thinks of the race. And Ruben says, 'Well, I mean, we're planning for Atlanta, but best-case scenario is we get to play you guys [in the National League Division Series].' So Nick told us that, and we're all like, 'What the fuck?' Who has the balls to say that? Obviously, we weren't running on all cylinders at the time. But you still had to beat Chris Carpenter. You still had to beat Albert Pujols and Lance Berkman or Rafael Furcal or Yadi Molina. We had dudes. It wasn't like some shitty team that came out of the blue and no one had ever heard of. Some people had picked us to win the World Series in the preseason. It wasn't some shit team. So a couple of us got wind of that, and it kind of lit a little fire in our ass entering [the NLDS] because we remembered Ruben wanted us. So for us, it was like: you wanted us? Here we are."

The Cardinals arrived in Philadelphia with a 23–9 record since August 24 and the Carpenter team meeting and the Adam Wainwright dinner speech. They believed they belonged. They also knew that every opponent from now on would be outstanding. You could even make the argument that the team they beat in the first round was the best of the teams they faced in October. "Every time we had a game, we had a legit chance to win," said Placido Polanco, the former Cardinals player who was a 2011 All-Star for the Phillies and won the Gold Glove at third base. "We had Roy Halladay. We had Cliff Lee. Cole Hamels. Roy Oswalt. We had Joe Blanton pitching. We had a really, really good team. It was kind of tough to face us in 2011. Good hitters, too. We had a good combination of veteran guys and guys coming up. It was a really nice group. I really thought we were going to make it further."

The Phillies, who won 102 games that year, had the lowest ERA in the National League, and it wasn't even close. As a team Philadelphia was at 3.02 (the San Francisco Giants were second at 3.20). In the Cy Young voting, the Phillies had the guys who came in second, third, and fifth. For the season the Phillies staff logged 18 complete games. The second-place total was seven. This was a stable of horses. Shoot, a stable of Secretariats. "That was as good of a staff as you could find around the league," the Cards' Daniel Descalso said. "But I think something that helped us and helped our offense was that we went into Philly in September, and we took three out of four from them. I think that gave us some confidence. So instead of being intimidated by that staff, which could happen to a lot of offenses, I think we recalled that series where we'd gone in and won. We had a boost headed into that place."

Halladay's ERA that season was 2.35, but in 2011 first innings, his ERA was 3.66. Sometimes in the small sample size of the playoffs, a stat like that is irrelevant. For Halladay, it defined his NLDS. Rafael Furcal led off the 2011 postseason with a Game 1 single off Doc. An aggressive Tony La Russa called for a hit-and-run, but as Furcal began to run, Allen Craig couldn't hit the pitch. Furcal, nevertheless, stole the base. But after Craig struck out, Halladay pitched around Pujols with a walk. Clean-shaven for this new season, Berkman came to bat and he smacked the first pitch he saw over the wall in right.

It was 3–0 Cardinals before the Phillies could get three outs (or even two). "The team takes on the identity of its leaders, so if you looked at Albert, Lance, Matt Holliday, Yadi, those guys never got too high, too low," Descalso said. "They never let the moment get too big or let the crowd affect them. So for us young guys, we were able to look at those veteran players and kind of take on that identity."

Back in St. Louis, in the heyday of the late 1990s, there was this magical locale where the currency was tokens. It was called The Infield Fun Center, but the soda-fueled kids in their Gap clothing just called it "The Infield." It had go-karts, mini-golf, video arcade, batting cages and was in Ellisville out in St. Louis County near Wildwood. Local ballplayers from nearby Lafayette High, including David Freese, would sometimes go there to take some swings.

And one Lafayette player even worked there. "Still have the T-shirt," said Ryan Howard at age 39 in 2019 in an interview for a *St. Louis Post-Dispatch* column. "It was great. In the day of age we live in now, you have all these different facilities that kids go to and work out and train and hit. We didn't really have a whole lot of those. For me I can go there and get six tokens for $5 and hit close to 200 balls. And for me it was more about the training aspect of it, seeing the speed."

It's extraordinary to think that Lafayette—just one of the many large public high schools in St. Louis—produced a World Series MVP in Freese, a National League MVP in Howard, and in subsequent years, Luke Voit, who led all of baseball in home runs in 2020. And on this 2011 day, Freese and Howard were opponents in the playoffs. The Infield was represented in the infield.

Howard's 2011 was the final top 10 MVP year of his career featuring triumphant oomph. It was the Philadelphia slugger's sixth straight season with 30 homers and 100 RBIs. (Incidentally and incredibly, 2011 was the first and only St. Louis season Pujols didn't have 100 RBIs; he had 99. And it was the only St. Louis season Pujols didn't hit .300; he hit .299.) Howard provided muscle in the heart of the Phillies lineup. "I remember how quiet [Howard's swing] is at the plate and still hitting the ball a mile," Polanco said of his teammate. "That tells you how strong that guy is."

With his manicured goatee and 3.39 ERA, Kyle Lohse allowed just one Game 1 run through five innings. But in the sixth with the Cards up 3–1, there were two on for Howard. The giant in red pinstripes loomed in the lefty batter's box. He spit on his right batting glove and rubbed his hands and gripped his bat and stared. Lohse's pitch No. 69 was creamed. This thing went 423 feet, and the Phillies led 4–3. "That stadium in Philly was a complete beehive," Cards coach Derek Lilliquist said.

Two batters later, Raul Ibanez hit a two-run homer. La Russa pulled Lohse, but it was too late. The Phillies scored five runs that inning and five more runs the next two innings. Oh, and after a subpar first inning, Halladay retired 21 straight Cardinals hitters—and only one ball even left the infield. The Phillies won Game 1 by the score of 11–6.

Was this going to be 2009 all over again?

In Game 2 the Cardinals were down 1–0 in the series and down 4–0 in the game. They weren't getting calls from the home-plate umpire, as La Russa continually chirped from the Birds' dugout. Heading into the fourth inning, Carpenter was done for the day, gassed by pitching on three days' rest. Meanwhile, Philadelphia's star starter Cliff Lee hadn't allowed a run. If Cardinals fans were to let themselves go there mentally, this sure seemed like it would end like the last playoffs did. The Cards missed the playoffs in 2010, but in 2009 they were swept in the NLDS, also losing the first two games on the road.

A difference here—Holliday wasn't in left field. In Game 2 in 2009, he was the culprit or victim of a missed fly ball, depending on how you detail it. Holliday had a monster year in 2011—like he did really every year he wore the birds on the bat. He was an All-Star in '11 and finished with a .912 OPS—second on the team behind Berkman's .959 and ahead of Pujols' .906. But he also endured multiple injuries, an appendectomy and even a moth that was stuck in his ear in the outfield. By the 2011 NLDS, Holliday suffered a tendon injury in his right hand and only started two of the games.

But down 4–0 in Game 2, the resilient Cardinals began to script a new narrative. They dinged Lee for three runs in the fourth, thanks in part to a Ryan Theriot double, and they tied the game off Lee in the sixth, thanks in part to another Theriot double. It was 4–4 and in essence a whole new ballgame. And the Cards had a bunch of momentum. They had scored the past four runs of the game, their bullpen was menacing, and Lee was laboring.

To lead off the seventh was the man who started for Holliday in left field—Craig. Though he was in his first full MLB season, Craig already had valuable postseason experience. He was the slugging sensation on the Cardinals' 2009 Triple A team, which won the Pacific Coast League championship. And in 2010 they made it to the final round of the PCL playoffs. Craig became close friends with Memphis teammates Descalso and Jon Jay, a friendship that became part of St. Louis lore in 2011. It was a friendship that grew on the field in Memphis—and the virtual fields of Barcelona and Manchester. "In Triple A we played a lot of *FIFA*," Craig said of the popular soccer video game. "In 2010 we were rooming together, and there wasn't a spare room for me when I was down one time, and I was sleeping on the couch. And *FIFA* helped me get through a few 0-for-4 games. I'd come home, and we'd play a bunch of *FIFA* and just talk shop about the baseball games while we were playing video games. It was an awesome way to decompress and get better at the same time. We were always honest with each other about how we were playing. And with *FIFA*, I'd stay up late and play and try to get better."

Each of the three was trustworthy with the glove, and each player also made offensive impacts on the 2011 Cardinals. Jay hit .297. Descalso hit .264 and had one of the bigger at-bats in Game 6 of the World Series. Craig's OPS in 2011 was .917 in his 219 plate appearances, and he played some of the season with a fracture in his kneecap. As a trio they combined for 59 doubles in 2011. "Obviously," Schumaker said, "we don't sniff the playoffs or win the World Series without those guys."

"I had heard that young guys can't play for Tony," Descalso said. "They usually have veteran players on the bench. We kind of broke that mold and passed all of Tony's tests. He can be intimidating for a young player at times, but he respected you if you showed up and played with no fear and knew what your job was. If you went out and competed, he had no problem with you. It was the guys who maybe weren't as prepared or maybe didn't compete like he wanted them to— they're the ones who had trouble playing for him."

In Game 2 of the NLDS, Jay had two hits. And there was Craig, starting in left for Holliday, batting in the top of the seventh of a 4–4 game. After six innings the Cards had nine hits against Lee, but none from Craig, who quickly found himself in a 0–2 count. He then fouled off a pitch and survived a curveball, which froze him…but was called a ball. Craig battled at the bat and then rattled his bat, drilling a ball to the deepest part of the ballpark. On the warning track, center fielder Shane Victorino tried to track it down but couldn't catch up to it. The ball bounced off the glove, and then Victorino bounced off the wall.

Craig had never tripled in the majors. Even when he retired after 1,831 at-bats, he'd only hit three triples. But here—in the biggest at-bat of his life—he tripled. And Pujols promptly drove him in with a hit. The Cards led 5–4.

Jason Motte closed things down with a four-out save. And while Craig's triple was the game's big hit, the St. Louis relievers were the biggest storyline—and a sign for what was to come. After Carp's three innings, six relievers combined for the final six innings. And they didn't walk a batter and allowed only one hit (the "they" being Marc Rzepczynski). The jovial Octavio Dotel, also part of the Colby Rasmus trade, picked up the win.

The series was tied 1–1. The series was now a series.

• • •

Game 3 brought out the Clydesdales and the shadows at Busch during an afternoon affair. Jaime Garcia pitched well, but Cole Hamels pitched even better. A Garcia homer allowed to—of all people, the innocuous Ben Francisco—was the difference in the game. It was a three-run shot, and the Philadelphia Phillies won Game 3 by the score of 3–2. The Cardinals would need to win the last two games to win the series.

And in the elimination Game 4, Skip Schumaker would produce two hits—yet the at-bat people remember is one where he got out.

Some ballplayers are so superstitious they're superstitious about talking about superstitions. Others, like the character Michael Scott in *The Office*, might not be not superstitious, but are "a little stitious."

As for the battling, glove-wriggling, Red Bull-chugging Schumaker, "You wouldn't believe how superstitious I am," he shared in 2020. "Superstitions before every game? We could be here all day. I used to have to adjust my batting gloves before every pitch. I was almost like Nomar Garciaparra. I'd have to touch my hat a certain way, had to touch the plate a certain way. There's a lot of things that I had to do before each game as far as superstitions go. I had the same meal for breakfast. I had a million peanut butter and jellys before games. That was my pregame snack. A sandwich and a Red Bull at 6:30 before every night game."

So if there was any Cardinals hitter to be the batter when an animal ran past home plate, it was, of course, the superstitious Skip. A couple weeks prior, bullpen coach Derek Lilliquist had a conversation with a ground crew member that sounded like a scene from *Caddyshack*. "The funny thing was," Lilliquist shared, "Billy from the ground crew kept telling us about a squirrel. 'This damn squirrel keeps coming out here and burying something in the grass almost every day, whether the team is here or not.' It didn't dawn on me then, but I knew a squirrel was out on the field during the day at times. And then, lo and behold, there's a squirrel out there during the game."

In Game 3 a squirrel quickly darted across the field but not near any action. A day later in Game 4, Schumaker was at-bat in the fifth, as the Cards led 3–2. The count was 1–1 when a squirrel again made an appearance. This time the little guy ran right in front of Schumaker and home plate—just a split-second after Roy Oswalt's pitch was caught. Schumaker hadn't swung, and umpire Angel Hernandez called the pitch a ball. "Roy threw a strike, by the way. That pitch was right down the middle," Schumaker said. "But he called it a ball. And Oswalt is like, *What the fuck happened?* Angel tells him it was a squirrel and that the pitch was a ball. And Oswalt says, 'What, does a fucking moose have to run by for that to be a strike?'"

There was quite a hubbub in the moments after. The squirrel ran into the stands, scampering through the green seats and then up the stairs. Oswalt and Phillies manager Charlie Manuel argued with Hernandez. Some onlookers might've been confused and thought Hernandez had called for time after the pitch, as if the squirrel had interrupted the at-bat, but no, Hernandez had simply called a ball. Oswalt mouthed the word "wow," as he gathered himself for the next pitch. Then Schumaker flew out to center on the next pitch. And Albert Pujols flew out to right.

Still, Twitter was atwitter with talk about the Cardinals' "rally squirrel." Someone even created a Twitter account for the squirrel. In the coming days, it became a thing. There would be rally squirrel T-Shirts, hats, and dolls. And an actual rally squirrel mascot was created to pal around with Fredbird at Busch Stadium. This squirrel was some sort of omen. Or some sort of something.

And then the very next inning after the squirrel, David Freese essentially saved the season. The third baseman entered Game 4 just 2-for-12 in the National League Division Series. No walks, six strikeouts. But earlier in Game 4, he finally had a postseason moment. He drove the ball to left and drove in two with the double. Down 2–1 in the game, the Cards suddenly led 3–2. That was the score when Schumaker came up in the fifth. And that was the score in the sixth when Freese returned to bat—and with Matt Holliday on first. Oswalt delivered an inside fastball, and Freese deposited it over the center-field wall onto the green rectangle lawn. Surely, it would go down as his greatest homer to ever land there.

It was 5–2. And when Fernando Salas allowed a run in the eighth, the score became 5–3. Freese's homer would thus prove to be the game-winning RBIs. And he had four total in Game 4.

Game 5 would happen. The Cards would throw Carp. The Phillies would counter with Doc. Chris Carpenter and Roy Halladay were former Toronto Blue Jays teammates. Fishing buddies. In the months after this classic duel, the two were part of a fishing excursion to the Amazon. The story of Game 5 sounds like a fish tale. "If you enjoy pitching," Carpenter said in 2020, "that game is something that people are going to talk about 50 years from now."

In 2017 Halladay tragically died in a plane accident. Thinking back to that night, Carpenter said, "There are definitely all kinds of mixed emotions that go on with that."

But in its own way, Game 5 is a keepsake for those who loved Halladay because even in defeat the start showcased his bristle and his brilliance. "It was a wonderful night, an epic game," Carpenter said. "And it's something I will always hold onto."

• • •

Skip Schumaker had started Games 1 and 4 of the series—both at second base. "Before Game 5 Tony called me in and said he wanted to start Nick Punto and second base," Schumaker recalled. "He knew I had some numbers against Halladay, but he said he wanted to start Nick at second. So I'm thinking, *I'm not playing.* He wanted Nick's glove at second base with Carpenter on the mound and all the lefties in the lineup. It made total sense to me. Then Tony told me he was going to start me in center field instead—and that I'll be hitting second. He told me, 'Furcal is going to get on. You've got to do what you can to make something happen.'"

Sure enough, the leadoff hitter Rafael Furcal got on. Just like in Game 1 against Roy Halladay, Furcal opened the game with a hit. But this was a smash—all the way to the outfield wall, off the advertisement for the Turkey Hill, a dairy in Lancaster County, Pennsylvania. Furcal kept trucking, the relay transition wasn't crisp, and Furcal slid head-first into third for a triple. "Luckily, for me, Tony always had a knack for putting guys in the right spots at the right time," Schumaker said. "He put guys in positions to succeed. For whatever reason, I saw Halladay okay. He wasn't a comfortable at-bat by any means, but I saw Halladay okay. So I felt good about starting against Halladay. I knew we were going to get him twice if we went five games…I felt good about getting on base for the big games. I knew we weren't going to score a ton of runs, but I knew I could get on base. Rafael hits a triple. I come up, and my whole thought process was: ground ball up the middle. Let me get him in. So I was just trying initially to get a good pitch to hit in the middle of the plate. But I wasn't getting it. Halladay wasn't nibbling because he doesn't nibble. He was putting every pitch where he wanted it nine out of the 10 times. It was some of the nastiest stuff I've ever seen. So I'm just battling, trying to put something in play. That was my whole mind-set."

Ten pitches. Six fouls. That at-bat lasted three minutes and 25 seconds. "He ends up hanging a curveball—something I never really hit in my career—and I was fortunate to send it down the line," Schumaker said.

He drilled it. The lefty Schumaker pulled it into the right-field corner. RBI double, Cards up 1–0. There had yet to be an out recorded in the first inning, and all the scoring that would happen in the game had occurred.

What happened next was performance art. Perhaps it was specifically like a hip-hop battle with two masterful emcees—one unleashing lyrics of poetry and potency, only to be matched greatness for greatness by the other man. Back and forth, back and forth. "Two great pitchers just competing their faces off," Cards reliever Jason Motte said. "It was crickets the rest of the game."

After the first inning, Halladay pitched seven scoreless innings. He allowed just four more hits, striking out seven, walking one. His day was over after eight innings and 126 pitches thrown. And the score remained the same—1–0 Cardinals. "Roy was a student of the game," said Placido Polanco, the Philadelphia Phillies third baseman who went 0-for-3 against Chris Carpenter in Game 5. "I never played with a guy who studied the other team more than he did. He studied days in advance about the lineup, how each guy hits. What a true professional. And then he had his cutter, his curveball, his fastball. Everything he threw was so good."

That same evening Carpenter pitched with an urgency and a certainty. He allowed only three hits the entire game. Not one walk either, though he hit one batter, which happened in the fourth. And with that runner on and two outs, Shane Victorino singled. That made it first and third for Raul Ibanez, who had 84 RBIs that season.

Inside the Cardinals' clubhouse, as they did for many of the games during the season, traveling secretary CJ Cherre watched the game with video coordinator Chad Blair. "And in the fourth inning, I'll never forget this," Cherre said, "There were men at first and third, two outs, and Ibanez came up. He crushed it. Chad and I at the same time said, 'Ah, fuck.' We thought it was gone. Berkman kept going back and back and he looked up, and the ball landed in his glove. Later on, I know somebody from the Phillies, and he came in and said if that ball is hit in the middle of the summer, that's a home run. But it was a cool night and it just didn't carry. After that you can feel your heart racing."

Carp would only let on one more base runner. Chase Utley singled in the sixth—and Yadier Molina threw him out trying to steal. But because of the 1–0 score, the tying (or a go-ahead) run was at the plate every single time a Phillies hitter was at the plate. But Carpenter sneered at fear. The Cards were going to do it. Carp was going to do it. "Game 5," St. Louis general manager John Mozeliak said, "perhaps the greatest pitching performance I've ever seen in person and in a game that mattered."

There were two outs in the bottom of the ninth, but the batter was Ryan Howard. The St. Louis native was all that stood between St. Louis and a playoff series victory. With the count 2–2, Carp whipped in a curveball. Howard grounded to second base and fell to the ground. He ruptured his left Achilles tendon. Punto corralled the grounder at second and tossed it to Albert Pujols at first.

Molina and the infielders came at Carpenter from all sides, and the pitcher unleashed a primal scream with his mouth opening impossibly wide. A three-hit, no-walk, 1–0 shutout against his dear friend to win a playoff series on the road. The Shredder shredded Carpenter's jersey. Huddled as one on the field, the Cardinals chanted: "Happy flight!" And the headline the next day in the *St. Louis Post-Dispatch* read: PHILLIE-BUSTER.

Game 6 Story No. 7

Of all the weeks, it happened the week Dr. Daniel Wann was visiting colleagues of his hyper-specific field. After a day of lectures at a conference, they went to a sports bar in Huntsville, Texas. Psychology professors sat amongst psychotic sports fans. It was October 27, 2011. Texas fans fixated on every Game 6 pitch. Each Cardinals out meant the Rangers were one out closer to their first World Series championship. "And then David Freese hit the triple to right field," Wann said. "The silence in that bar became deafening."

That lack of noise was so impactful that it became overwhelming. "We're half-looking at the TV and half-looking at all of the fans in the room," Wann said. "It was fascinating. I said, 'I should hand these fans a questionnaire and I could write my dinner off on my taxes.'"

Wann is a distinguished professor of psychology at Murray State University. The 2020–21 school year was his 30th year at the school. For a living he studies sports fandom. He's devoted his professional life to answering the question: why do we care so much? "I got my PhD in social psychology from the University of Kansas," Wann said. "And when I was there, one of our first assignments was to talk to the other grad students about their research. Every time I talked to them, they would just tell me how boring it was. I knew I didn't want to do something boring. I was brainstorming about what I wanted to study, and there was no one—and I mean no one—who was doing research on sports fans. I found that strange because something like 75 percent of our country is sports fans. So I approached a faculty member, and she said it sounded interesting. No one was doing anything on it. So it went from there."

In St. Louis so many people adore the Cardinals. But what's the psychology behind it? Why do fans behave so emotionally when it comes to their Cardinals? It all seems quite normal behavior to those who live it, but look at it from this peculiar perspective: imagine explaining our culture to an intelligent alien lifeform:

ALIEN: What do you do for fun?

ST. LOUISAN: Sports!

ALIEN: Oh, so you play sports?

ST. LOUISAN: No, no, we watch others play sports.

ALIEN: Oh, you mean like family and close friends?

ST. LOUISAN: No, actually it's people we've never met and probably never will.

ALIEN: So for fun you spend time watching strangers accomplish something?

"To that alien," Wann said, "who would probably look at me like I was an alien, I would say: 'Well, do you have theater on your planet?' They'd say, 'sure.' 'Well, are you in the theater?' 'No, I go and watch it.' 'Are they your friends on stage?' 'No, they're actors.' 'Aha!' And besides sports, there are other pastimes where humans are just as passionate. Good Lord, look how long people will sit outside in the rain waiting for a new *Star Wars* movie. And you think baseball fans dress up? We're amateurs compared to those people. The difference, of course, is that you can go see *Star Wars* a thousand times, and the ending is the same. You can go see a thousand Cardinals games. It's never same story. But with sports, I've spent about 30 years studying why fans do what they do."

So why do fans do what they do? "How much time do you have?" Wann said with a chuckle. "There are a lot of ways that you can tackle that question. You can look at motivations or drivers of fandom. We know some fans will consume sport because of a desire for escape, or some fans will consume sport because they like the aesthetic or the artistic form of the game. I'm watching something on Facebook now about the all-time best catch in baseball. They thought it was Jim Edmonds [and his famous catch for the Angels, diving backward full extension to haul in a ball]. Baseball fans, we look at that and say, 'That's art. That's like ballet.' So we know that there are these drivers for consumption, but I think at the end of the day, the reason people are so interested in following sport as a passion is because doing so meets basic human psychological needs. There are needs that we have at a very basic human level, that are psychological in nature, and sport fandom can help meet that. So for example, we have a very powerful need to belong. We've evolved to be social creatures. Well, what's a more social activity than sport fandom? No one goes to Busch Stadium and doesn't talk to people. And you go with friends or family. It's a shared experience. It's something they have in common and it makes them feel as though they belong, as though they fit in.

"So if you're a Cardinals fan in St. Louis or O'Fallon or Wentzville, and it's the summer of 2011, and you're walking around with a Cardinals hat on, there's no way that you feel alone. Everywhere you go, you feel [accepted by others]. You might not know their name. You don't know what their job is or who their family is. But you still feel as though you know them and you fit in. So one very powerful need is this sense of belonging. Another powerful need that's met by fandom is: meaning in life. It gives us a sense of purpose. If you talk to Cardinals fans and you ask them to reminisce about the 2011 season, you'll hear them saying things that let you know that they weren't simply watching this on TV. They weren't just going, 'Okay, the Cardinals are on, and I'll watch and whatever.' No, it meant something to them. It gave them a sense of purpose. They'd wake up in the morning and think about how Game 3 is later that day. It gave them meaning.

"And one more thing with sports—and this is really important during a baseball season—is it gives you structure. Talk to baseball fans [during the first months of the 2020 pandemic]. Ask them what's missing in St. Louis. They'll tell you it's summer, so I'm supposed to get up, go to work, come home at 6:00, and then turn on the game at 7:00. Listen to people that are 50 to 60 years old and ask them about summers growing up as a kid. 'I came home and at 7:00, I turned on Jack Buck and Mike Shannon on the radio. That's what you would do.' So there's a need for a sense of structure, a sense of normality and normalcy. That's really missing in people's lives right now. Cardinals fans aren't just missing the baseball and the stadium. They're missing the fact that they can set their calendar by it."

The yearning for a championship is central to the shared quest of a team's fans. In 2011 Cardinals fans were in it together. They'd been all in on this wild ride—from 10½ games out to Game 162 to Game 5 to knocking off the Milwaukee Brewers to Game 6. This inexplicable and exhilarating journey toward bliss. "When the championship occurs," Wann said, "because being a fan of the team is so central to who we are, it's such a central component of our identity. We are naturally going to feel a sense of accomplishment ourselves, particularly if we've been waiting 50 years for it to happen. 'I've earned it because I've put in the blood, the sweat, the tears.' Listen to Red Sox fans. They say they went through all of that, 'I deserve this. I've paid my dues.' You haven't done anything. You have yet to make a plate appearance."

Wann's perspective on sports fandom isn't solely based on research. The doctor is a Chicago Cubs, Kansas City Royals, and Kansas City Chiefs fan. He understands the longing for a championship simply by existing in modern America—let alone his fancy degree. "We did this study a few years ago," he recalled. "I was at home one night watching TV and a Klondike bar commercial comes on. It goes, 'What would you do for a Klondike Bar?' For some reason, maybe it's the fact that I'm a Cubs fan and a Royals fan who was horrifically frustrated at that point, but I thought to myself: *What would I do for a championship? What would I do to watch the Cubs win a World Series?* So I got a hold of some of my colleagues, and we came up with these crazy scenarios. Would you go without showering for a month? Would you cut off one of your fingers? Would you wear the same underwear for a year?

"And here's what we found. First of all, you'd be shocked at what people would admit to doing to win a championship. But the two things that predicted their willingness to engage in these crazy activities: one was their level of identification. And that makes sense. If you're not a big Cardinals fan, you go to one game every other year—you're not wearing the same underwear for 20 days to see them win a championship. But if you're a season-ticket holder, you'll wear the same underwear for the rest of your life. So the more identified you were, the more you felt a connection to the team, the more likely you would believe you would do these things. But also, and this was fascinating, the longer it had been since that fan's team had won a championship, the more likely they were to be engaging in those things. So if I asked Cubs fans in 2013, 'Would you cut off your pinky for a Cubs World Series,' they'd have said, 'Where's the knife?' You ask that same person now, they'd say: 'Well, we did just recently win one.'"

The 2011 World Series made David Freese a forever 11-letter, goose bump-grower of a noun. His name tingles bones, turns adults into kids, and neutralizes societal status. It doesn't matter if you're rich, poor, successful, or scuffling, everyone's idolization of Freese is similar. This hero worship is remarkable, especially considering most Cardinals fans don't know Freese, have never met Freese. But they speak of him in this reverence, as if he did this thing for them personally that no one they actually know could reciprocate. And then you add the fact that he's from St. Louis, and it takes the idolization to a special place. And when it comes to the two-out, two-strike triple, the fact that the stakes were so high and the odds were so low made the accomplishment gobsmackingly important. It was personal. It's so weird, right? A stranger in your life can do something that is so intimately personal to you. "It mattered to the fans," Wann said. "How many people's lives were changed because David Freese placed a piece of wood at the right spot, at the right time twice? When people lift up the teams that we love in such a dramatic fashion, then those people become these icons that represent these magical moments to us.

"No one cares about the outs that David Freese made in the postseason. None of that matters. To them, he was responsible for so much happiness that they had not only that game, but the next game and the next several months after that—and it continues now. Sit a Cardinals fan down and ask what they remember about the 2011 World Series. They're going to smile. You're going to put them in a good mood. It doesn't matter how their day has been. 'Man, I got a flat tire coming home, then I got stuck in traffic.' That's a bummer. Hey, can you tell me about the 2011 World Series?' Their smile would light up a room. David Freese is the reason for that. He's the person that is sort of attached to that overly powerful and positive memory. You do that and you get elevated to icon status.

"One of the best predictors of a fan choosing a sport hero is the similarity that they feel with that player. It is the best predictor. Similarity in any numbers of ways, whether it's gender or race or ethnicity or hometown or what college they attended. So my wife, Michelle, she loves the Cowboys. And she's an Ohio State fan. So she *loves* Ezekiel Elliott. A couple of years ago, we were at a conference in Dallas, and it was being held in their training facility. We got to go on this very special tour of the locker rooms. They had security everywhere, and we were told not to sit in their lockers. All of a sudden, I hear, 'Ma'am, you can't sit there.' I look over, and she's having a seat in Zeke's locker. I knew then I married great and I should keep studying this stuff. So why would she like Zeke? Because they went to the same school. When we were first starting to date, she told me she liked the Patriots because one of the players, Matt Light, was from her hometown of Greenville, Ohio, and he was still very actively involved in her hometown in Ohio. So it makes perfect sense that the fans are already going to like David Freese because he's one of them. He's from St. Louis. And then you add on his performance in Game 6? He should have run for mayor or something."

CHAPTER 8

THE 2011 NLCS

Revenge is a dish best served with curds. So the Cardinals headed to Wisconsin for a couple weekends and exacted vengeance via victories against the Milwaukee Brewers. The National League Championship Series matchup was delicious—the National League Central champion Brewers against the second-place Cardinals, who so often won the division. Finally, the Brewers prevailed as the top team in the division in 2011, but they had to overcome the Cards, yet again, if they wanted to reach the World Series.

Incidentally, the Brewers hadn't been to the World Series since 1982—back when they were in the American League and lost to, of course, the Cardinals. And in the last 2011 game between the two teams, a certain someone threw chew in the direction of Chris Carpenter, inciting both teams to rush the field. "We wanted Nyjer Morgan so bad," Skip Schumaker said. "We wanted him so bad. Nobody wanted him more than Chris Carpenter or Yadi, but all of us were really looking forward to that series after him saying that we'd be watching them from the couch. We wanted them as much as anybody. I've had some rivals everywhere I've played, but there was nothing like this one, where we wanted a team so bad."

The Cardinals sure hit like it early on—five runs in the first five innings against Zack Greinke. But in the bottom of that fifth inning, Milwaukee proved why they had the best home record in the majors. Down 5–2 Milwaukee scored six times. Tony La Russa described the onslaught as "bam, bam, bam." Unpredictable in the postseason, Jaime Garcia got the Game 1 loss.

What happened next was almost like something out of a different league. Like an NBA player who can control the offense with the shots he takes, Albert Pujols took over a Major League Baseball game. His homer, three doubles, and five RBIs in Game 2 was like, well, something out of a different league. His homer came in the first inning. He had that look. On the swing prior to the homer, he ripped a ball foul. And then on the homer swing, he adjusted perfectly with his hands and catapulted the pitch. It was 2–0 Cards before some Milwaukee fans could get the sauerkraut on their sausages. The Cards put up a dozen and won 12–6.

They flew a happy flight back to St. Louis for the first National League Championship Series since 2006. But perhaps there was an omen on a different flight. Headed to St. Louis for the home games, some Cardinals fans took American Airlines flight…1982.

Carp picked up the win in Game 3, and David Freese picked up three more hits—six for the series already. Oh, and he had six RBIs. "I don't know if I've ever seen anyone as locked in as Freese was in that whole postseason," Adam Wainwright recalled. "It wasn't just the World Series, as people remember. He won the NLCS MVP, too. The guy could barely get out. I'll tell you what that does for an entire lineup that already has Albert Pujols, Lance Berkman, and Matt Holliday in it. You've already got three boppers that you've got to contend with. And that's not even considering that you've got Furcal and Molina and a lot of quality at-bats in there. But three MVP-type players that you usually pattern your game around, and all of a sudden, you throw this other guy in there who is hotter than all of them? So now you find yourself having to pitch to those other guys because you can't have anyone on base for David. That was an incredible lift for our lineup. If you look at teams that win the World Series, they almost always have three dudes in the lineup. You had Rolen, you had Edmonds, and you had Pujols.

You had Berkman, Holliday, and Pujols. These teams that win, they have three guys. You can take two guys out of the lineup and just pitch to everyone else. But if there's three, you can spread them out a little bit and now you can't pitch around both of them. But David was extremely intense. That whole month, I just remember he had this look in his eye when he showed up to the field. There was nothing cracking that."

St. Louis lost Game 4 in St. Louis but got after Greinke again in Game 5, and the Cards led 4–1 in the fifth. But Garcia again got in a jam. This set up the at-bat that defined the series. When Freese did get his NLCS MVP trophy, he said it should go to someone else. He said the bullpen was the MVP of the NLCS. In game after game, the relievers were resplendent. And so, La Russa and Dave Duncan made an intriguing decision there in Game 5 with the series tied. They pulled Garcia in the top of the fifth.

In came Octavio Eduardo Dotel, the ageless fire-stomper. There were two on and two out in the 2–2 series. In the 4–1 game, the tying run was at the plate in the form of Ryan Braun, the PED-enhanced slugger who won the MVP that year. "St. Louis has defied every law of baseball to get here," Hall of Fame pitcher John Smoltz said on the TBS broadcast during the at-bat. "This formula—you can't imagine if it continues like this that it bodes well for them because this was a game Garcia could've easily given them six to seven innings. He was one out away."

Also in the broadcast booth, former All-Star pitcher Ron Darling remarked: "The use of the bullpen almost feels like a robbing-Peter-to-pay-Paul kind of thing."

But over the years against Braun, Dotel had fared well. As bullpen coach Derek Lilliquist said: "If you put a heart monitor on him out on the field, it'd probably be close to resting heart rate."

And in the at-bat, Dotel worked Braun low and low and also lower and lower. And then came the 2–2 pitch—an elevated slider that Braun swung through. The strikeout terminated the Brewers' inning, their hopes, and maybe, in essence, the Brewers' season. The Cards won Game 5 by the score of 7–1. The bullpen yet again gobbled up innings. It allowed just one run in 13 innings in Games 3 through 5. "Our bullpen was so important, and once our bullpen got going, that's what really did it," outfielder Adron Chambers said. "Mitch Boggs, Dotel, Arthur Rhodes. Our bullpen was so good. I think that gets overlooked."

That bullpen helped the Cardinals hold slugger Prince Fielder to a 1-for-14 stretch in the final four games. Rickie Weeks only had a .250 OBP in series. And Morgan? He went 2-for-12 with a walk in the series.

And so came Game 6—the first of two that October. Freese dominated this one as well—this time in the first of the innings. His first-inning homer in Milwaukee made a 1–0 game a 4–0 game. In *One Last Strike*, La Russa gave credit to hitting coach Mark McGwire, who worked with Freese on getting the front foot down sooner, "so he could lever off it."

The Brewers did battle back. But the Cards just kept slugging. They could feel it. And apropos enough, St. Louis starter Edwin Jackson lasted only two innings, so the bullpen finished out the final seven with Jason Motte recording the final out: a K of Mark Kotsay.

The 2011 St. Louis Cardinals, 10½ games back of the wild-card in late August, earned the wild-card and won the National League pennant. On Milwaukee's home field, they jumped and hugged and chanted: "Happy flight!" "Looking back on it," the Cards' Ryan Theriot said, nearly a decade later, "it seemed like it was a team of destiny."

Game 6 Story No. 8

She walked outside her house as a wife and walked back in as a widow. "She found dad," Darren Cook said of his mother, Jo. "He'd gone out to spread some ice stuff on the driveway."

Darren began to sob. It had been nearly a decade, and that did not matter. Re-telling the story, he was back in it. Back in his Boca

Raton, Florida, kitchen, he prepared for a presentation and finished the knot on his tie. "I picked my phone up off the counter and I saw a voicemail from my brother and thought: *That's weird*," he said of February 1, 2011. "I picked it up, and he told me that Dad had a massive heart attack and didn't make it. I was in the kitchen and then I was on the floor. Dad and I were chatting via email that morning."

Dennis and Jo Cook, married for 53 years in Florissant, Missouri, raised their boys on Cardinals baseball, as if it was a parenting method. Dennis' favorite player was Bob Gibson; he liked how Gibson never backed down. Darren still remembers his first game at Busch Stadium in 1966. "Ray Washburn was pitching," he said. He remembers attending the 1987 World Series in Minneapolis. "It was so loud, I couldn't hear myself think."

And he remembers the first game he attended in the 2011 season, a spring training game that doubled as an escape because it just felt like the day after his dad died was being repeated over and over. "I was pretty much destroyed. And exhausted," Darren said. "My dad loved sports. I told myself: 'You better get your ass off the couch and get out and do something.' So I went up to Jupiter [40 miles away] and bought a ticket to the game. I sat behind home plate next to this guy who was retired Navy. It was such a nice afternoon. Matt Carpenter was just coming up. He wasn't even a regular roster player yet. And I'm sitting third row, watching Albert Pujols."

By late August the grieving Cooks soon also grieved over the 2011 season. Their beloved Cardinals were 10½ games out of the playoffs. And then the magic began. If only dad could see this. "A hot streak for the ages!" Darren said. "Squeezing in on the last day of the season? Only to be followed by the rally squirrel? Charmed. Destiny. Fate."

The Cook boys had to get mom to the World Series. Jo was 73 years old and had been alive for 12 of the Cardinals' 17 World Series seasons at that point, but she never once attended a game in the Fall Classic. So her sons bought two tickets for Game 6—one for mom and one for Darren's brother, Jeff. "They sat in upper right-field seats," said Darren, who was 51 in 2011. "To this day, one of my most favorite pictures of those two is them sitting in the seats. Somebody took a picture of them before the game. You can see the excitement and happiness in my mom."

Darren again began to sob. "So my wife and I," Darren said, regrouping himself over the phone in the summer of 2020, "we were watching the game at the beer garden in Boca Raton. If you can't tell from this conversation, I'm not the stoic one in the family. I pretty much wear my emotions on my sleeve. So Game 6 was a roller coaster. I was a nervous wreck. I wanted the Cards to win obviously. But more so, I wanted them to win for my mom. Get a win for mom. Of course, it also meant the team would go to Game 7."

Darren and his wife watched that one at the bar, though Darren seldom sat. And he nervously gnawed on Bavarian pretzels. Ninth inning. Two outs, two on, two strikes. When David Freese hit the triple, Darren didn't just jump. "I launched myself into the air, my arms up high."

He hugged his wife as they jumped up and down in unison. "They were down to the last strike!" Darren recalled. "It was euphoric...And then the homer? Delirium."

And mom saw it in person. "I spoke to her the next morning—first thing," Darren said. "And Mom says, 'Oh my gosh, I can't believe it!' To this day, that sentence is still in my head. I had this conversation with her not more than two weeks ago, and the same tone and same excitement and same joy was in her voice as it was then...I don't want to say it was cathartic for her, but for the first time in a while, all the breaks went right. Maybe that's how I would put it."

The next night Darren and his wife went to the same bar. Same seats. Same outfit. Darren was draped in his Cardinals pullover. As Allen Craig squeezed that final fly ball, Darren thought of his mom and dad—and his mom without his dad. And Darren couldn't believe Dad didn't get to see this—though here's thinking that his dad probably caught the game from above. "You miss him every day," Darren said. "But it's times like those when the memories come back. I would give anything to have one last conversation. That would have been a great one to have. To talk about winning the World Series with my dad, that would have been great. That's what gets me today. I'd give anything for one more conversation."

CHAPTER 9

TEXAS HOLD 'EM

Tony La Russa's Ultimate Baseball. Released in 1991 for disk operating systems, this computer game became a staple of childhoods and paired best with Crystal Pepsi and Spree. *Tony La Russa's Ultimate Baseball* gave users access to managerial options and tips from La Russa himself. It offered expansive statistics—like the back of a baseball card on a screen—as well as access to classic team rosters. And it was the first to feature "an innovative 'fly ball cursor' which, for the first time in computer gaming gives players an accurate and controllable method to catch fly balls," per Stormfront Studios promotional material of the game.

Mark Lowe was born in 1983, grew up in Texas, and grew up with the game. "Oh yeah—when I was growing up, I had this computer game," said. "There were all these old-timers that were in there. The Cardinals would have Rogers Hornsby and Stan Musial. Bob Gibson. They had all these studs from the organization all in one team. So I just learned about them and I could go back and look at their stats. Then you play the game and you find out the guys who are really, really good—and the guys that are just okay. So I got fascinated with just learning the names and learning the history of these teams. Actually, my mom and dad both grew up in Illinois. Belleville and Ellis Grove, a small town by Chester. And so in my grandmother's house, there'd be all these St. Louis Cardinals books and World Series books, and they had old VHS tapes of the Cardinals and the Royals in the 1985 World Series. And so we would go to their house—and not a whole lot to do at grandma and grandpa's house—so I'd just pop those in and sit in the TV room and just watch old World Series games."

Lowe went to college at the University of Texas-Arlington and then moved away until a job took him back to Arlington in 2010. "I feel very blessed to have a dream as a little kid, and it actually came true," said Lowe, who pitched for 11 seasons in Major League Baseball. "So maybe *Tony La Russa's Ultimate Baseball* has something to do with that."

And in 2011 the Texas Rangers' Lowe played for his home-state team in the World Series against Tony La Russa's team. And just like from those VHS tapes from 1985, the 2011 World Series also featured the Cardinals in a seven-game battle. Lowe himself was out there a couple times for Texas against St. Louis. He even got to pitch in the 11th inning of a key game.

• • •

In St. Louis, October is an experience. In the summers when its steamy and dreams are stirred, October is a destination. But when you reach the fall and the Fall Classic, October is a location—you're there, you're in it, you're feeling the postseason, you're feeling feelings other months cannot provide. And there are horses! Clydesdales, these majestic creatures that stride in cadence and make you think of yesteryear and, of course, beer. For each St. Louisan that first World Series October is a rite of passage, be it in the 1940s with the Swifties, the 1960s with El Birdos, the 1980s with the Runnin' Redbirds, or the 2000s with MV3. And in 2011 a new generation of St. Louisans experienced their first World Series, which isn't the same as being alive during a World Series. You could've been two years old in, say, 2006, and while a World Series championship happened in your lifetime, your first World Series memories were made when you were seven in '11 and you were introduced to fall in full—October in St. Louis when the Cardinals were still playing.

And because Texas Rangers pitcher C.J. Wilson allowed a three-run homer in the All-Star Game in July, Texas Rangers pitcher C.J. Wilson had to start Game 1 of the World Series at Busch Stadium. Home-field advantage in the World Series went to the league that won the All-Star Game, so there were Wilson and the Rangers—with a regular-season record better than St. Louis'—in St. Louis. And if there was to be a Game 6 or 7, they'd be back.

October 19, 2011. Game 1 of the World Series. The Cardinals, by many measures, were statistically the best offensive team in the National League. And in the National League Championship Series, they averaged an absurd 7.1 runs per game. But their World Series opponent saw their offensive absurdity and raised them like it was a game of Texas Hold 'Em. The Rangers had six players with an OPS of .821 or higher; the Cards had three. And the sixth guy, Nelson Cruz (.821 OPS), slugged six homers in the American League Championship Series, winning the series MVP. "I felt like every time we stepped on a baseball field, we were hands down the better team," Rangers pitcher Mark Lowe said. "A lot of the other teams knew that, too, coming in. Sometimes you just can just tell during batting practice that the other team was deflated and done just watching us take BP. There was not a weak link one through nine in the lineup. There was no breath of fresh air. I've pitched against teams that had that feeling. Maybe there's a few guys you can pitch around and get to the next guy. Well, you couldn't do that. You had to go after every single guy. When those guys were hot, I've never seen anything like it. I've never been on a team that could throw up five runs, and it felt like 30 seconds. Especially in the hot summer in Arlington, where the ball is just flying to right-center. You've got Nelson Cruz hitting opposite field homers into the upper deck. That happened. Mike Napoli was doing the same thing. That whole lineup."

And the Rangers were hungry. They won the pennant a season prior but lost the World Series to the San Francisco Giants. This sure seemed like it would be their year.

Chris Carpenter was the first Cardinals starter to face the gauntlet in gray. There was a chill in the air because, of course, there was. At first pitch it was 49 degrees. Ian Kinsler, who had played college ball at the University of Missouri, batted first for the visitors. He drilled Carp's four-seam fastball toward third base. David Freese dove to his right, but his glove only deflected the ball. Base hit. Of course, the World Series featuring these two powerful teams began with a ball hit so hard it couldn't be fielded.

Kinsler had 30 stolen bases that year and he was caught stealing just four times. But the American League didn't have Yadier Molina, who extinguished the stealing Kinsler with a perfect throw to second. And with the stadium still buzzing, the pitcher Carpenter then made the play that best-encapsulated himself as a ballplayer—and it wasn't even a pitch. Elvis Andrus struck a chopper between first and second. First baseman Albert Pujols backhanded the ball with the glove on his left hand. And with his body falling back, he tossed the ball toward first base—but it was about five feet in front of first base.

Like a football wide receiver, a sprinting Carp dove headfirst, catching the ball in midair. And momentum just carried Carp full speed across the base for the out. Carpenter's timing was perfect. But it was also a crazy dangerous play, as the sprinting batter stepped on the base just inches from Carp's pitching hand as Carp's body slid across. "Well, he's an old hockey player and he's tough as nails," Adam Wainwright said of Carpenter. "The guy could run right into a brick wall and then stare the brick wall down with total confidence that he could run through it the next time. He's not scared of anything. But I think in that moment, you don't care about your personal well-being at all. You don't care if someone steps on your hand, and if they do, who cares? It's just cleat marks. In that moment the only thing that mattered to him was getting that out. Nothing else crossed his mind. The mind-set he taught me over the years was just patented Carp—this is what we need in the game right now, and I have to make this play. And he did it."

Both Carp and Wilson settled in, each allowing two runs in the first five innings. With these offenses, for all intents and purposes, this was a pitchers' duel.

• • •

Allen Craig's play-on-words works better said aloud than in print, but it was still appreciated. Asked about his tortoise, Craig said: "I had wild hair, no pun intended. It was back in 2007, the year after I got drafted. I've always been a fan of reptiles and what not. I decided I wanted a pet that can live a long time. And I think that tortoises are awesome. My wife and I went into a local pet store and picked out a small tortoise. He could fit in the palm of your hand. And we just raised him up from the time he was very small to now when he's really big."

Craig's closest friends on the Cards, Jon Jay and Daniel Descalso, loved that their buddy had a pet tortoise. "So they told Chris Carpenter one day in Chicago," Craig recalled. "They went up to him and said, 'Carp, did you know that Allen has a tortoise?' Carp was like, 'What?' He got all serious but kind of funny. He confronted me about it. At that time being a young player, a guy like Chris Carpenter comes up to you and wants to find out about your tortoise—it's a funny moment. That was it on my end. But it just kind of took off. People ran with it. As our team had more success and I was having success, it just became a thing."

Word spread to the media—and on social media—about Craig's pet tortoise, aptly named Torty. Around St. Louis, fans started making references to Torty while drinking Schlafly beers at Talanya's or JP

Fields. And, naturally, a Twitter handle soon emerged—@TortyCraig gained more than 21,000 followers and would tweet delightful comments about hanging out with "Master Allen" and their adventures, be it procuring sprinkled donuts or hobnobbing with Cardinals players. "At the time," Craig said, "I remember thinking this is crazy. It's just a pet tortoise. I didn't think it was that bizarre or whatever. But it took. People rallied around it. The people in the city of St. Louis really enjoyed it. So I was okay with that. It was fun."

Even Tony La Russa, generally pretty serious during press conferences, had some fun discussing Torty. After the rally squirrel made its National League Division Series appearance during Skip Schumaker's at-bat, La Russa joked to the media that "I think that the squirrel is attached to Craig's tortoise…It's my understanding that the squirrel was the tortoise's pass to the game, and they're supposed to be here tomorrow together…Maybe they have a suite so they won't be running on the field. I've never met it. I actually want to meet the tortoise. The squirrel, too."

The tortoise lives on in St. Louis sports lore. And the tortoise lives on. Those things don't die. In 2020 Craig said that Torty was still with their family in Southern California. Might still be in 3020.

As for Torty's Master Allen, he got the huge triple in the National League Division Series in Game 2. And in Game 1 of the World Series, he found himself up in a key moment yet again. With the score 2–2 in the bottom of the sixth, David Freese, as David Freese was wont to do, hit a line drive to the opposite field. On second with a double, Freese went to third on a wild pitch. After Yadier Molina struck out, Nick Punto walked. First and third. Carp was up.

What would La Russa do? He decided to pull his starter, acknowledging that this moment right then could be the Cards' last chance to take the lead. Craig pinch hit, and the Texas Rangers countered by pulling their own starter, C.J. Wilson, and bringing in Alexi Ogando. He threw fast. Craig faced 97, 96, and 97 again. And then, on a 1–2 pitch, the righty Craig hit 98 to the opposite field. Nelson Cruz slid, and the ball hit his glove—and popped out. And @TortyCraig tweeted: "HOOOOOOORAY MASTER ALLEN!!!!!!!!"

La Russa used five relievers to get the final nine outs. They allowed a combined one hit.

The Cardinals won Game 1. The last time a game-winning RBI in a World Series came from a pinch-hitter? Kirk Gibson's homer against La Russa's Oakland A's team in Game 1 of 1988, when Jack Buck said on the broadcast: "I don't believe what I just saw!"

In Game 2 of the 2011 World Series the very next night, Craig found himself again pinch-hitting in a tie game…again with Freese on third…and again with Ogando coming out of the bullpen. And again, Craig singled in Freese. Again, to the opposite field. @TortyCraig tweeted: "Woooooooo! Merry World Series, Master Allen!"

And like Carp provided in Game 1, the Cards got another excellent start. "This goes unlooked a lot of the time, but Jaime Garcia threw seven innings of shutout baseball in a World Series against the Texas Rangers," Adam Wainwright said. "That is no small feat."

Fernando Salas and Marc Rzepczynski combined for a runner-less eighth. Jason Motte came in for the save. The Cards were going to go up 2–0. Happy flight to Texas. And then…disaster. Hit, steal. Hit, error. Sac fly, sac fly. The Rangers took a 2–1 lead in the ninth—and took Game 2 with them all the way back to Texas.

Everything just gets bigger in the playoffs. The pitches. The hits. The nerves. The emotions. And it's for everyone involved from players to managers to fans to broadcasters to reporters. In the Game 2 loss, Albert Pujols made a ninth-inning error, which advanced a runner who later scored. After the game, journalists waited for Pujols in the Cards' clubhouse. Pujols remained in the players' lounge, which was closed off to the media. Even if no one told Pujols the reporters were waiting there for him, the superstar knew that reporters wanted to interview him after seemingly every game. So surely after a World

Series game, they would. But Pujols went home. Some reporters were particularly angered—how could the biggest star in baseball skip out on a postseason postgame interview? Imagine this happening in the NFL or NBA? Reporters reported this. Some columnists opined about Pujols' lack of accountability. And with everything just bigger in the playoffs, the story blew up.

The next day at the off-day workout in Texas, Pujols met with the media. "To try to rip somebody's reputation for something like this I don't think is fair," Pujols said. "But you know what? I don't throw rocks at you guys. You guys are human. You guys make mistakes just like I do."

A prickly Pujols was ticked. He was also hitless in the first two games of the World Series. And the Cards really should've won Game 2. To La Russa's credit, he tried to lighten the mood of his club by pushing an unlikely button involving Rangers president Nolan Ryan. As the manager explained in *One Last Strike*, the Cardinals were told to schedule their workout to end at 4:00 PM. In the clubhouse beforehand, La Russa was told by Katy Feeney, the beloved and longtime MLB executive, that the Rangers wanted to start their workout at 3:30 PM. "A few guys were milling around and could overhear me," La Russa said in *One Last Strike*. "So I said to Katy: 'That's unacceptable. We already moved our flight up to earlier this morning because of what we'd been told. Tell them: no way.' And then I paused to consider my next comment. 'And tell Nolan Ryan that I'm not Robin Ventura either.' I was, of course, making reference to the White Sox player who charged Nolan after being hit by a pitch, slipped while going after him, and found himself in a headlock, and punched on the top of the skull a few times. I heard a few guys laughing, and before I knew it, the story spread among them. They added on by saying within earshot of me: 'Hey, let's go watch Nolan kick Tony's ass.' A few suggested they'd form a circle around me, schoolyard-style. Never underestimate the power of humor, especially when you offer yourself up as a target for a joke—or a punch, for that matter."

Everything fell into place. The Cards calmed, and in the first inning of Game 3, sure enough, Master Allen homered. The Ballpark at Arlington wasn't known for keeping the ball in the park. It was a launching pad in the Texas air. The Rangers averaged more than six runs per game at home. Broadcaster Tim McCarver said on FOX: "Get used to that home-run ball, folks, because I think you're going to see a lot of that in these three games."

After Craig's at-bat, Pujols was up. It would be the only time all night he got out. What some people overlook is that Game 3's final score wasn't indicative of the game that was Game 3. It was tight for a while there. Twice, Matt Holliday was part of crucial plays. First, he was incorrectly called safe on a play at first base. Later, he threw out a runner at home from left field.

In the fifth inning, the Rangers scored three runs, cutting St. Louis' lead to 8–6. In the top of the sixth, Pujols Pujolsed. He obliterated a baseball into the orbit. His three-run homer made it 11–6 Cards. The next inning Pujols homered again. "When he comes up to the plate with two homers already, nobody was really saying it, but we're all looking at each other and thinking to ourselves, *Albert's gonna get a third one here*," Cardinals infielder Daniel Descalso recalled. "And sure enough, even in this big blowout, he got it."

Pujols' third homer in the game made the score the final score 16–7. "We were witnessing history," Descalso said. "We knew it in the moment, just watching from the dugout at how he was locked in that night."

After the debacle of Game 2 came Pujols' spectacle of Game 3. He hit three homers in a World Series game, something only done at that point by Babe Ruth and "Mr. October," Reggie Jackson. And then Señor Octubre.

• • •

The beautiful thing about a series is that it is just that, a series of games, a mosaic of storylines. That's also the infuriating thing about a series—it doesn't necessarily matter how dominant you are in just one particular game. You can blow out a team one night but face a hot pitcher and get shut out the next. And such was the case in Game 4 of the 2011 World Series. After scoring 16 runs with 15 hits, the Cardinals didn't score a run and got just two hits while enduring the wrath of Derek Holland's left arm. The young man with the wispy mustache whipped up a hell of a Game 4, tying the series 2–2.

So, about Game 5. It will be always remembered as the bullpen phone game because of the rarity and unfathomability with what happened. But that's the thing with sports—we remember the conspicuous moments of failure. But we often overlook the subtle times where an opportunity was there and not capitalized perhaps earlier in a game. Such is hindsight, such is sports analysis. And the fact is: the Cards only had seven hits in Game 5 and botched two hit-and-runs.

But we remember the bullpen phone.

Just like in the series opener, Chris Carpenter and C.J. Wilson started and started well. By the eighth inning, both had been replaced. By the bottom of the eighth, it was a 2–2 game in a 2–2 series. With Octavio Dotel on the mound for St. Louis, the inning's leadoff hitter, Texas Rangers veteran Michael Young, doubled. As Tony La Russa explained in the inning breakdown in *One Last Strike*, it was then that he first called the bullpen. It was preposterously loud out at the stadium. Bullpen coach Derek Lilliquist didn't hear the ring at first. He finally answered. La Russa said to get lefty Marc Rzepczynski "up" and righty Jason Motte "going easy."

Dotel struck out Adrian Beltre for the first out and then he intentionally walked Nelson Cruz. La Russa went to the mound and signaled for the lefty. Rzepczynski entered the Texas-sized pressure-cooker. The lefty faced a lefty hitter, David Murphy, who grounded the ball right back to the mound. But the ball ricocheted off Rzepczynski's glove, and all the runners were safe. Bases loaded, one out. The batter was the scorching hot right-hander Mike Napoli. La Russa asked pitching coach Dave Duncan to call up the bullpen. "Tell Motte to get ready. We can stall."

Duncan called and then broke the news to La Russa: "Motte's not even throwing. Nobody's up."

So instead of the righty Motte against the righty Napoli, the pitcher would be the lefty Rzepczynski. La Russa got on the phone and told the bullpen to "get Motte going."

Still, La Russa wasn't incensed because he liked Rzepczynski's stuff against righties and lefties. In 2011 righties slugged just .383 off Rzepczynski (though lefties slugged just .221). Well, in this moment, Napoli slugged off Rzepczynski. He drilled a ball to the wall, driving in two runs with a double. Texas 4, St. Louis 2.

At this point, it appeared that Napoli would be frontrunner for World Series MVP. Rzepczynski stayed in the game and struck out the lefty Mitch Moreland. Two outs, runners on second and third. The batter was Ian Kinsler, a righty, so La Russa walked out to the mound and signaled for the right-handed pitcher to come out of the bullpen. And, indeed, the righty who had been warming up in the bullpen came to the mound. It was Lance Lynn. "What are you doing here?" La Russa famously said to Lynn.

Somehow, in the same inning, the Cardinals made two miscommunications from the dugout to the bullpen. First, Motte wasn't ready to face Napoli. And now Motte wasn't ready to face Kinsler, but Lynn was—and neither La Russa nor Duncan had said for Lynn to warm up in the first place.

In fact, to make matters worse, Lynn had thrown 47 pitches in Game 3, so he was deemed off limits for Games 4 and 5. Rules stated a pitcher who entered the game must face one batter. So, instead of risking a Lynn injury, La Russa had Lynn intentionally walk Kinsler. Finally, mercifully, Motte was ready in the bullpen. La Russa brought him in to pitch with the bases loaded to Elvis Andrus. Motte struck out Andrus. Inning over.

But the question that lingered was: would Motte have struck out Napoli? Down 4–2 in the ninth, the Cardinals couldn't score. The Rangers were up 3–2 in the 2011 World Series. Game 6 in St. Louis would be Wednesday, October 26. Until it wasn't.

Game 6 Story No. 9

In St. Louis it's a question asked on first dates and business lunches, in line to check out at Schnucks, or while getting a Busch at Busch. It's an icebreaker and a way to instantly bond.

It's the new "Where did you go to high school?" "People always ask, 'Where were you for Game 6?'" St. Louis native Andrew Doerhoff said. "I tell them I was under water in a steel tube."

EM1 (SS) Andrew Doerhoff of the United States Navy didn't even know what happened in Game 6. He was on a submarine. The USS Topeka. "A fast-attack submarine, its mission is to spy on people," said Doerhoff, who was 26 in October of 2011. "We go places where we're not supposed to be without people knowing that we're there. In my position I wasn't privy to what exactly our mission was. That's a need-to-know basis. I worked in the propulsion plant…My responsibility was to operate all of the electrical equipment. Electrical operator was my position when I was on watch. All of the pieces of electrical equipment like generators, motors, pumps, things like that were my expertise."

In the fall of 2011, the men and women on the USS Topeka prepared the submarine for an early 2012 deployment. They'd be gone for six months, so they had to test all of the on-board equipment. These testing missions in the Pacific Ocean near San Diego would sometimes take one to two weeks. Other times they'd take six weeks. Sure enough, the day after Game 1 of the 2011 World Series, they headed out to sea.

As a boy in St. Louis, Doerhoff's favorite player wasn't a player; he was a wizard. "I was just raised by my mom. So we didn't go to a ton of games, but I watched on TV and fell in love," Doerhoff said. "When I was younger, the place she worked at, Ozzie Smith was a part owner of a temp agency. And they had a business meeting or a luncheon, but my mom brought me to it. So I got to meet and talk to Ozzie Smith for a few minutes. He took time to talk with me. I don't know how my mom got me in or how many kids were there, but there weren't very many."

Doerhoff grew up in the Maryland Heights area of St. Louis. He attended Pattonville High, the alma mater of another homegrown Cardinals third baseman, Scott Cooper, from the 1995 team. "I intended to go to college, but that didn't really work out," Doerhoff said. "I joined the Navy instead. It was more of a lack of motivation than anything, not the smarts part. I tested well for the Navy and joined the naval nuclear program."

Doerhoff served from 2006 to 2014 while stationed in San Diego. In 2011 he passionately followed his hometown Cardinals, enduring July and August, embracing September and October. "I had a feeling about this team," he said.

But after the Game 1 win, he was underwater. "There's no cell service," he said. "The only thing you have is email, and you only got it sparingly."

So on this ship that had an absurd amount of technology on it, he couldn't even find out the score of the baseball game? "Exactly!" he said. "If we were close to land, we had a slower-than-dial-up connection. So you could maybe load a page in 10 minutes or something. But that was only if you were close to land and if the hatch was open, when we pulled into the port in San Diego to get people or supplies. But the submarine is pretty thick steel. Nothing gets through it. No cell service gets through it. So I had no idea of what was going on in the World Series...It was brutal."

Speaking during the 2020 pandemic, Doerhoff referenced the bubble that the National Hockey League players lived in. There had been articles about how rough it was for those guys away from their families, living in a hotel, day after day. "The articles were feeling sorry for them," he said. "I can't buy into that even a little bit with my experience. They have no idea what isolation is."

Finally, on October 28, 2011, the *USS Topeka* returned to shore. Doerhoff didn't know how the World Series played out, but one thing he knew—Game 7 was scheduled for October 27, so the season would be over upon their return. "When I came up," he said, "the first thing I do is turn on my phone and look to see who won. Maybe we won the World Series. And I saw that Game 7 was in a few hours. I was blown away." Because of the rainout, Game 6 was moved to the 27th and Game 7 to the 28th.

Imagine Doerhoff trying to comprehend all of this after all that time on the submarine…then imagine his emotions when he realized he could watch Game 7…then imagine his emotions when he saw how the Cardinals got to Game 7 in the first place. "I see that Game 6 ended in extras. So I go in and I'm reading the game recap and I find out that it was an instant classic," he said. "I'm watching videos of Freese hitting a triple and Berkman and the walk-off by Freese. It was crazy. I could feel anxiety watching it…I think I was resigned to the fact that I had missed it all. It felt like I won something when I came up. Something that I had lost, I had found or gained again. It was like a gift from the sports gods. I knew that I had to take this opportunity. It wasn't going to come again. We miss a lot of things being in the service. I didn't have a family. I wasn't married. I don't have kids. This was something that was important to me, something similar to a family thing that might be important to other sailors."

When they would get to shore, their work was just beginning. Huge responsibilities awaited that involves long cables and shutting down the reactor. Sometimes it would take five hours to finish. But this day was one unique circumstance, "I told my boss I was leaving early," Doerhoff said. "'I'm leaving.' That's what I said. 'This is a once-in-a-lifetime opportunity. I want to see it. This is very important to me.' My boss was not happy."

Doerhoff went to a bar in Mission Valley. Some Cards fans happened to be there. "I'd had a few drinks and I was feeling good," he said. "So when we won, I ended up running around the bar and high-fiving every single Cardinals fan."

To this day, Doerhoff is still jealous of his friends who actually attended Game 6. When he watches highlights nearly a decade later, "it still gives me tingles."

CHAPTER 10

GAME 6

During the uncertain and unnerving spring of 2020, as the coronavirus cruelly spread across the country, families quarantined in their homes, together yet so alone. Sports networks re-aired feel-good footage from classic sporting events, pixilated pick-me-ups from the past. One night the MLB Network showed Game 6 of the 2011 World Series. Turned out that Lance Berkman's four daughters had never seen the full game. "So we all sat down and watched it," said the former Cardinals outfielder, who turned 44 in 2020. "And it was funny because I know what happens, but I was still getting nervous watching that game. It brought back so many emotions. My palms are sweaty, and my wife was getting nervous, and the girls are like, 'Wait a minute!'"

Game 6 forever does something to you—even if you've already experienced it. Heck, even if you've already played in it. "Success or failure in baseball is such a razor's edge proposition," Berkman said. "And you realize, looking back on that thing, it's like, man, we could have lost that game 100 ways. It seemed like we just probably should have lost, but somehow we didn't."

But first came the rain. Well, actually it didn't rain much during the rainout. The lack of rain remains one of the great ironies in St. Louis sports history. Major League Baseball postponed Game 6 from Wednesday, October 26 to Thursday October 27, which gave Chris Carpenter an extra day of rest for a potential Game 7. After all those times of disregarding schoolkids' wishes for snow days, Mother Nature made good on all St. Louisans' prayers at once (and kept them relatively dry, to boot). "We got Chris Carpenter because of that," Skip Schumaker said. "That is a big deal. I talk to guys that were on the Rangers and they ask, 'How did you guys do that? How did you get a rainout and there was no rain?'"

The two days off between Games 5 and 6, though, also gave Texas Rangers slugger Josh Hamilton extra time to rest his nagging groin. Hamilton had just three hits in the entire World Series to that point, but then got three in Game 6 alone, including the extra-innings home run that appeared to be the Game 6 homer we'd all remember.

October 27 was already a special date in St. Louis Cardinals history. Five years prior, Adam Wainwright got the final out to win the World Series against Sean Casey, Placido Polanco, and the rest of the Detroit Tigers. Thanks to the 2011 drizzle-out, October 27 would get a chance to add to its résumé.

For lunch in St. Louis the day of Game 6, Jason Motte went to Carl's Drive In located on Route 66 and not to be confused with (but often is) Carl's Deli, which is just four miles away. Carl's Drive In appears almost miniature. The tiny roadside cube is basically just a door, a counter, a grill, another counter, and another door. "It's a good little spot," Motte said. "We kind of found it by accident, driving around one day. We ended up going there maybe once a homestand, once a month. We're normal people, we've got to eat, too. And it's a good spot. I'd never know if I wanted a small root beer or a large, and Kelly behind the counter would be like: 'Come on.' So I'd end up getting the large and also fries and a triple burger with cheese. Kelly would always give us a hard time and stuff like that. We came in there before Game 6, and she said, 'When you guys win tonight, you're going to have to come back tomorrow.'"

The game that night would feature high drama but was not always an artistic masterpiece. Just ask an expert on the latter like Dan Zettwoch, who also has a particular appreciation for homegrown talent on the St. Louis Cardinals. He was raised on Triple A baseball in Louisville, Kentucky, where the Redbirds called home from 1982 to 1997. And as an artist, he enjoyed the creation of the major leaguer, ultimately colored in resplendent red. He came to St. Louis in 1995 to study art at Washington University. "I was a dual-major of art and math actually," Zettwoch said. "But one semester of Wash U calculus and I was like, 'Art's pretty awesome. I'm going to stick with that.' I was always a big Cardinals fan. The thing that turned me into a super fan was moving here, going to art school, and listening to all the games on radio in the Delmar Loop. Working all those nights in the studio, I'd listen to KMOX."

He became a successful freelance illustrator and cartoonist. At one point he was commissioned by the Missouri History Museum to do 35 wall-sized murals for the exhibit called "A Walk In 1875 St. Louis." His fondness for the Cardinals led to multiple pieces of art, including an homage to the famous quotes of Mike Shannon, the Cards' down-to-earth radio broadcaster who sometimes said things from another planet. "That piece was born out of all those years working and listening to him," Zettwoch said. "I'm a big fan. That's actually what I like about baseball. I'm not in it for the dignified, classy. I'm here for the weird folk stories and the humor and the kind of oddball side of it."

Mrs. Z was from Cardinals Country, too. Leslie Zettwoch hailed from Little Rock, Arkansas. The two were newlyweds in 2011, living in the charming St. Louis area called Webster Groves. An hour before first pitch they decided to—what the heck—just check Stubhub. Sure enough, "we scooped up a couple of tickets and went straight down there," Dan said. "My wife and I were in the right-field bleachers— probably like two rows up from the bullpen."

As he awaited the first pitch, Game 6 was a blank canvas. If Texas won, the Rangers would be world champions for the first time. The Cardinals were in a spot they didn't want to be, but they were in a spot that seemed fitting for them to be. The 2011 team, 10½ games out in late August, played its best baseball when its opponent was adversity. And another good omen psychologically was that everyone seemed to be accepting the blame for the Game 5 tumult. There was accountability—from Tony La Russa through the lineup and the staff. The players weren't callowing; they were ascending.

In the broadcast booth, Joe Buck looked down upon the vast green with the Arch mowed into the outfield and then the actual Arch looking down upon the outfield. He was on a work trip, but he was home. The son of the Hall of Fame broadcaster Jack Buck, Joe became a legendary broadcaster himself. Raised a Cards fan in St. Louis, he would play in the bowels of old Busch with Ted Simmons' kids in the 1970s. The night Don Denkinger blew the call, Joe watched on a transistor TV with the front-desk attendant at St. Louis Country Club, while Joe skipped a high school dance inside a ballroom. He became the broadcaster for the Louisville ballclub in 1989, when Zettwoch was a teenager in town, and by 1991 there were two Bucks working St. Louis Cardinals games.

In 1996 at age 27, Joe Buck called his first World Series for FOX. By 2011 he was as much an October staple as pumpkin spice. "Glad you're with us," he said at 7:06 Central Standard Time, as the southpaw Jaime Garcia uncoiled from his windup. "Should be a fun night."

Sellout crowd, a crisp 53-degree October night with, indubitably, something in the air. When people talk about Game 6, many will say it was the best game in Cardinals history, World Series history, or possibly, depending on their audaciousness, baseball history. But they'll also point out that Game 6 began as one of the worst games the sport has seen professionally played. Five errors were committed in the first six innings, including a pop-up that popped out of David Freese's glove and dropped upon his noggin. Garcia was pulled after just three innings. Matt Holliday was picked off third base—and injured himself in the process, forcing the All-Star's removal.

After six innings the score was 4–4. It was a sloppy ballgame but still a ballgame. But in the seventh, La Russa actually did call for Lance Lynn out of the bullpen—and Lynn allowed leadoff back-to-back homers. Adrian Beltre. Nelson Cruz. These homers seemed ceremonious, coronating the new kings of baseball, as the Rangers took a 6–4 lead in the seventh. Alec Baris, the boy whose birthday was the day of Game 162, began to cry. He was at Busch with his older brother. "All the noise was just sucked out of the building. I thought it was pretty much impossible for us to come back at that point," Baris said. "Even in that game with everything going on, everything just kept swinging back toward the Cardinals. But in that moment, I felt all hope was lost. Me being that middle schooler at the time, literally my whole personality was watching baseball, watching the Cardinals and rooting for them. So the tears just flowed."

Then, off Octavio Dotel, the Rangers got their seventh in the seventh. "There was a whole row of Texas Rangers fans in front of us," recalled the artist Zettwoch from the bleachers by the bullpen. "Behind us there were some very aggressive Cardinals fans who were riding those guys the whole time. We were kind of stuck in between. That was a weird battle zone. We had that feeling of being like—we're not leaving no matter what. But also you were definitely feeling like it was over, that that was it. I remember being cold. I went to the gift shop and bought a hoodie to wear. Of course, that's now my good luck hoodie. I remember the Allen Craig home run was the first spark of hope."

In for the injured Holliday, the clutch Craig cut the Texas lead to 7–5 in the bottom of the eighth. "I think about Allen Craig a lot," Zettwoch said, "because he was such a big part of that. I remember the Rangers fans hated him because he was killing them that series. Every time he came up, he had a clutch hit. Those fans were like, 'Who is Allen Craig? He's killing us.' We didn't know either. We just knew he had a pet turtle that lives in his backyard."

Craig, Daniel Descalso, and Jon Jay, the old minor league roommates who talked baseball deep into the nights while playing video games, were now all in the game, the biggest of games. "Tony likes to make moves that aren't necessarily conventional," Descalso said. "We had only two guys left on the bench, and he sent Gerald Laird in to hit [in the pitcher's spot]. But they brought out a righty from the bullpen, and it was a case of, 'Boom! You're going in.' So Tony sends me up for Laird, and our bench is now empty in terms of position players."

Bottom of the eighth, two outs, down two. With a runner on first, the pinch-hitter Descalso singled for his first hit of the World Series. With runners on first and second, Jay singled for his first hit of the World Series. With the bases loaded, Rafael Furcal came to the plate. Busch Stadium brimmed with loud cheers and silent prayers, some hands waving towels, other hands in front of mouths (or inside them). The fans were coated by nerves, and their shivering had nothing to do with the cold. Furcal, the hero of so many moments in September and October, fearless against Cliff Lee and Roy Halladay, here in the at-bat of a lifetime.

Crappy ground-out to the pitcher. To the ninth.

And another La Russa double-switch meant Furcal's night— and possibly his season—was over. "I didn't really anticipate double-switching into the game," Descalso said. "At that point I hadn't played a whole lot of shortstop since we traded for Furcal. So he makes the last out, I got back to the dugout, and Joe Pettini, the bench coach, says, 'You're playing short.' I'm thinking, *Oh, shit.* So I go grab my glove and get out there. Think I took a few grounders and made a few throws, and I'm just standing there thinking, *Wow, I'm playing shortstop in the World Series.* I wasn't anticipating any of that. I was probably the fourth shortstop on the depth chart at that point with Theriot, Punto, and Furcal. I got a ground ball like the first inning I was out there. I bobbled it a little bit, but I made the play, and that settled things down for me."

Motte didn't allow a run in the top of the ninth. Still 7–5. And so, with closer Neftali Feliz on the mound, the Rangers were three defensive outs from the World Series championship. Nasty Feliz. His stuff was so good. He was the American League Rookie of the Year in 2010 and had 32 saves in 2011. "I did see some beer being carted toward the visiting clubhouse," said KMOX radio reporter Tom Ackerman, who was inside the secondary stadium studio behind the entrance to the green seats. "And I did see some Rangers family members starting to make their way downstairs toward the Rangers' clubhouse."

Ryan Theriot struck out swinging. The Rangers were two outs away. Albert Pujols came to bat in what could be his final time for St. Louis. Eleven seasons with the Cardinals possibly ending in '11 but likely without No. 11. Without a chance to say good-bye, Pujols spoke to the fans the best way he could—he crushed the shit out of a Feliz fastball for a double. It was Pujols' first hit since his third homer back in Game 3.

As Lance Berkman came to bat, Tim McCarver said on the FOX broadcast: "The Rangers are in their no-doubles defense, which is similar to football's prevent defense."

Feliz walked Berkman. First and second, one out, bottom of the ninth, 7–5 Texas. Craig, who homered in his last at bat, came to bat. Feliz struck him out. The Rangers were one out away.

In the Cardinals bullpen, the phone rang. La Russa called Derek Lilliquist to send a sobering but important message. If the Cardinals lost, the pitchers still needed to come onto the field to acknowledge the fans. In the Rangers bullpen, Mark Lowe felt like he was "about to throw up." He and his teammates were one out from making history, the first championship for this proud franchise in his home state. "I'm sitting next to [reliever] Mike Gonzalez and just trying to get a view over the fence," said Lowe, who pitched in 52 games with a 3.80 ERA for the 2011 Rangers. "I mean, just that feeling of like a little kid, so excited. It's like Christmas morning. Here we go. This is what you dream of as a little kid, and this moment is right here in front of you. You're literally one pitch away from having that."

"And it comes down to the hometown kid," Joe Buck said on the broadcast. "David Freese."

The FOX cameras caught a woman hiding her face in a white rally towel and a man wearing his ball cap inside out and backward. And the cameras caught Rangers executive Nolan Ryan, the most fearsome ballplayer of his time, maybe any time, gently nibbling on his famous right hand.

First pitch, outside slider, 86 mph for ball one. At his apartment in South County in St. Louis, 21-year-old Anthony Holmes got off his couch. "I remember praying to God. I was on my knees praying, 'Please!'" Holmes said. "My girlfriend, she was just sitting on the couch. She's not a huge sports fan. She was laughing at me at first. I was literally on my knees. I wanted that World Series so bad. I just loved the Cardinals and I loved that Cardinals team."

Second pitch, slider over the plate, 84 mph for a called strike one. Draped as Don Draper, Jon Hamm crammed beside other *Mad Men* cast members into the tiny trailer of actor Jay Ferguson, who happened to be a fan of the Texas Rangers. "They'd knock on the door and say, 'We need you on set,'" recalled the St. Louis native Hamm. "And we'd all tumble out of the trailer, run back to the set, shoot whatever we needed to shoot, run back to the trailer, and watch the World Series… Sprinting, I mean sprinting. In dress shoes and '60s suits."

Third pitch, fastball, 97 mph, swinging strike two. This was the culmination of emotion. This was it for Cardinals fans, this season, this maddening, magical season—from Wainwright to Berkman to Joplin, from the Rasmus trade to 10½ out to Nyjer Morgan, from Adron Chambers to Rafael Furcal to Game 162, from Game 5 against Halladay in Philly to the Game 6 elimination of Milwaukee to Game 5 phone follies in Texas. It all came down to this pitch to Freese because the Rangers, champions never before, were one strike away.

Fourth pitch, fastball, 98 mph, in play. The magic-maker Freese swung dutifully and beautifully, driving the baseball to the opposite field. The righty hit it to right field in such a way that it was almost as if he's wasn't supposed to do that. That ball isn't supposed to go that way, as if he broke the game, as if he found a glitch, as if he created this chaotic scenario that didn't have a clean outcome. The ball sailed as the right fielder Cruz flailed. "From where I'm sitting and the height I was at 14, when Freese hit the ball in the air, I couldn't see it," said Baris, the middle schooler. "So I had to listen for the crowd. That gave me chills right away."

The ball bounced off the wall and bounced on the warning track and rolled onto the green outfield grass. "We couldn't see it, but we saw the ball coming back," said Zettwoch, who was in the bleachers with his wife. "It was madness, of course. It was so loud, and everyone was jumping around and everything. It was disorienting. Everyone was losing their minds. Everyone was losing their minds, but at the same time, I'm such a sensitive artist type that I was already starting to feel for the Rangers fans in front of me. Not really, but kind of. They were so heartbroken. I still think about them. One of them had this Rangers flag tied around his neck like a cape, and he just looked so sad. I didn't feel too bad for him for too long."

With two outs and two strikes in the bottom of the ninth inning and Texas on the brink of winning Game 6 and the World Series, Freese tripled and drove in two runs to tie the game at 7–7. It was a big moment, one might say. "Jay's crestfallen," Hamm said of Ferguson, the Rangers fan and fellow cast member. "And I'm running around doing a victory dance. Literally, the trailer is bouncing…It's just a really great feeling to have your team pull something out in that way and you think, *That should not have happened.*"

Two things are sometimes forgotten. First, the very next pitch to Yadier Molina was an outside breaking ball that catcher Mike Napoli had to block. If he didn't get his body in front of that thing, the wild pitch would've lost Texas the game right there. Second, Molina got some good wood on his next swing, too. He also sliced it to right field toward the surely frazzled Cruz. But Cruz tracked it down to finally get that third out of the ninth—two runs too late.

As the 10th inning began, Rangers reliever Lowe really started feeling the chill in the air. "They had a little bike out there in the bullpen for us to ride, and I was coming off a hamstring injury. It was really important for me to constantly stay warm," Lowe said. "In the meantime, you're locked into this game…I'm staying ready. And I'm feeling the emotions. At the same time, I have to stay ready. I have to stay in this mental state and I've got to go in and do my job if called upon."

Motte returned to the mound for St. Louis. Missouri was a state of delirium. Ian Kinsler popped out on the first pitch. Elvis Andrus singled on the second pitch. And then there's Hamilton. "It's all part of the story," Motte said. "Some people remember, some people don't, but I went back out and pitched the 10th inning. And that's when Josh Hamilton hit the two-run home run off me and put them back up again by two. I remember when Hamilton hit it, I literally thought to myself on the mound, *Man, I just lost the World Series.*"

In 2020 felony charges against Hamilton forever changed his reputation. But back in 2011, the redemption story of Hamilton was a feel-good one. He was the top pick in the draft who succumbed to drugs and addiction—only to amazingly return to the game after three years off and ultimately make it to the majors and become an All-Star and then an MVP. "I just remember my heart dropping into my stomach a bit," Descalso said. "It was extreme high to extreme low in a matter of a few minutes."

"It was miraculous that we came back from a two-run deficit," Berkman said, "and against their closer who was really good. Then you're thinking we go down two runs again the very next inning and you're like: there's no way. It's practically speaking as a baseball player. You have enough experience to know that—hey, this is not looking good. The chances of us coming back twice from two-run deficits are not good against a talented team. So when Hamilton hit that home run, I thought, *Well, they deserve it. They had a great year, they got a great team.* And then you start thinking, *Okay, well, wait a minute, am I coming up next inning?* You start thinking about your offensive inning and what you need to do to try to tie the game again."

Up in his suite, the bespectacled general manager John Mozeliak watched Game 6 unfold with a pad of paper in front of him. For him there was an additional layer of thickening plot. He was one of the only few people who knew that La Russa was retiring after the World Series. "Throughout the ebb and flow of that game, multiple times I was writing what I was going to tell the club on Tony's departure," Mozeliak said. "On the sheet of paper, I was writing down what I thought the messaging should be. One time I even rolled it up and threw it out in the trash can—and then I had to pick it back up."

Down 9–7 in the bottom of the 10th, Descalso would lead off for St. Louis. "I kind of had to get over [the Hamilton homer] pretty quick," said Descalso, who before that night had one hit in the entire postseason. "I'm thinking, *I just need to get myself on base.* I thought I was going to be facing Neftali Feliz, who had given up the triple to Freese the inning before. This is one of the best closers in the league, throws high 90s, 100 mph. But I get into the on-deck circle and I see Darren Oliver coming in from the bullpen. And no offense to Darren Oliver, but he was a left-handed pitcher who throws 88 or 89. I'd much rather face him than their closer. So I had a little bit of extra confidence going up there, even though I'd never faced him before. I was telling myself, 'Have a good at-bat. Find a way to get on base.' I knew if I could find a way to get on base and the tying run comes to bat, we at least have a shot."

The Rangers were, again, three outs away. And sure enough, Descalso smacked the eighth pitch of the at-bat into right field for his second hit of the night. Jay was next. Descalso's dear friend sliced a pitch the opposite way for a little fly ball single. What was happening? Two on, no one out, for the pitcher's spot. And all the Cardinals had on their bench were pitchers.

So, La Russa sent up Edwin Jackson to bat for Motte. But after the Rangers met on the mound, La Russa pinch hit Kyle Lohse for Jackson. That's right—La Russa pinch hit for the pitcher with a pitcher, and before a pitch, pinch hit that pitcher with another pitcher. Wonder if this scenario ever arose in the computer game, *Tony La Russa's Ultimate Baseball*? But Lohse did the job with a sacrifice bunt—albeit dangerously since the bunt was in the air—and the runners advanced to second and third.

The Rangers were two outs away. Scott Feldman came in to pitch. The unlikely Feldman, who pitched in just 11 games for the '11 Rangers, would potentially be the guy in the photo, the pitcher who got the historic final out of a franchise's first World Series. Theriot went to the plate. Signed back in the offseason all those months ago, Theriot infused the clubhouse with personality. He contributed with his glove and bat. And in this—the biggest at-bat of his life—Theriot hit a chopper to third base, which drove in Descalso. Theriot was thrown out at first, and Jay remained at second. So Texas was still leading 9–8 with two outs in the bottom of the 10th inning.

The Rangers were one out away. The batter, of all batters, was Pujols. Texas promptly took the bat out of the slugger's hands, intentionally walking Pujols and creating a force-out situation with Jay on second and Pujols on first. The fans were running out of fingernails. La Russa again called the bullpen to remind them to thank the fans if they lost.

Then came the 35-year-old Berkman. Clean-shaven to begin the playoffs in Philadelphia, he now sported a beard speckled with gray.

He'd accomplished so much in baseball at that point—six All-Star games, four top five MVP finishes, five postseasons, and more than $100 million in salary. He even got to be the Triple A New Orleans mascot. But he had never won the World Series. "That was the one at-bat of my life where I feel like I had just total concentration," Berkman said. "There was no other thought other than, *Hey, just see the ball, get a great look at the ball.* And I wasn't worried about making an out. I wasn't thinking about, *You got to do this or that or what the defense was doing.* The focus was so pure, maybe to a point that I've never gotten to before or since in my life. So, Matt Holliday had hurt his hand in one of the previous games and he wasn't swinging the bat very well as a consequence. Tony told me that I was going to be hitting fourth behind Albert. Well, Albert hit three homers in Game 3. So from that point forward in the series, the Rangers decided they weren't going to pitch to him at all. So I knew that whoever was hitting right behind Albert was going to be in the grease at some point.

"When we were transitioning from Game 5 to 6, we had the rainout. The worst part about the playoffs is the off days when you're sitting there agonizing and thinking about what might happen. So I knew that I'd be hitting behind Albert and I just had this funny feeling that the season is going to come down to one of my at-bats. So I prayed. 'Lord, If that happens, just don't let the moment be too big. Let me be able to focus and concentrate. I'm not praying for success. I'm not praying for a hit. But Lord just let me be able to focus and really concentrate on what I'm doing and just use the ability that you've given me.' And what's crazy is that when I was in the dugout in the 10th inning, I was a nervous wreck. But I just knew: here it comes. I got in the on-deck circle, and the place is going nuts. And when you see him start to intentionally walk Albert, you just know that: okay, it's on me now. And from the second I took that donut off my bat and as I was striding up to the plate, it was like, I can't explain it, but just a calm and focus. I've never really had that level of focus before.

In my life. And you can just see it. When I watched it the other night [with my wife and daughters], I can see on my face this incredible calm focus. The first pitch was a fastball, kind of up and in, and I took a huge rip at it. There was no fear, there was no tentativeness. It was all focused aggression, and what's great is the competition was pure because he didn't make a bad pitch. If you go back and watch that at-bat, every pitch he threw was either a ball, or it was like right on the corners. He was making really tough pitches."

In fact, he made four tough pitches, and the count on Berkman was 2–2. The Rangers were, again, one strike away. "He jammed me. It broke my bat," Berkman said of the 2–2 pitch. "But I was able to hit that little line drive into center field to score the tying run. It was just great competition. It's a moment that obviously in my life I'll never forget."

Jay scored the game-tying run. For the first time in the history of Major League Baseball, a team was down to its final strike twice and didn't get out. On the broadcast Joe Buck said: "In the air to right-center, this game is tied! Going to third is Pujols, and it's 9–9." Then, he sat silent, while the raucous crowd noise spilled and filled living rooms across the city and across the country. Buck waited for 43 seconds and then he said: "They just. Won't. Go. Away."

"It's a feeling," said Lowe, who was in the Texas bullpen, "of complete disappointment. And to have that twice? It was a lot of emotions. A lot of emotions going on—and some feelings I'd never had before."

Feldman, mercifully, got the third out when Craig grounded out. To the top of the 11th, 9–9 in Game 6. "The one guy that I have to mention who sort of embodies the spirit of that whole team was Jake Westbrook," Berkman said. "You've got to keep in mind this dude was like the ace of the Indians. So he's used to being the dude. And when he got traded over the previous year, he had a great run with the Cardinals if you go back and look. He was very effective. He was a starter in the rotation the whole year in 2011. And he didn't have like an All-Star type year, but he had a solid year as a starter. Well, then he gets left off the playoff roster in the NLCS. A lot of guys would have sulked and said, 'They're doing me wrong or this and that.' Then he was a late add to the World Series roster. They stuck him in the bullpen, which is a role that he hadn't pitched in period. But he just kept himself, got ready to pitch, and knew that he may have to make a contribution. And sure enough, there he was in the top of the 11th and he gets three big outs for us. He ended up being the winning pitcher that game. His attitude about the whole thing was unbelievable, just completely selfless, completely team-first. And we had so many guys on that team who were that way. That was a huge reason that we were successful, but I feel like that little anecdote with Jake sort of encapsulates or captures the spirit of that. I've coached in high school for four years and I told that story every year, just trying to demonstrate the type of commitment to the team that comes from a winning ballplayer. I mean, that's a winning mentality right there. It kind of gives me chills to think about that."

Westbrook finished off the top of the 11th, and Game 6 remained tied 9–9. The leadoff hitter for St. Louis was the third baseman Freese. The PA system blared the LL Cool J song "Mama Said Knock You Out," the emphatic anthem that opens with: "DON'T CALL IT A COMEBACK!"

Lowe—the 6'3" righty with blond hair sprouting out from the back of his cap—was brought in to pitch for Texas. Of all players for Lowe to replace in the double-switch, it was Cruz. "You're anxious every time the bullpen phone rings," Lowe said. "And then you get in the game, and you throw that first pitch, and you're in. It's over. It completely leaves, and you have this tunnel vision that comes in. You don't hear the crowd and you're just focusing on your job and what pitch you're throwing. That's where I'm at that moment. Once I come in, everything that's going on is history."

Coming out of the commercial break, FOX showed footage of previous history. Other great Game 6s—Carlton Fisk in 1975, Reggie Jackson in 1977, Mookie Wilson and Bill Buckner in 1986, Kirby Puckett in 1991, and Joe Carter in 1993. "This is already a classic," McCarver said.

A stat flashed on the screen—the Cards were the first team to score runs in the eighth, ninth, and 10th innings of the same World Series game. To lead off the 11th, Freese took three straight balls from Lowe. Then strike one, which sure looked like ball four. Foul ball. Full count. "Whenever I came out into an inning," Lowe said, "if you get the first guy out, the inning becomes a lot easier as a reliever. If you just get the first guy, if anyone gets on base, you're one pitch away from getting out of the inning with a double play. So that was a big focus of mine there. I was thinking, *Let's get this first guy.*"

Lowe threw a change-up. As soon as Freese's swing connected with the ball, Freese looked up—like we all did—to see just what was in store. If you look closely, his mouth made an unusual shape—half agape, half smiling. "Freese hits it in the air to center," Joe Buck said on the broadcast, as he suddenly channeled his father, repeating Jack's famous line after Puckett's homer. "We will see you tomorrow night."

Home run. Cards won Game 6 by the score of 10–9. The stadium erupted with volcanic euphoria. And simultaneously, 45,000 humans had one of the greatest moments of their lives. "I had a bat and a helmet in my hand. I was in the hole," Descalso said. "So my bat goes flying. My helmet goes flying. There's a couple of great pictures of four or five of us getting to home plate in various states of jumping. There's a great shot of Gerald Laird just ecstatic right next to me. It was pandemonium."

Of all the celebrations, each unique, one stood out, as Laird looked like he pulled an oblique. The stout catcher jubilantly ran with high knees toward home plate, ultimately jumping forward with both arms in the air—but toward no one. He landed and just jumped again, almost Leprechaun-like.

The middle schooler Baris, who cried when Texas took the big lead, recalled "hugging, jumping for joy, complete strangers just coming together. I do not remember a single person's name in our section, but during that game, we were all family."

Tony Dattoli was the coach at Meramec Community College who gave Freese his return to baseball. "It was one of those situations where I couldn't stop smiling," Dattoli said. "I had never been so happy for one person. And there was that feeling again of: that's my guy! It was unbelievable. I wouldn't trade that experience for anything. I was there at the game with my boys, and it was so special."

From Ferguson's *Mad Men* trailer, Hamm experienced Freese's homer. "Buck makes the call: 'We will see you tomorrow night.' I'm screaming and freaking out," Hamm said. "And Jay is holding his head in his hands. He's despondent."

In Venice, Italy, Greg Fugate and his wife spent Game 6 up at 6:00 AM, "getting text updates on really spotty Internet. It was random who would get the next update. Freese was stuck with two strikes for four to five minutes before the next update would come in. We have a picture from the next morning from a gondola and we are both grinning like idiots because of the baseball game. We then listened to Mike Shannon call the winner while drinking a Budvar in Zurich."

In Milwaukee, Patrick Quinn was in his strange new house by himself. His wife and her mom—both big Cards fans—were driving separately to Wisconsin. "They were listening on the radio, and I'm all alone watching the game," Patrick said. "I couldn't believe what I was seeing with the comeback, the slide into third, and eventually the game-winning homer and then all of, 'We will see you tomorrow night!' I was immediately brought to tears. I thought of Jack Buck's call from back in the day, and it hit me. Wow. What a moment and I have no one to celebrate what I just saw! My wife came in the door, and we hugged. I admitted to some tears—and I'm a die-hard Cubs fan!"

In the PICU at Mercy Hospital in St. Louis, Jenny Kuchem and her husband watched Game 6 with their four-year-old daughter, who underwent an invasive sinus surgery. It was their 10th wedding anniversary. "The nurses or techs that came in," Kuchem said, "they, of course, would take great care of our daughter, but then there would always be a pause to watch a little bit of the game. Our four year old had a huge thing for Lance Berkman and she was in her hospital bed cheering and saying, 'Go Big Puma!' The nurse that we had at the surgery had tickets that night to go with her boyfriend. Six weeks later our daughter had to go back in for another sinus surgery, and we had that nurse again. She told us she got engaged that night at Game 6. The day is synonymous with the game, the wedding anniversary, and the stress and worry about our chronically ill daughter having surgery. Whenever I watch that game's highlights on YouTube, it makes me tear up."

In the maternity ward of Mercy Hospital, Rachael and Matt Lampe watched the baseball game they had tickets to. Their first date—back in 2005—was the night Pujols hit his famous playoff homer off Brad Lidge. On that very date in 2008—October 17—they were married. In 2011, nine days after their anniversary, they planned to go to the Cards game, but it was rained out and postponed until the next night. Alas, they had plans. Rachael was being induced into labor. "Even my doctor was like, 'Do you want us to move it?'" Rachael recalled in 2018. "And I was like, 'No.' It was my first baby. Maybe I'm not supposed to be there, you know? Everything happens for a reason."

She gave birth at 8:53 PM and watched the Freese heroics with her husband and newborn, Joshua Stephen Lampe. The baby's middle name was after Matt's beloved brother. "But," Rachael said with a laugh, "We almost changed the middle name to David."

"Yep, we discussed it that night," Matt said. "Stephen would've understood."

In New York City, the playwright Ken Ferrigni was already having a nice day. For starters it was his birthday. And his play *Mangella* was sold out that night at the Drilling Company Theater on the Upper West Side. "The cast sang me 'Happy Birthday' on the way to the bar, where I was just in time for Freese's triple," Ferrigni said. "I got hammered, I screamed myself hoarse on the Upper West Side when he homered and slept in a cab on the way home—the sort of magical memorable day when everything went righter than you thought it could."

· · ·

He'd arrived inside the quiet. Mark Lowe finally returned to his St. Louis hotel room. The escape awaited him under the white sheets. But he remained awake. And he did what he'd always do after a game in a hotel in Oakland, Kansas City, or Baltimore. "I always rewatch the games," he said. "Good or bad."

So, after giving up a walk-off homer in Game 6 of the World Series, he sat in the quiet and relived giving up a walk-off homer in Game 6 of the World Series. Lowe watched the six pitches—even the sixth pitch. "I watched my outing, and that's the last time I've seen it," Lowe said in 2020. "Other than moments when you're watching TV, and they're showing playoff history, and it comes up."

Finally, he got under the covers, but as the clock showed well past midnight, Thursday wouldn't go away. "It was tough laying in bed that night," Lowe said, "as you're just kind of finding a place to relax and keep your head from spinning."

His story is history—or at least the other side of it. He threw a change-up, which analytics show was his fourth best pitch in 2011. But in that scenario, Lowe said, "That change-up was the right pitch to go to. And I remember shaking off Napoli two, three times to get to that. And as a pitcher, I've learned over the course of my career up to that point that when you throw a pitch that isn't the pitch you wanted to throw—and you give up a home run or a base hit—you take that pitch home with you that night and you can't sleep because you didn't throw the pitch that you wanted to throw. It's more of a conviction thing. If it's your pitch, you're going to have so much conviction on that as opposed to saying, 'All right, let's give that a try.' And so for me, that is the only saving grace I have from that World Series. Was I disappointed? Absolutely. I felt like I let my team down. But at the same time, I know that my teammates know how much effort I put in every single day. I threw the pitch that I wanted to throw. So I could go home that night. I could look myself in the mirror that night and for the rest of my life, knowing that I wouldn't have done anything different because I could throw that same pitch today in the 3–2 count to Freese, and he swings and misses. Sure, granted some time has passed. But that's just baseball."

Lowe was 28 that night. He'd pitch in 165 more games. But David Freese has him forever frozen on that mound in 2011. He's always in the highlight. "When you give up a home run, you kind of know," he said. "But the ones over your head to center field are the hardest ones to gauge because that's a lot deeper. Sometimes they fall short. So that one going over my head, I knew it was going to be close. You can hear the backspin on the ball going over your head, and it had some steam on it. I thought that it wouldn't have gone as far as it did, the way that sounded going over me. But we can all watch the video and know exactly what happened. That was a pretty tough feeling to swallow right there, just to have that moment. As a kid you put yourself in those situations and you always come through. Bottom of whatever inning, full count, here's your pitch, and he swings and misses."

After the pitch, after talking about the pitch to the media, after trying to wash off the pitch in the shower, Lowe left the losing locker room to see his family. "My grandfather was there," Lowe said. "That was the last time I saw him. I just remember just walking with him in the tunnel. We're all kind of quiet. They were understanding of how I was feeling about that letdown. He tried to kind of play it off, but I don't think anybody could truly do that the second you leave the locker room. I just remember him saying that he's proud of me regardless of anything and happy that he could be there. It was a pretty awesome experience to have in there, and the last time you see him, you're pitching in a World Series. My last memories of him are walking in the tunnel with me at Busch Stadium."

Lowe went on to pitch for five more MLB teams and four minor league teams. Over the years the guys got to talking about their careers—perhaps in the clubhouse or over beers. He'd mention he was on the Texas teams that went to the 2010 and 2011 World Series. "They'd say, 'Oh, you were on that team?' And then they just keep digging," Lowe said. "They keep asking about those teams and then they ask who's the one that gave up the homer to David Freese, and I look at them and I wonder—who set them up? Somebody is messing with me, right?

"But that's a moment that everybody remembers. Somebody has to be on the sour side of it, and that just happened to be me that night. But I wouldn't change it for the world. It was a moment that really gave me some perspective on the game of baseball. That even though you do all the right things, it doesn't mean that you're always going to finish on top. You have to really take every game separately, every pitch separately, every moment separately. And you just have to live on the good moments and you just have to let the bad ones go because it's a game of nothing but failure. And you get addicted to the success. And I think at that moment [after Freese], I became addicted to success, just knowing that feeling and just knowing I didn't ever want to feel that way again. So I worked really, really hard that offseason to maintain what I had finishing that [regular season] because I felt really strong. It was a learning lesson for me to go through that. I feel in life it's taught me so many lessons."

He did face Freese five total times in his career in the regular season. Against Lowe, Freese was 1-for-5 with a double, RBI, and two strikeouts. But they've actually never met. "I really wanted to," Lowe said. "I was hoping that our paths would cross because he was hopping from team to team the same time I was. But I'd be lying if I told you every time he came up to the plate I didn't think about it. I completely changed how I went about facing him from there on out. After that, all I did was throw fastballs down and in and sliders down and away. That's it. Definitely never threw him another change-up."

• • •

Along with his wife, the artist Dan Zettwoch "kind of spilled onto the street after the game. We had some other friends who were at the game in different parts of the ballpark. We met up and we're hugging, asking about what happened in this section or that section. We were hearing about all the weird superstitious things that people were doing to summon up any good will from the baseball gods. I remember looking at Twitter when I got home that night. People that weren't even St. Louis fans were saying it might have been the craziest game ever."

Zettwoch decided to take the Game 6 experience and make it art. "The win expectancy chart was a big thing, and I was into the blogs at the time that would keep close track of that kind of statistical information," he said. "So I thought of incorporating the win expectancy chart with some funny vignettes from the game. I watched it back a few times in its entirety. I even found the KMOX feed at one point to hear that. It was like sketching and reportage in a way to capture the game in one image…I was sketching and figuring out how I can cram as much information as possible into this one poster. And then I ended up drawing it and then soap screening in my basement. That's how I do my prints. It's kind of an old-fashioned printmaking technique of soap screening where you have to print each color at a time. If you look at it, it's just three colors. There's navy blue, red, and yellow. You have a stencil for each one. You create the stencil and then you squeegee and push the ink through. Each one is handmade."

The result was an eye-popping piece that made it an eye-watering print. "The Greatest Game Of All-Time" screamed across the top of the horizontal work of art. And it really did have everything—from the pop fly that landed on David Freese's head to the David Freese fly ball that landed on the lawn. He knew he wanted to make about 100 so he had fun with the numbers and made 111 first-print editions. In total, he's made about 500. "I have sold at least one to a Texas Rangers fan who begrudgingly wanted to somehow remember it, even though they lost," Zettwoch said. "David Freese has a couple. Someone brought one to him at a signing event, and he was like, 'What is this?' So his agent somehow got in touch with me, and I went over to his office one time and signed some for him. And he signed a couple for me and my wife. So actually mine is made out to 'Dan and Les, from No. 23, David Freese.'"

Originally from the Lake of the Ozarks, Ryan Binkley lived off the Delmar Loop during 2011—not far from where Zettwoch spent his 10,000 hours at his college art studio. Binkley distinctly remembered the two-strike count on Freese in the ninth and "thinking, *God damn it, this thing is over*. It's just too much of a wall to climb. Then he hits a fly ball that was long enough to go out, and Cruz misplayed it like a clown…And then the homer? I think it's pretty badass that somebody could be from here, kind of just a part of the team, but just has a moment like that that instantly defines a career. It's got to be one of the coolest sports stories ever."

And so when Binkley and his brother opened a bar, they paid homage to that night. It's called Game 6 Honky Tonk Joint and located in downtown St. Louis on 4th Street or walking distance from Busch. "We wanted it to feel local," Binkley said. "We landed on Game 6 because it was easy and something that if you're a Cardinals fan, that's all you need to say, and you get positive stories and excitement. And it's sort of like 9/11; everyone knew where they were and they can tell you about watching the game or if they were at the game. Everyone had their story."

They specialized in live country music, as Binkley's brother used some old Nashville connections to get some strong acts. Inside the joint, which is an old brick building that's literally 100 years old, is a framed Freese jersey; *St. Louis Post-Dispatch* pages on display; and even red, white, and blue bunting like at the ballpark during the playoffs. On the bar's Twitter profile, it's advertised as "St. Louis & Nashville's love child. Cardinals baseball & live honky tonk music. Makin' every night feel like Game 6 of the 2011 World Series."

• • •

During the day of October 27, 2011, David Huyette sent a text (though, clearly, he didn't edit the text before sending it): "Jeremy & I goign to world series game Look for us catching the careds winning home run!"

Huyette had two tickets in the Busch Stadium bleachers, so he invited Jeremy Reiland, a new buddy whom he met at a bachelor party. The evening got off to an inauspicious start, however, when Reiland showed up for the Cardinals' Game 6 of the World Series in a Chicago Cubs shirt. "I was actually kind of angry with him because I thought he'd be getting harassed, and people are going to want to beat us up," said Huyette, who at the time was 39 and a radiologist in Alton, Illinois. "The thing was everyone felt sorry for him and said basically that he was never going to see a World Series game anyways, so he might as well be there."

The experience was extraordinary. After Jake Westbrook kept Texas from scoring in the top of the 11th, Reiland hustled up the stairs to use the restroom. He stood at the top of the steps for the first batter, looking down at Huyette in the seats. During the late innings, they had joked about a big home run landing on the grassy area to their right. So as Freese prepared for his at-bat, Huyette jokingly prepared to jump onto the grass. "He was even joking around, putting his leg up on the railing like he was going to jump the fence," Reiland recalled. "So he's just looking at me, and then, sure enough, the very next pitch…"

"I heard the crack of the bat," Huyette said. "And I could tell from the trajectory that it was going to go to center there. At that point I heard the crowd start cheering, and then it all went silent. I don't remember jumping the fence. I had knee trouble at the time. I don't know how I got over it so easily."

Huyette was on the grass before the ball was. A few other fans tracked it, too, but weren't as close as Huyette to where it would land. "It was basically like the whole world got quiet, and the ball thudded in the grass in front of me. All I heard was the thud," he said. "And then I took it."

He snatched it with his left hand and tumbled forward onto the grass. Nobody else jumped on him—until the second Huyette stood up. He gripped the ball in his left hand into his chest, raised his right hand, and, sure enough, Reiland was there to hug him. "I ended up jumping the fence at the very top," Reiland said. "So with the batter's eye, it's a real steep grass slope. I'm watching the ball and I'm running down the hill. And I slipped. If you watch the replay, I have a black jacket on at that time. I slipped, and it looks like I'm sliding down next to Dave like I knew he had the ball. I honestly didn't know. I was just trying to get there. So I slip down the hill and roll over and see Dave with the ball in his arms. He kind of looked at me, and then I jumped on top of him, celebrating."

In the moments after, the guys posed for a picture with a man and a young boy who sat near them during the game. It was then that a plain clothes cop approached him. The cop asked if they wanted to go to the clubhouse. "But then he said to me," Reiland shared, "'I don't know if they're going to let you in with your Cubs shirt though.' So Dave said something like, 'Well, we'll just keep the ball if they're not going to let him in.' So he radioed down to security as we're walking down there, and they said, 'Fine, we'll let him in.'"

"My phone started dying," Huyette said, "but I called my mom, I called my best friend, and I called my lawyer. And my lawyer didn't answer. So we went down to the clubhouse and we were sitting outside the door. Jeremy saw Frank Thomas walk by and talked to him for a second. [ESPN reporter] Tim Kurkjian was sitting down and writing notes about everything right outside of there. So I asked Tim: 'What should I do with the ball?' And Tim said, 'That ball needs to be in the Hall of Fame.'"

They hung out in a small waiting area by the main clubhouse doors, and Freese suddenly appeared. Freese, Huyette, and Reiland—in his Cubs shirt—posed for photos with the baseball. Freese gave Huyette a bat, signed his autograph on there with his jersey number, and a message: "Dave, thanks for the home run ball." The Cardinals also gave Huyette a ball signed by the entire 2011 team. "So we went to the Lumiere Casino," Huyette said, "and we're walking all around there with the bat and the ball, telling the story to anyone who would listen. I ended up getting home around probably 4:15 or 4:30 and I got my first phone call to come do interviews downtown for morning shows. So I was like, 'Okay, yeah!' I changed into a clean shirt and grabbed a couple of Red Bulls and walked out the door. I called Jeremy. He had just pulled into his driveway. He said okay too and never even went into the house. So he's still wearing the same shirt the next day! We're starting to do interviews between 5:00 and 6:00 AM on no sleep. We brought the ball and bat everywhere we went."

Channel 5 even coordinated with the Cardinals to have them come into the stadium during the day. "They basically had us reenact the whole thing," Huyette said. "We were in the stadium alone with this camera crew. They wouldn't let us onto the field, but we got onto the warning track. It was pretty cool to walk around the stadium before Game 7 with nobody in it."

Another TV station coordinated a taped interview at a local AutoZone, and the folks there gifted Huyette and Reiland two 15th row tickets to Game 7. It wasn't just Freese living a fairy tale; it was also the guys who got the Freese home-run ball. Back downtown, they kept charging their phones in Reiland's car because radio stations and reporters kept calling. They estimated they did 30 total interviews. They didn't even go home. They just stayed downtown before attending Game 7 for free. "And the day was just perfect, probably 75 degrees," Huyette said. "So we were walking around—me with a Cardinals red shirt on and Jeremy in his Cubs shirt. And I think people had seen the pictures online because we were getting looks everywhere we would go. Their first thought was: *Why is he wearing a Cubs shirt?* And then their eyes would get big, and then we knew we were getting recognized. It was so strange. People asked to take pictures with us, and we didn't even know if they knew our names, but they just knew that they had seen us in pictures with David Freese."

"So a week later," Reiland said, "the Cubs mailed me a picture out of the blue. They took a photo of the Wrigley Field marquee that said: 'Jeremy Rieland. No. 1 Cubs fan in Cardinal territory.'"

Game 6 Story No. 10

"What a fucking night that was!" Game 6 was one of the more memorable moments of Sean Casey's baseball life, even though the former All-Star didn't play in the game, have a favorite or former team in the game, or for that matter even attend the game. But that night he got to experience St. Louis via the eyes (and liver) of a true fan and dear friend. All these years later, Casey speaks of October 27, 2011, with gobsmacked bliss. "There was an energy that was so different—and only a World Series game in St. Louis could provide that," said Casey, who hit .302 in 12 MLB seasons. "And the way it happened, to send it to a Game 7 at the brink of elimination, the energy in St. Louis that night was like nothing I'd seen. I've played in a World Series. Maybe as a player it was something I felt, but just city-wide, the energy that was created and the buzz and excitement was something I've never felt."

The voice on KMOX Radio told folks to go crazy, and Greg Amsinger's relatives started going crazy, but on the TV screen, the batter was still up. Amsinger was six and cramped inside the living room in a South St. Louis brick house, where his grandpa refused to listen to the national TV broadcast. "I'm wondering what the hell is happening, and then all of a sudden, Ozzie Smith hits a home run," Amsinger recalled of Game 5 of the 1985 National League Championship Series. "Did something magical just happen? I don't understand. How did this guy on the radio know it was going to happen?…I fell in love with the game from there."

Now a studio host for MLB Network, Amsinger is undeniably and unabashedly St. Louis and speaks of his city with something like a Parisian's pride. He grew up in the Bevo Mill area and grew up on '80s and '90s Cardinals baseball, his soul forever carpeted with Astroturf. "I was as passionate of a Cardinals fan as you could find at a young age," he said. "I could tell you starting lineups. I could tell you lineups of the teams they played against. I just was obsessed with baseball. I created my own baseball card dice game. This is no joke. My friends would come over and play it. I had all the rules. It was a probability game. I did probability stats before that was a thing. I was like eight. I had sheets that would come out for leadoff guys. So based on slugging percentage, here are different rules. The probability of dice. This was my psychotic nerd brain."

As seen on TV, Amsinger is energetic and opinionated. An aspiring broadcaster, he began almost a decade of dues-paying after his 2001 graduation from Lindenwood University in St. Charles, Missouri. He worked at a TV station in Terre Haute, Indiana. He went on to host shows such as the *World Series of Video Games* and *The #1 College Sports Show*. Finally, in 2009 the MLB Network launched. Amsinger was the perfect fit—a confident, fast-talking personality with a childlike love of baseball and the aforementioned "psychotic nerd brain." "It gives me goose bumps," said Amsinger, who was 32 during the 2011 World Series. "When the network started in 2009, I was there for the launch. First All-Star game we ever covered was

in St. Louis. So the grand marshal is Bob Gibson. I'm doing the red
carpet show with Harold Reynolds and I'm interviewing Bob Gibson.
Then comes Albert Pujols. Like it's in St. Louis, my hometown, and
our first All-Star is there. Our first MLB Draft in 2009, we got one
kid to show up. Only one. Some kid from Jersey, and no one knew
for sure if he was going to go in the first 30 picks. We thought he
was going to go 19th, and once he didn't, we were like: oh no. We
can't keep showing this kid with his family. Ended up being Mike
Trout. And then, 2011 happens. World Series in St. Louis, and it's the
greatest World Series of all time."

In the hour before Game 6, Amsinger cohosted MLB Network's
live pregame show along with Casey. But Amsinger wasn't on for the
postgame show. That night the gig went to Matt Vasgersian. So after
the pregame show, Amsinger, Casey, and a few other TV types went
to Ruth's Chris Steakhouse with their boss, network president Tony
Petitti, who later became the chief operating officer of Major League
Baseball. They had a private room with a TV and succulent steaks for
entrees. "MLB Network is picking up the tab, so we get some wine
flowing," Amsinger said. "But everyone leaves because the game is
over [with the Texas Rangers up 7–4 in the eighth inning]. I'm the
only Cardinals fan at the table, so I can't leave until the game is over."

So, Amsinger asked Casey to stay with him. The boys had a
growing friendship. And there were drinks and a ballgame on. So
Casey stayed. "And then, all of a sudden," Casey recalled, "shit started
happening."

A base runner in the ninth. Another base runner. And then with
two on, two outs, and two strikes, David Freese tripled. "Greg was
running around screaming, 'Oh my God! Oh my God!' said Casey, who
was 37 at the time. "It was like I saw 12-year-old Greg Amsinger. Oh
my God, little Greg over here. He was going bananas. I was excited,
too. I was excited for him. Obviously, I'm not a huge Cardinals fan.
But I'm a Greg Amsinger fan. And this guy is so freaking excited…
It was such a connection for me and him. We're the only ones there.
We're hugging. This is unbelievable!"

For the extra innings, Amsinger made the call—they just had
to go to Mike Shannon's. The two hustled over to the famed St.

Louis sports bar just in time for the roller coaster of the 10th inning. "St. Louis, they're such rabid baseball fans, and this was one of the biggest, greatest games in baseball history," said Casey, who made three All-Star Games and played primarily for the Cincinnati Reds, but also the Cleveland Indians, Pittsburgh Pirates, Detroit Tigers, and Boston Red Sox from 1997 to 2008. "So the freaking city was electric where Greg and I were. And being at Shannon's together, it started to get a little crazy. But it was a good crazy. I think I was hugging many different Cardinals fans. They'd come over yelling, 'Sean Casey! Greg Amsinger! Blaaaaaaah.' I'm giving everyone hugs. All of a sudden, Greg and I were just two kids and we were mixed in with Cardinals fans really enjoying the energy."

Casey was so famously friendly that he was nicknamed "The Mayor" during his playing days. A hero to many in Cincinnati, the St. Louis fans also respected the way he played the game. Casey recalled making a diving play and getting cheers from the crowd at Busch Stadium. A great play, after all, is a great play. Though Casey's 2011 trip to St. Louis "certainly felt a little weird" because the last time he was there he lost the World Series. It was literally a half-decade to the day—October 27, 2006—when Casey was at the bat in the ninth inning of Game 5.

Looking back, the 2006 World Series felt like a buzzsaw since the Detroit Tigers won just a lone game. But consider that in Game 5, the Cards led just 4–2 in the top of the ninth. If the rookie closer blew it, the series would've gone back to Detroit for at least a Game 6. And Kenny Rogers would've started that game—and he dominated the Cardinals in the Game 2 Detroit win.

So there was Casey in the top of the ninth against Adam Wainwright. "It was one of my favorite at-bats ever in St. Louis," said Casey, who went 9-for-17 against the Cardinals in that World Series. "He got me 0–2. I would have been the second out of the ninth in Game 5 when they won it. I remember stepping out and I had never heard a crowd—or a sound—like I heard right there in St. Louis. It was deafening. It was like a deafening cheer. When I got to 0–2, I worked him to 3–2 and ended up getting a double. But I just remember that at-bat. I could take you through every pitch. It was just so amazing how loud the crowd got in St. Louis."

Casey was many things, but one he wasn't was fast. So the Tigers pinch ran a fellow named Ramon Santiago. Soon, Santiago was joined on the bases by Placido Polanco—Albert Pujols' close friend—who Waino walked. But with the tying run on first, Wainwright struck out Brandon Inge, who was joined in final-out infamy five years and one day later by Texas' David Murphy.

At Mike Shannon's bar for Game 6 in 2011, Casey was having a blast. "I can't remember how many drinks in we were. That's all you need to know," Casey recalled. "We were definitely feeling good."

He and Amsinger actually discussed using their press passes to go into Busch Stadium and watch after the Cardinals tied the game in the 10th inning. "Superstitions kicked in." Casey said. "The former ballplayer in me came out. We can't go. The mojo is too good for us to go in."

And so Amsinger and Casey were amid the plastered masses at Mike Shannon's. Freese, of course, homered in the 11th inning to win Game 6. "I'm suddenly a Cardinal fan or something," Casey said. "I'm a Cardinals fan. Me and Greg are having the greatest night ever. And then I think after that we end up going out on the town and drinking all night."

"We just take off running," Amsinger recalled. "Sean Casey and Greg Amsinger ran the streets of downtown St. Louis, literally hugging random strangers. And Sean Casey, you would have thought he played for the Cardinals for 20 years. That's how he reacted…It was the most hilarious thing ever. Just losing our minds that we saw the greatest World Series game ever together, it's a memory Sean and I will always have."

After a win for the ages, and surely a hangover for the ages, Amsinger was back on the pregame show for Game 7 the next night. The postgame plan was to have Vasgersian host if Texas won, but the energetic Amsinger was earmarked to host if his hometown team won. Late in Game 7 inside the makeshift green room, he gave a bear hug to Keith Costas, a researcher for MLB Network, a St. Louis native, and the son of Bob Costas. And then Amsinger headed to the right-field corner behind the outfield wall with the anchor desk on wheels. "We're standing behind the outfield wall, and there's this little black and white TV in the tunnel," he said. "So I'm watching the last three outs. I'm so locked in that I'm standing there, and the game ends, and I have no idea who this person standing next to me is. I turn and I'm about to hug the person standing next to me. This is no joke. It was Fredbird. I hugged Fredbird. I legit hugged Fredbird. Then we're on the field, and everyone's going crazy. I'm hearing fans saying stuff like, 'Amsinger! Lindenwood!' I'm hugging fans as I'm walking out. I felt like I'd just won the World Series. I sit down at the desk and I turn to Harold Reynolds, Al Leiter, Dan, and Kevin Millar, I tell them, 'Guys, this is one of the top 10 greatest nights of my life.' They all laughed, and as we opened the show, Albert Pujols and Tony La Russa ran up on the set. It's the last time they're seen in Cardinals uniforms…To say that's a dream come true is bogus. No one could ever dream that up. There's not a kid that could even dream that that would happen. It's beyond a dream come true."

CHAPTER 11

TASTING VICTORY

The tradition began in Philadelphia way back in Game 2, when Cliff Lee was hanging strikes on the edges, and the season was hanging on the edge of the cliff. "Here man, eat some fruit snacks," Kyle McClellan said to Adam Wainwright. "We need some runs."

Down 4–0, the Cardinals scored five to win 5–4. "We looked at each other," McClellan said. "We were like—they're magical fruit snacks. So that was our thing the whole playoffs. We ate massive amounts of fruit snacks, probably hundreds of thousands of calories of fruit snacks."

Which brought them to Game 7 of the World Series. "I had a mouthful of fruit snacks," Wainwright recalled of October 28, 2011. "And Kyle and I were counting down outs."

The Game 7 starter would be Christopher John Carpenter, the man who gave the speech, the man who won Game 162, the man who out-dueled Roy Halladay, the man who sacrificed his body for a Game 1 out, the man who allowed only two runs in seven Game 5 innings. The rainout gave Carp three days' rest between Games 5 and 7, but as Tony La Russa admitted in 2017, Carp was the Game 7 starter all along. "The only question was," La Russa said, "without the rainout would he have pitched on two days' rest?"

In that very game against Lee and the Philadelphia Phillies, Carpenter learned a lesson that he utilized in Game 7 of the World Series. In that National League Division Series game, Carp started on three days' rest for the first time in his career. He got banged around.

219

He told La Russa he wasn't feeling as strong as normal, so he put extra effort behind each pitch. Messed up his mechanics. He told La Russa if he ever pitched on three days' rest again, he would "pitch with what he had," as explained in *One Last Strike*. Sure enough, it happened just 26 days later.

Before Game 7 La Russa reminded the Cardinals of a spring training visitor the previous year. Mike Eruzione arrived at Cardinals camp and shared stories about his 1980 U.S. Olympic hockey team. Everyone remembers beating the Russians. But not everyone remembers the squad beating Finland. The game against the Soviets put America in the gold medal game the very next day. Had to win that one, too. The legendary coach Herb Brooks famously told the boys that if they lost, they'd take it to their graves. So here were the Cardinals the day after Game 6, recognizing that Game 6 would only matter if they won Game 7.

There's a narrative out there that the Texas Rangers were done for even before the first pitch. After all, how do you recover after losing Game 6 the way they lost Game 6? But Texas scored two runs in the top of the first against Carp. "You definitely don't want the momentum to stay with them at all for any length of time," Lance Berkman said.

With two outs in the first, Albert Pujols walked. Then, Berkman himself walked. "Now batting," Busch public-address man John Ulett announced, "No. 23, third baseman, David Freese." The fans would've given him a standing ovation—except that they were already standing, so they just gave him this overtly raucous and rocking ovation.

Starter Matt Harrison got two strikes on Freese, but at this point with Freese, it was unclear who had the advantage in that situation. Freese connected on a fastball, which carried into the gap in left-center field. He did it again. This time, tying Game 7 in the first 2–2. "To me," Berkman said, "that kind of gets lost in the shuffle. They jump out to a lead, and we come right back? At that point, we're like 'We're winning, we're winning this thing.'"

Carp didn't allow a run in the second or third, and after Ryan Theriot flew out to start the Cards' third, left fielder Allen Craig came to bat. The previous night Matt Holliday suffered a hand injury that ended his season. "You dream as a kid of a chance to play in the World Series and in a Game 7," Holliday said. "It was frustrating. But at that point, you're kind of feeling like Allen Craig is a really good player, and we still have a really good team."

Just like Freese the previous night, Craig drilled a ball the opposite way to right field. Nelson Cruz chased it, but this one went over the wall. With a 3–2 lead, Carpenter pitched a scoreless fourth and fifth, too. In the bottom of the fifth, the Cards scored two more runs yet didn't get a hit (walk, hit batsmen, ground-out, intentional walk, regular walk, and yet another hit batsmen). Carpenter pitched a scoreless sixth—Craig helped by robbing Cruz of a potential homer—and La Russa even let Carp hit in the bottom of the inning. But when David Murphy doubled to start the seventh, La Russa walked to the mound. The ovation for Carpenter was personal. Here was the man, 36 years old in 2011, who literally pitched more innings than any player in the National League (237⅓). And he had just pitched a quality start in Game 7 of the World Series.

In its final showcase of autumn, the St. Louis bullpen lived up to its reputation one last time. Yadier Molina drove in a sixth run with a single in the seventh. And in the ninth with a 6–2 lead to preserve, Jason Motte trotted onto the field. "We did go back to Carl's that day for lunch," Motte said of the burger spot. "We're a little superstitious, us baseball players. It had to have been the Carl's that helped us win. And it ended up being one of the best nights…I remember walking out of the bullpen and taking everything in more than I had in the past. *Man, this is pretty cool.*"

In the ninth inning, McClellan and Wainwright chewed fruit snacks, while a few fans chewed their own fingernails. Cruz, who could've caught the final out of the World Series, flew out. Mike

Napoli, who then would've been the MVP of the World Series, grounded out. As Murphy came to the plate, Joe Buck said on FOX: "Nobody, and I mean nobody, could've expected the Cardinals to be in this position, even midway through September."

Murphy did not swing at strike one. "I just remember standing out in left field and looking up into the crowd," Craig said. "They're chanting 'Let's go Cards. Let's go Cards!' over and over again. It just gives me goose bumps to this day remembering that and feeling that moment."

And then, Motte unleashed a heater, and the lefty-hitting Murphy hit a fly ball the opposite way to left field. "Back is Craig," Buck said, as the left fielder squeezed the final out in his glove. "What a team! What a ride! The Cardinals are world champs in 2011!"

They did it. They won championship No. 11 in '11. "When it finally happened," Wainwright said, "it was just pandemonium. You're just running and you don't know where to go or who to hug and you just realize you're going to jump into everyone and hug everyone. You're going to scream as loud as you can for as long as you can. And that's what we did."

"After the final out was made," Motte said, "I turned to Yadi and was like, 'Hey, come get some, baby!' He was running out, and I remember going to put my arms around him, as he's jumping in the air, and then next thing you know, I'm getting sideswiped from the rest of the bench! And I completely had blinders on. I hadn't been looking at anyone else, just seeing Yadi. And I know my joy and my emotion in that moment was pretty awesome, but for me I got to see Yadi's face. He's got that smile, running out at me, and it's one of those things I'll never forget, baseball-wise. It's burned into my mind."

They were champions—all of them. Pujols and Freese, Carp and Yadi, Skip and the skipper, Theriot and Furcal, Big Puma and The Shredder. They were floating on the field—one final happy flight.

Jon Jay, Daniel Descalso, and Craig, the Memphis roommates and St. Louis champions, each fielded the final three outs of the ninth inning. "One of your best friends is in center field, one of your other best friends is at third, we're all on the field closing out the World Series together," Craig said. "Right after I caught it, the first thing I remember is looking to my left, and Jon Jay was running full speed at me. We jumped into each other's arms and then ran full speed into the infield together just screaming at each other, 'We did it!' Everything that we had talked about in the minor leagues and how it was all about winning and being a part of the St. Louis Cardinals on a championship team, it actually happened."

Craig carried the ball from the final out into the clubhouse. He put it in his locker. But the next day, when he heard La Russa was retiring, "I immediately went and got it and gave it to him," he said.

• • •

As a boy in the 1980s, Kevin Willmann was infused by fandom for the St. Louis Cardinals, these soaring, scoring Birds who turned Astroturf baselines into a runway. "In the backyard playing Wiffle Ball, my brother and I took turns trying to be Willie McGee," Willmann said. "It was—who got to be Willie McGee that day?"

By 2011 at age 34, Willmann was the owner and chef of FarmHaus and he was named in *Food & Wine* magazine's "Best New Chefs, Class of 2011." But he'd never cooked up anything like this before. As they watched Game 7 in the FarmHaus kitchen, the superfan Willmann's idea was to try to get into Busch Stadium after the game. Not just the stadium itself, but the Cardinals' clubhouse. They would put on their chef jackets and bring reinforcements of their signature meatloaf for the clubhouse catering setup.

Willmann had become close friends with Mike Emerson, who owned the St. Louis barbecue joint called Pappy's, which did some catering for the ballclub. Because of this friendship, Willmann actually got a tour during the season of the Cardinals' kitchen and catering setup in the clubhouse. "So we knew the lay of the land," Willmann said. "I knew Pappy's was there. And I had a big ol' jug of Pappy's barbecue sauce in the basement. Mike had given it to me to use in a collaboration sauce we used to serve in our meatloaf. So I went down and grabbed the barbecue sauce and showed it to everybody in the kitchen. Everybody just started smiling. I think at that point we knew it was going to work. We loaded up and we tried to make it as real as we could. So we vacuumed individual portions of meatloaf and put them into hotel pans, these stainless steel pans, so that they would be hot with building water on top. We had some legit-looking, real props. We put our chef coats on. The four of us came up to the gate, and I know somebody is going to get in trouble for this, but they let us in. We said, 'We're here with reinforcements,' and I pointed to Pappy's on the jug of barbecue sauce, and they waved us right in. I think the statute of limitations is up on us getting into too much trouble."

They kept just thinking to themselves—*we're supposed to be here, we're supposed to be here.* They made their way through the door, right past more security, and right into the players' lounge and the kitchen. They were in. This was incredible. Insanity. "We started cutting out little sections of meatloaf in the hotel pans, warming up the barbecue sauce," Willmann said. "Sure enough, I saw one of Pappy's pans had run out of barbecue so I came over there and took it out and put our meatloaf down. Here comes Matt Holliday, and I grab a set of tongs and put it on his plate. I'm handing Matt Holliday the meatloaf and I'm shaking. I set the first one down and I'm looking at him. This is Matt Holliday. He's giant. He keeps looking at me so I grabbed another piece. It was just awesome. We were there for probably five more minutes before somebody came over, and I heard the intercom, 'FarmHaus, I don't know how they got in here.'

"Somebody came up to us and said, 'What the hell are you guys doing?' I got in his ear immediately. 'We had to do it. I'm so sorry, I take full responsibility. Chance of a lifetime. We went for it. I promise we didn't touch anything. We'll get the hell out.' It was then that it dawned on me that I might have gotten someone in trouble here. He looks at me and says, 'Did you take anything?' I said we didn't. And he goes, 'Take a beer and get the hell out of here.' He gave us all one of the beers—2011 World Champion Budweisers. So at this point we just abandoned everything. All of our pans and everything. We just walk out. But as we're leaving, one of my cooks sees David Freese. He was just getting away from it all for a second. My cook goes, 'Can I get your autograph?' And the only thing Eric had was his paycheck in his pocket. So David Freese signed his paycheck, and they took a photo. It was just total elation. We got out. They didn't even escort us out. They're just like, 'Get out of here.' A legendary moment."

• • •

When the man who gave St. Louis that rare feeling would return home, St. Louis would try to give him one in return. John Ulett would announce the next batter for the Pittsburgh Pirates or the Los Angeles Dodgers, and Yadier Molina would coolly call time and walk toward the pitcher's mound to let the homecoming king stand at home alone. There was David Freese, and they would cheer. And would they cheer. So loud, so genuine, so appreciative. This man made Game 6, Game 6. "I just remember smiling," said Dodgers broadcaster Joe Davis, the man who replaced Vin Scully—and thus has a personal appreciation for what a legend means to a town. "You smile seeing the ovations and you smile knowing the guy and how much it would mean to him. I know the St. Louis fans see themselves as the Best Fans in Baseball, and when you see things like that, it's hard to argue. They know what their standing ovations mean to a guy like that. It's true. It's true that they can make such an impact by showing their appreciation. It was the same way when we saw Pujols return last summer."

Indeed, Albert Pujols received similar adulation in 2019 during his first games as a player back at Busch Stadium. So much changed right after Allen Craig caught the 27th out of the 2011 World Series. Pujols signed as a free agent with the Los Angeles Angels. And Tony La Russa retired from managing, though in October of 2020, he agreed to return to the game as manager of the Chicago White Sox.

Also in October of 2020 after another postseason appearance by the Cardinals, John Mozeliak took a few quiet moments to reflect on the legacy of Freese. "What his success did was it really allowed us to have a pretty good decade of baseball," said Mozeliak, whose team made the playoffs in six of the nine seasons after 2011. "Had we not maybe qualified for the postseason, had we maybe lost Game 6, it could have definitely put this organization on a different trajectory. As you recall, we had two major things happen that offseason: we had Albert Pujols file for free agency and ultimately signing for Anaheim and we had Tony La Russa stepping down. So when you look back on what that playoff run meant, it culminated in a World Series championship. It allowed perhaps players to leave here more at peace with their decisions if they decided to leave. Obviously, it allowed Tony to step away on top…Say we had lost Game 6. And then the next day we announce Tony stepping down. And then within a few months, Albert leaves the Cardinals. There's probably a lot more people asking, 'what's going on,' than the fact that we had [won the pennant]. And then not only had we won, but we felt confident that we still had a good, quality core of players around us that—if we could add to it, we could still be successful. And, of course, 2012 we were a game away from going to the World Series. And 2013? We went to the World Series. It just positioned us perhaps very differently than had we lost."

But they won, unfathomably and incredibly, thanks to a boy who grew up to help his favorite team, his hometown team, win the World Series. "I know he had some times of struggle—he put some self-imposed obstacles in his way—but I think 2011 was the baseball gods giving him a gift," said Tony Dattoli, Freese's coach at Meramec Community College. "David is a great kid. He's a great father, a great human being. One of the most generous people I ever met. And 2011? It couldn't have happened to a better person."

Game 6 Story No. 11

Inside the stadium's concrete concourse, it was drab and gray and felt cold even in August. "But then you walk through the corridor and out into the open," John Nagle recalled, "and there's the green. Just the expanse of it, the real rich color of the Astroturf. Just walking through there, you're like, 'Oh my goodness.' Both mom and I were just like, 'Wow. Here we are.'"

John's first Cardinals game was August 13, 1987. He was 12, and his mother, Linda, drove the 67 miles from small-town Sullivan, Missouri, to downtown St. Louis. That feeling of walking into Busch for the first time is—for many Cardinals faithful—similar to that of a first kiss. It's memorable, unmistakable, and unforgettable. The sun-drenched green field and the coliseum of red seats. The feeling of spotting your favorite player in the flesh, draped in the gleaming white of the home uniforms. The waft of the grilled hot dogs. The welcoming organ music, which sounded like the soundtrack to a carnival or maybe even a religious gathering. "After that first game," John said, "I was hooked."

That summer he mowed lawns for money to spend on baseball cards. He would go to a local store called Town & Country and buy packs of those famed, 1987 wood-framed Topps design, hoping to get Cardinals players.

After high school John took a year off before getting his associate's degree in drafting. He worked at a couple of companies. Lost his job in 2001. Got divorced in 2002. Finally latched on to a job at a suspension parts warehouse in St. Clair, Missouri. And that's where he worked in 2011.

John was a Junior. John Sr. died when his son was just five. John became a dad to John III, who loved the Cardinals, too. It's what kids did.

At the Cardinals Care Winter Warm-Up before the 2011 season, John brought a game-used ball from 2005, the final season at the old Busch Stadium, the site of his baseball baptism. Chris Carpenter started that 2005 game he attended. And on that 2011 day, John and his son actually met Carp. Got him to sign the ball. Sure enough, a Channel 5 cameraperson caught the sweet interaction. "My phone was blowing up!" John recalled. "People [were] saying: 'I see Johnny on the TV!' So that's kind of how 2011 started off for us. It was really cool."

For about two years, John had developed a relationship with a woman over Facebook. Shaley lived in Rolla, Missouri, about 40 miles away. He loved the escape of chatting with Shaley. She stirred something in him. That September of 2011, they finally met. The first date was at a restaurant. But the next few were Cardinals-related. Shaley wasn't into baseball, but she was into John, so she took to the sport. He warned her: "I become quite a different person during the playoffs."

But neither of them had any idea what that would truly mean. They watched Game 4 and Game 5 of the World Series together. But before Game 6, he thought he had food poisoning. "I told my boss," John said. "'Hey, I need to go get checked out. Something's wrong.'"

On the day of Game 6, John was told he needed to have his gallbladder surgically removed. "And they did warn me that there could be complications," he said. "I was kind of a big guy."

Imagine this emotional hurricane. At the beginning of the day, he thought it was a bout with food poisoning. By nighttime he was in a hospital bed, enduring pain, stress, and anger. And he had to share a hospital room with a chatty man that was annoying him. John watched Game 6 "until David Freese dropped the ball" in the fifth inning. Texas Rangers hitter Michael Young doubled home that batter in the next at-bat, and the Rangers took the lead. "I got so mad," John said. "'They don't want to win. This is it. I'm going to bed.' It was an emotional day."

Around midnight nurses came into the room to do some blood work. That's when the roommate told John about David Freese. And Lance Berkman. And David Freese. "It would be the perfect Game 7 situation," John recalled. "So I was pretty excited about that."

Surgery was at 1:00 PM. But the doctor discovered the gallbladder was gangrenous. There was major tissue damage. "So they had to scrap the laparoscopic plan and ended up cutting me open," John said. "Like a big, 10-inch incision. So I ended up being under for a lot longer than they had planned. And when the surgery was over, I wasn't breathing on my own. They had to put me on a ventilator. When I woke up, I had a tube down my throat basically."

His mother was by his bedside with nurses. It was late into the night. "She was like, 'Don't try to talk,'" John recalled. "They said, 'You ended up having a really rough surgery, but you made it through.' I'm trying to talk, and they go, 'We'll get you a piece of paper and a pen.' I was really weak. And I just wrote: 'WS?' My mother looked at it and was kind of confused. She didn't know exactly what it meant. Then she said, 'Oh, World Series?' I nodded. 'Oh yeah, they won! They won!' I gave her a thumbs up and then literally just went right back out and to sleep."

He was at the hospital for another week and a half. Shaley would make the drive every day "to come take care of me," John said.

He was smitten by this woman. They knew each other well but hadn't spent too much time actually together. These nights were precious. Once he was out of the hospital, John proposed to Shaley. She said yes. The fall of 2011 changed his life forever.

"But I started having complications from the original surgery," he said.

There was some leakage. So they needed to put a stent in. He said it was a normal procedure. That day he returned from the procedure to his mother's house, John III was there. "And the first time I ate something, I kind of had an almost out-of-body experience," John said. "Something happened. I went into shock. And so my family rushed me to the hospital. And what happened was there ended up being a blockage…They call it pancreatitis. And this was a particularly bad one. They said there was a 50/50 chance I would make it. When my father died, he was 37 years old, and so here my son watches me nearly die. And I was 37 years old."

When Shaley got the call that John had a 50/50 chance, she was in the midst of shopping. For her wedding dress. "They almost kind of put me in a coma," John said. "They gave me so much medication. I was in the most pain I've ever been through in my life. I want to say it was like two or three days before I can remember anything."

He survived. But weeks later he was back in the hospital again due to pancreatitis. This time in St. Louis. This time for three weeks. And every day after work, Shaley made the one-hour, 40-minute drive from Rolla to St. Louis. "And it got to be that she was as much a regular as I was in there," John said. "I didn't have anyone in the room with me, but there was another bed. And she would spend the night and then leave early in the morning to go back to work in Rolla. And so they would put her up in the bed and then they pushed the bed close to mine so we could sit there and watch TV and hold hands."

John's body was cruelly uncooperative. He'd survive one bout and soon begin a new one. "There ended up being what they call an ERCP," he said, "where they go down through my mouth and they cut holes in my stomach and then go to the pancreas and different areas that needed to be worked on. I think they did like three of those while I was in the hospital, three or four. I know I went on a feeding tube at some point because I couldn't eat. And honestly from there on, I didn't really eat much for the next year to the end of 2012. Being a big guy, I lost like 100 pounds. I was getting pretty close to 400 pounds. I think at my lowest I was 264 at the end of that year. It was a terrible way to lose weight. It was good to be lighter. But because my pancreas was damaged, I ended up with diabetes. And I have chronic pancreatitis to this day.

"We had set a date for our wedding on March 2, 2012. Even during that time, I was having a hard time just standing up…There were some pretty low times. There were times where I honestly wished that it would have killed me because of the pain that I was going through. But when Shaley would come and visit, it's like all that went away while she was there. I'm not exaggerating to tell you a story. That's really the way that it was. We've talked about it quite a bit. And a lot of people said that. I had a friend, who was a nurse, who said, 'I'm really surprised you made it because not very many people make it. I think it was Shaley.' We had talked about putting off the wedding because I was so sick. But as I told everybody, 'We might as well keep it because I feel so much better when I'm with her.'"

They were indeed married that March day. John's mother was there. John III was the best man. "I felt amazing," John said.

After the wedding the couple lived together in Rolla, then in Sullivan. In 2020 they moved to nearby Salem. "I still have health problems, but for the most part, everything is doing well," John said in the fall of 2020, "compared to at least 2011 and 2012."

They got a cat. And some guinea pigs in the backyard. And they watch the Cardinals—their Cardinals—on television. "Because of the World Series in 2011, because of me and all that, she became a superfan," John said of Shaley. "And they were playoff bound every year at that time. She's kind of surpassed me in some ways because she'll go, 'Can you believe so-and-so is only batting .212 this year?'"

Since their anniversary is during spring training, they annually celebrate at spring training. "Baseball brings back a lot of memories…it takes me back to when I was a kid." John said. "It's a lot of emotion. I'm kind of an emotional guy, especially after everything that happened to me. Anytime I watch Game 6, I usually tear up. It takes me back to that time—the greatest and worst time of my life… But it really is a cool story for us. It's kind of like we lived happily ever after."

CLOSING REMARKS

Ten years? It is crazy how fast time flies. It definitely does not feel like it was that long ago. It feels like yesterday we were out on that field doing what we did with an awesome group of guys. Time flies, but it is really cool to think back on.

It was a team thing in 2011. We just went out and handled our business. When it comes to sports, I know people say that all the time, but it really was just that—a team thing. Everybody truly did pick everyone else up. We did not come from 10½ games back solely because Chris Carpenter threw a really good Game 162, Albert Pujols' greatness, or Yadier Molina's leadership. It was a purely a team thing and it was every single person. Guys went out and picked each other up day in and day out. It was players who were called up in September, like Adron Chambers, contributing to big wins. It was bullpen guys going out there, trying to put together scoreless innings. It was guys at the plate grinding, giving us strong at-bats. It was always who will be next to step up?

There is no better example of this than Game 6. We were down by a few runs, but we battled and did not let them pile the runs on. Then the hitters came out and—*wham*—David Freese tied it up. I went back out in the 10th inning and gave up a homer. I was thinking, *Crap. I might have just lost us the World Series because now we are two runs down again. I can't do anything about it now, so I might as well lock it in and get these next two guys out.* I did, and what happened when we came to bat? Daniel Descalso, Jon Jay, Lance Berkman. They picked me up. Jake Westbrook took the mound in the 11th and threw a shutout inning. Freese went out and hit a walk-off. As much as it is the old cliche that it takes a team, it really did take a team. It truly was everybody picking each other up. If someone was having a bad day, they knew we had them. We had the I-got-you mentality, and it was awesome to be a part of it.

When I sit back and think about 2011, all the little moments, the ones that do not stand out as much as those really big moments, come back. It was an amazing group of guys who did something very, very special. Some special things came out of that World Series as well. I would like to think our charity work would have happened regardless, but our family's foundation is one of those special things that came out of me being a part of that World Series-winning team. My wife's grandfather was diagnosed with stage 4 lung cancer in 2010, a year before the World Series. In 2011 he was still with us, and we had the idea of doing our first charity event that offseason. We were 10½ games back at the end of August, and I was thinking, *Well, I guess we will have some time this offseason to do this event.*

But we kept winning and winning, so we held off planning the event until 2012. It is crazy how it all worked out. Our foundation, the Jason Motte Foundation, uses that same I-got-you mentality the 2011 team had. Through our efforts to strike out cancer, the Motte Foundation has raised hundreds of thousands of dollars to help cancer patients, research, and treatment facilities. We got them, those cancer patients and their families, and I cannot help but think part of that has to do with our success in 2011.

I always tried to keep baseball as what I did. I never tried to make it who I was. I am a normal guy, who just happened to throw a baseball. I probably could not write a book or perform surgery because I had a different skillset. It is funny and amazing to look at everything that came with throwing a baseball. What a ride it led me on. It led me to the Cardinals, it led me to that team in 2011, and it led me to those guys who know that I still have them. It's still a team thing—10 years later.

—Jason Motte
St. Louis Cardinals reliever (2008–14)

ACKNOWLEDGMENTS

The journalist Eli Lederman was imperative to the process of making this project a reality. A 2020 graduate of the University of Missouri School of Journalism, Lederman joined me on this journey—he helped with the interviews, the transcribing, the research, and the editing. His work ethic was impressive, and his outside-the-box thinking infused creativity into the book. Frankly, I don't know if I could've pulled this off without Eli's help.

At Triumph Books Jeff Fedotin was a friendly, hard-working, and optimistic editor. It was my third book with Jeff, and each time the experience has been delightful. And thank you to Josh Williams, Noah Amstadter, and all the other talented folks at Triumph Books for believing in me and helping me.

My wife, Angela Hochman, is the most understanding and most compassionate person I know. I began working on this book the same month our first child was born. Each day was an adventure wrapped around another adventure. Thank you, darling, for your understanding and your strength. You're a warrior.

My parents, Jere and Josette Hochman, taught me to appreciate writing, storytelling, the beauty of baseball, and the St. Louis Cardinals. And here we are.

I'm so lucky to be the brother of Emily Hochman. I learn from her. She exudes integrity. She believes in what's right in this world—and isn't afraid to say it. And she laughs at a good 85 percent of my jokes.

To all the people interviewed for this book, thank you for your time and your candidness. Your quotes are the lifeblood. And Chris Carpenter and Jason Motte were kind enough to share their stories as sections in the book. How cool is that?

Roger Hensley, the sports editor of the *St. Louis Post-Dispatch*, was gracious enough to allow me to write this book. And thank you, Roger, for bringing me home in 2015.

Thank you to the *Post-Dispatch* staff from the 2011 baseball season—notably the writers Rick Hummel, Bernie Miklasz, Derrick Goold, Tom Timmermann, Jeff Gordon, Dan O'Neill, the late Joe Strauss, and the late Bryan Burwell. Your coverage of the season was helpful reference point during the course of my research and writing.

Thank you to Drew Green, for going with me to Game 6.

Thank you to Michael Slonim, for going with me to Game 7.

And lastly, to my daughter, Olsen Hochman. I wrote this book with the hope that it would make you proud of your dad.

Bibliography

Books

La Russa, Tony and Hummel, Rick. *One Last Strike.* HarperCollins (2012).

Hochman, Benjamin. *The Big 50: St. Louis Cardinals.* Triumph Books (2018).

Periodicals

ESPN The Magazine

Jackson Free Press

Los Angeles Times

St. Louis Post-Dispatch

Sports Illustrated

The Denver Post

The New York Times

The Times-Picayune

USA TODAY

Websites

baseball-reference.com

cardinals.com

espn.com

fangraphs.com

mlb.com

nj.com

pujolsfamilyfoundation.org

scribd.com

si.com/vault

vivaelbirdos.com

yahoo.com

youtube.com